THE BOOK OF WITCHES
LARGE PRINT EDITION, ENHANCED READABILITY

OLIVER MADOX HUEFFER

ALICIA EDITIONS

CONTENTS

Foreword   v

I. On A Possible Revival Of Witchcraft   1
II. A Sabbath-General   20
III. The Origins Of The Witch   47
IV. The Half-Way Worlds   64
V. The Witch's Attributes   92
VI. Some Representative English Witches   121
VII. The Witch Of Antiquity   135
VIII. The Witch In Greece And Rome   150
IX. From Paganism to Christianity   175
X. The Witch-Bull And Its Effects   202
XI. The Later Persecutions In England   221
XII. Persecutions In Scotland   248
XIII. Other Persecutions   270
XIV. Philtres, Charms And Potions   296
XV. The Witch In Fiction   320
XVI. Some Witches Of To-Day   338

Bibliography   359

FOREWORD

Lest any reader should open this volume expecting to read an exhaustive treatise on witches and witchcraft, treated scientifically, historically, and so forth, let me disarm him beforehand by telling him that he will be disappointed. The witch occupies so large a place in the story of mankind that to include all the detail of her natural history within the limits of one volume would need the powers of a magician no less potent than was he who confined the Eastern Djinn in a bottle. I have attempted nothing so ambitious as a large-scale Ordnance Map of Witchland; rather I have endeavoured to produce a picture from which a general impression may be gained. I have chosen, that is to say, from the enormous mass of material only so much as seemed necessary for my immediate purpose, and on my lack of judgment be the blame for any undesirable hiatus. I have sought, again, to show whence the witch came and why, as well as what she was and is; to point out, further, how necessary she is and must be to the happiness of mankind, and how great the responsibility of those who, disbelieving in her themselves, seek to infect others with their scepticism. We have few picturesque excrescences left upon this age of smoothly-running machine-wheels, certainly we cannot spare one of the most time-honoured and romantic of any. And if anything I have written about her seem incompatible with sense or fact, I would plead in extenuation that neither is essential to the firm believer in witchcraft, and that to be able to enter thoroughly into the subject it is above all things necessary to cast aside such nineteenth-century shibboleths.

I would here express my gratitude to the many friends who have assisted me with material, and especially to Miss Muriel Harris, whose valuable help has done much to lighten my task.

I. ON A POSSIBLE REVIVAL OF WITCHCRAFT

To the superficial glance it might seem that he who would urge a revival of witchcraft is confronted by a task more Herculean than that of making dry bones live—in that the bones he seeks to revivify have never existed. The educated class —which, be it remembered, includes those who have studied in the elementary schools of whatever nation—is united in declaring that such a person as a witch never did, never could, and never will exist. It is true that there are still those —a waning band—who, preserving implicit faith in the literal exactitude of revealed religion, maintain that witchcraft—along with Gardens of Eden, giants, and Jewish leaders capable of influencing the movements of sun and moon—flourished under the Old Dispensation, even though it has become incredible under the New. Yet, speaking generally, the witch is as extinct in civilised men's minds as is the dodo; so that they who accept as gospel the vaticinations of racecourse tipsters or swallow patent medicines with implicit faith, yet moralise upon the illimitability of human superstition when they read that witch-doctors still command a following in West Africa, or that Sicilian peasants are not yet tired of opening their purses to sham sorcerers.

Were the reality of sorcery dependent upon a referendum of our universities—or, for that matter, of our elementary school mistresses—it were at once proclaimed a clamant imposture. Fortunately for the witch, and incidentally for a picturesque aspect of the human intellect, the Enlightened, even if we include among them those who accept their dogma as the New Gospel, are but a small—a ridiculously small—item of the human race. Compared with the whole population of the world, their numbers are so insignificant as to be for all practical purposes nonexistent. There are villages but a few miles beyond the boundary of the Metropolitan Police District, where the witch is as firmly enthroned in the imaginations of the mobility as in those of their ancestors three centuries ago. There are many

British legislators who would refuse to start an electioneering campaign upon a Friday. I myself have known a man—and know him still—a Romney Marsh-lander, who, within the last decade, has suffered grievously—himself and through his children—at the hands of witches whose names and whereabout he can detail. And I have known a woman—she kept a lodging-house in the Kennington Road—who, if not herself a witch, was yet the daughter of one, and of acknowledged power. It is true that, if the daughter's tale—told to me in the small front parlour in intervals between the crashing passage of electric trams and motor-lorries—may be accepted, her mother's gifts were put to no worse use than the curing of her Devonshire neighbours' minor ailments.

There is no need to go fifty, nor five, miles from London to find material for a revival in Black Magic. Scarcely a week passes but some old crone is charged before a Metropolitan police magistrate with having defrauded silly servant-girls on the pretence of telling them their futures. You cannot pass down Bond Street during the season without encountering a row of sandwich-men—themselves preserving very few illusions—earning a meagre wage in the service of this, that, or the other Society crystal-gazer, palmist, or clairvoyant. Who has not seen some such advertisement as the following—quoted from a current journal—proffering information about the future, "calculated from astrological horoscopes," at the very moderate charge of half-a-crown. The advertiser—in deference to modern convention he is described as a "Professor" rather than a sorcerer—further protests his mastery of Phrenology, Graphology, Clairvoyance, and Psychometry. And this advertiser is but one of many, all seeking to gain some humble profit by following in the footsteps of Diana and Mother Demdyke of Pendle Forest.

Are there not a hundred and one select Societies, each with its band of earnest adherents—many with official organs, published at more or less regular intervals and commanding circulations of a sort—openly furthering "arts" such as would, two centuries ago, have entailed upon their members the charge of Witchcraft? Is not spiritualism exalted into an international cult? The very existence of such a coterie as the "Thirteen Club," with a membership sworn to exhibit, *hic et ubique*, their contempt of degrading superstitions, is the strongest testimony to their ubiquitous regard. Most curious fact of all, it is in America, the New World, home of all that is most modern and enlightened, that we find superstitions commanding most implicit faith. It is only necessary to glance through the advertisement pages of an American popular magazine to realise how far the New World has outstripped the Old in its blind adherence to this form of faith. Nowhere has the Hypnotic, the Mesmeric, the Psychic Quack such unchallenged empire.

In Lady Charlotte Bury's "Memoirs of a Lady in Waiting" we find an example of the belief in Witchcraft cherished in the most exalted circle in the nineteenth century. Writing of the unhappy Princess—later Queen—Caroline, wife of George IV., she says as follows:—"After dinner her Royal Highness made a wax figure as usual, and gave it an amiable addition of large horns; then took three pins out of her garment and stuck them through and through, and put the figure to roast and melt at the fire. . . . Lady—says the Princess indulges in this amusement whenever there are no strangers at table, and she thinks her Royal Highness really has a superstitious belief that destroying the effigy of her husband will bring to pass the destruction of his Royal Person." We laugh at this instance of Royal credulity; yet is not the "mascot" a commonplace of our conversation? Madame de Montespan, it is recorded, had recourse—not without success—to the Black Mass as a means towards gaining the affections of Louis XIV. It is but a few years since the attention of the police was directed towards the practices of those —Society leaders for the most part—who had revived, in twentieth-century Paris, the cult of Devil worship. The most widely circulated London newspapers of the day gravely discuss in "special articles" the respective value of various mascots for motorists, or insert long descriptive reports of the vaticinations of this spiritualist or that wise-woman as to the probable perpetrators of mysterious murders. This is no exaggeration, as he may prove for himself who has patience to search the files of the London daily Press for 1907. And, be it remembered, the self-proclaimed mission of the contemporary Press is to mirror the public mind as the most obvious way of instructing it.

Under these circumstances it is easy to credit the possibility of a revival of the belief in witchcraft even in the most civilised countries of the modern world. What is more, it is far from certain that such a revival would be altogether deplorable. Granted that oceans of innocent blood were shed in the name of witchcraft—the same might be said of Christianity, of patriotism, of liberty, of half a hundred other altogether unexceptionable ideals. And, as with them, the total extinction of the witchcraft superstition might, not impossibly, have results no less disastrous than, for instance, the world-wide adoption of European fashions in dress. This quite apart from any question of whether or no witches have ever existed or do still exist. Even if we grant that superstition is necessarily superstitious in the more degraded sense of the word, we need not therefore deny it some share in alleviating the human lot.

A very large—perhaps the greater—share of human happiness is based upon "make believe." The world would be dull, miserable, intolerable did we believe only what our unfeeling stepmother Science would have us believe. It is already perceptibly less endurable—for those unfortunate enough to be civilised—since we definitely abandoned judgment by the senses in favour of algebraical calculations. While it might be too much to say that the number of suicides has increased in proportion to the decline of witchcraft, it is at least certain that superstition of whatever kind has, in the past, played a notable part in making humanity contented with its lot. The scientist has robbed us of Romance—he has taken from many of us our hope of Heaven, without giving us anything to put in its place; he reduces the beauty of Nature to a formula, so that we may no longer regard a primrose as a primrose and nothing more; he even denies us the privilege of regarding our virtues and vices as anything more than the inevitable results of environment or heredity. Every day he steals away more and more of our humanity, strips us of yet another of the few poor garments of phantasy shielding us from the Unbearable. He is indeed the Devil of modern days, forcing knowledge upon us whether we will or no. And we, instead of execrating him after the goodly fashion of our forefathers, offer our happiness upon his altars as though he were indeed the God he has explained away. And why? Purely on the faith of his own asseverations.

Why should we accept the scientist more than his grandmother, the witch? We have no better reason for accepting him than for rejecting what he tells us are no more than idle dreams. Let him discover what he will, it does but vouch the more decidedly for the illimitability of his, and our, ignorance. It is true he can perform apparent miracles; so could the witch. He pooh-poohs the arts that were so terrible to former generations; our posterity will laugh at his boasted knowledge as at a boastful child's. Already there are world-wide signs that whatever his success in the material world, mankind is ready to revolt against his tyranny over the Unseen. The innumerable new religious sects, the thousand and one ethical fads, the renaissance of so many ancient faiths—the Spiritualist and the Theosophist, the Christian Scientist and the Cooneyite, the Tolstoyan and the Salvationist—laugh at them individually who may—are all alike outward and visible signs of the revolt of man against being relegated to the insignificance of a scientific incident. And among such troubled waters witchcraft may well come into its own again. For it, as much as any, has brought happiness out of misery. Consider the unsuccessful man. Under the *régime* of enlightenment he can find no one to blame for his sorrows, nor anywhere to look for their solacement. Everything works according to immutable laws; he is sick, poor, miserable, because the Law of the Inevitable will have it so; he has no God to whom he can pray for some capricious alleviation; he cannot buy good fortune from the Devil even at the price of his soul—there is no God, nor Devil, nor good fortune nor ill; nothing but the imperturbably grinding cog-wheels upon whose orbit he is inevitably bound. Were he not a happier man if he might find an old-time witch whose spells, being removed, would leave him hope, even though fulfilment never come? Undoubtedly. We have been told that had there been no God, it would have been necessary to invent one. Yes, and along with Him a Devil and good and evil spirits, and good luck and bad, and superstitions as many as we can cram into our aching pates—

anything, everything that may save us from the horrible conception of a machine-like Certainty, from which there is no escape, after which there is no future. Surely it were better that a few thousand old women be murdered in the name of superstition, a few millions of human beings butchered in the name of religion, than that all mankind be doomed to such a fate.

Be it remembered, too, that even the witch has her grievance against the learned numbskulls who have undone her. For the witch-life was not without its alleviations. Consider. Without her witchcraft she was no more than a poor old, starved, shrunken woman, inconsiderable and unconsidered, ugly, despised, unhappy. With it she became a Power. She was feared—as all mankind wishes to be—hated perhaps, but still feared; courted, also, by those who sought her help. She was again Somebody, a recognisable entity, a human being distinguished from the common ruck. Surely that more than outweighed the chances of a fiery death. Nor was the method of her death without its compensations. Painful indeed it was, though scarcely more so than slow starvation. But if she knew herself innocent, she knew as well that her short agony was but the prelude to the eternal reward of martyrdom. If she believed herself, with that poor weary brain of hers, sold to the Devil, what a world of consolation in the thought that he, the Prince of the Powers of Darkness, scarcely inferior to the Almighty Himself, and to Him alone, should have singled her out as the one woman whose help he needed in all the countryside. And this being so, was there not always the hope that, as he had promised, he might appear even at the eleventh hour and protect his own. If he failed, the witch had but little time to realise it and all the Hereafter, full of infinite possibilities, before her. Few witches, I think, but would have preferred their grim pre-eminence, with its sporting interest, to being made the butt of doctors little wiser than themselves in the sight of infinity, held up to mockery as silly old women, cozening or self-cozened.

If witches do not in fact exist for us, it is because we have killed them with laughter—as many a good and evil cause has been killed. Had we laughed at them from the beginning of things it is even possible that they had never existed. But, as between them and Science, the whole weight of evidence is in their favour. There is the universal verdict of history. For untold centuries, as long as mankind has lorded it over the earth, their active existence was never held in doubt, down to within the last few generations. The best and wisest men of their ages have seen them, spoken with them, tested their powers and suffered under them, tried, sentenced, executed them. Every nation, every century bears equal testimony to their prowess. Even to-day, save for a tiny band of over-educated scoffers sprung for the most part from a race notorious for its wrongheaded prejudice, the universal world accepts them without any shadow of doubt. In August of the present year a police-court case was heard at Witham, an Essex town not fifty miles from London, in which the defendant stood accused of assaulting another man because his wife had bewitched him. And it was given in evidence that the complainant's wife was generally regarded as a witch by the inhabitants of the Tiptree district. Nor, as I have already pointed out, does Tiptree stand alone. Dare we, then, accept the opinion of so few against the experience, the faith, of so many? If so, must we not throw all history overboard as well? We are told that an Attila, a Mahomet, an Alexander, or, to come nearer to our own days, a Napoleon existed and did marvellous deeds impossible to other men. We read of miracles performed by a Moses, a Saint Peter, a Buddha. Do we refuse to believe that such persons ever existed because their recorded deeds are more or less incompatible with the theories of modern science? The witch carries history and the supernatural tightly clasped in her skinny arms. Let us beware lest in turning her from our door she carry them along with her, to leave us in their place the origin of species, radium, the gramophone, and some imperfect flying-machines.

Those same flying-machines provide yet another argument in the witch's favour. Why deny the possibility that she possessed powers many of which we possess ourselves. The witch flew through the air upon a broomstick; Mr. Henry Farman and Mr. Wilbur Wright, to mention two out of many, are doing the same daily as these lines are written. The vast majority of us have never seen either gentleman; we take their achievements on trust from the tales told by newspaper correspondents—a race of men inevitably inclined towards exaggeration. Yet none of us deny that Mr. Farman exists and can fly through the air upon a structure only more stable than a broomstick in degree. Why deny to the witch that faith you extend to the aeronaut? Or, again, a witch cured diseases, or caused them, by reciting a charm, compounding a noxious brew in a kettle, making passes in the air with her hands. A modern physician writes out a prescription, mixes a few drugs in a bottle—and cures diseases. He could as easily cause them by letting loose invisible microbes out of a phial. Is the one feat more credible than the other? The witch sent murrains upon cattle—and removed them. He were a poor M.R.C.V.S. who could not do as much. In a story quoted elsewhere in this volume, a sorcerer of Roman days bewitched his horses and so won chariot-races. We refuse him the tribute of our belief, but we none the less warn the modern "doper" off our racecourses. The witch could cause rain, or stay it. Scarcely a month passes but we read well attested accounts of how this or that desert has been made to blossom like the rose by irrigation or other means. But a few months since we were told that an Italian scientist had discovered a means whereby London could be relieved of fogs through some subtle employment of electricity. It is true that since then we have had our full complement of foggy weather; but does anyone regard the feat as incredible?

In all the long list of witch-attainments there is not one that would gain more than a passing newspaper paragraph in the silly season were it performed in the London of to-day. Why, then, this obstinate disbelief in the perfectly credible? Largely, perhaps, because the witch was understood to perform her wonders by the aid of the Devil rather than of the Dynamo. But must she be therefore branded as an impostor? Certainly not by those who believe in a personal Spirit of Evil. I do not know the proportion of professing Christians who to-day accept the Devil as part of their faith, but it must be considerable; and the same is the case with many non-Christian beliefs. They who can swallow a Devil have surely no excuse for refusing a witch. Nor is the difficulty greater for those who, while rejecting the Devil, accept the existence of some sort of Evil Principle—recognise, in fact, that there is such a thing as evil at all. For them the picturesque incidentals of witch-life, the signing of diabolical contracts, aerial journeyings to the Sabbath, and so forth, are but allegorical expression of the fact that the witch did evil and was not ashamed, are but roundabout ways of expressing a great truth, just as are the first three chapters of Genesis or the story that Hannibal cut his way through the Alps by the use of vinegar.

The conscientious agnostic, again, has no greater reason for disbelieving in witches and all their works than for refusing his belief to such historical characters as Cleopatra and Joan of Arc—eminent witches both, if contemporary records may be trusted. I pass over the great army of heterodox sects, Unitarians, Christian Scientists, and the like, many of whom unite with the orthodox in accepting the principle of Evil in some form or other, and with it, as a natural corollary, the existence of earthly agencies for its better propagation; while, for the rest, witchcraft stands in no worse position than do the other portions of revealed religion which they accept or do not accept, as their inclinations lead them.

It is sometimes held out as an argument for implicit belief in the Biblical legend of the Deluge that its universality among all races of mankind from China to Peru can only be accounted for by accepting Noah and his Ark. How much more forcibly does the same argument uphold the *bona fides* of the witch. Not only has she been accepted by every age and race, but she has everywhere and always been dowered with the same gifts. We find the witch of ancient Babylon an adept in the making of those same waxen or clay images in which, as we have seen, a nineteenth-century Queen of England placed such fond reliance. Witch-knots, spells, philtres, divination—the witch has been as conservative as she has been enduring. Every other profession changes and has changed its aspects and its methods from century to century. Only the witch has remained faithful to her original ideals, confident in the perfection of her art. And for all reward of such unexampled steadfastness we, creatures of the moment, deny that this one unchanging human type, this

Pyramid of human endeavour, has ever existed at all! Buttressed, then, upon the Scriptures, to say nothing of the holy writings of Buddhist, Brahmin, Mahometan, and every other religion of the first class, countenanced, increasingly though unwittingly, by the researches of science into the vastness of our ignorance; acceptable to orthodox and heterodox alike, vouched for by history and personal testimony of the most convincing, our rejection of the witch is based but upon the dogmatisms of one inconsiderable class, the impenitent atheist, blinded by the imperfection of his senses into denying everything beyond their feeble comprehension. To deny our recognition to a long line of women who, however mistakenly, have yet, in the teeth of prodigious difficulties, persevered in their self-allotted task with an altruistic enthusiasm perhaps unrivalled in the history of the world—to relegate those who have left such enduring marks upon the face of history to an obscure corner of the nursery, and that upon such feeble and suspect testimony, were to brand ourselves as materialists indeed. Rather let us believe —and thus prove our belief in human nature— that long after the last atheist has departed into the nothingness he claims as his birthright, the witch, once more raised to her seat of honour, will continue to regulate the lives and destinies of her devotees as unquestioned and as unquestionable as she was in the days of Saul and of Oliver Cromwell. It is to women that we must look chiefly for the impetus towards this renaissance. Always the more devout, the more faithful half of humanity, there is yet another peculiar claim upon her sympathies towards the witch. In days such as ours, when the whole problem of the rights and wrongs of women is among the most urgent and immediate with which we have to deal, it were as anachronistic as unnatural that Woman should allow the high purpose, the splendid endurance, the noble steadfastness in inquiry, of a whole great section of her sex—including some of the most deservedly famous women that ever lived—should allow all this not only to be forgotten, but to be absolutely discredited and denied. Persecuted by man-made laws as she has ever been, and as eternally in revolt against them, there could be no more appropriate or deserving figure to be chosen as Patroness of the great fight for freedom than the much-libelled, much-martyrised, long-enduring, eternally misunderstood Witch.

No. The time has come when we can appreciate the artistic temperament of Nero; when Bluebeard is revealed to us in the newer and more kindly aspect of an eccentric Marshal of France;

when many of us are ready to believe that Cæsar Borgia acted from a mistaken sense of duty; and that Messalina did but display the qualities natural to a brilliant Society leader. Surely among them all not one is more deserving of "whitewashing" than that signal instance of the *femme incomprise*, the Witch. We may not approve all her actions, we may not accept her as an example to be generally followed; let us at least so far escape the charge of narrow-mindedness and lack of imagination as to pay her the tribute, if not of a tear, at least of respectful credulity.

II. A SABBATH-GENERAL

It is wild weather overhead. All day the wind has been growing more and more boisterous, blowing up great mountains of grey cloud out of the East, chasing them helter-skelter across the sky, tearing them into long ribbons and thrashing them all together into one whirling tangle, through which the harassed moon can scarcely find her way. The late traveller has many an airy buffet to withstand ere he can top the last ascent and see the hamlet outlined in a sudden glint of watery moonlight at his feet. Those who lie abed are roused by the moaning in the eaves, to mutter fearfully, "The witches are abroad tonight!"

The witch lives by herself in a dingle, a hundred yards beyond the last cottage of the hamlet.

The dingle is a wilderness of brushwood, through which a twisted pathway leads to the witch's door. Matted branches overhang her roof-tree, and even when the moon, breaking for a moment from its net of cloud, sends down a brighter ray than ordinary, it does but emphasise the secretiveness of the ancient moss-grown thatch and the ill-omened plants, henbane, purple nightshade, or white bryony, that cluster round the walls. He were a bold villager who dared venture anywhere within the Witch's dingle on such a night as this. The very wind wails among the clashing branches in a subdued key, very different from its boisterous carelessness on the open downs beyond.

There is but one room—and that of the barest—in the witch's cottage. The village children, who whisper of hoarded wealth as old Mother Hackett passes them in the gloaming, little know how scant is the fare and small the grace they must look for who have sold themselves to such a master. She sleeps upon the earthen floor, with garnered pine-needles for mattress. She has a broken stool to sit on, and a great iron pot hangs above the slumbering embers on the clay hearth.

It wants still an hour to midnight, this eve of May Day, when there comes a stirring among these same embers. They are thrust aside, and up from beneath them Something heaves its way into the room. It is the size of a fox, black and hairy, shapeless and with many feet. From somewhere in its middle two green eyes shed a baleful light that horribly illuminates the room. It moves across the floor, after the manner of a great caterpillar, and as it nears her the witch casts a skinny arm abroad and mutters in her sleep. It reaches the bed, lifts itself upon it, and mumbles something in her ear. She awakes, rises upon her elbow, and replies peevishly. She has no fear of the Thing—it is a familiar visitant. She is angry, and scolds it in a shrill old voice for disturbing her too soon. Has she not the Devil's marks upon her—breast and thigh—round, blue marks that are impervious to all pain from without, but itch and throb when it is time for her to go about her devilish business? The Thing takes her scoldings lightly, twitting her with having overslept herself at the last Sabbath—which she denies. They fall a-jesting; she calls it Tom—Vinegar Tom; and they laugh together over old exploits and present purposes.

A moonbeam glints-through a hole in the thatch. Where the witch has lain now sits a black cat, larger than any of natural generation—as large, almost, as a donkey. It talks still with the witch's voice, and lingers awhile, the two pairs of green eyes watching each other through the darkness. At last, with a careless greeting, it bounds across the floor, leaps up the wall to the chimney opening, and is gone. The shapeless Thing remains upon the bed. Its sides quiver, it chuckles beneath its breath in a way half human, yet altogether inhuman and obscene.

The black cat is hastening towards the hamlet under the shadow of the brushwood. When she comes within sight of the end house, she leaves the path and strikes out into the gorse-clad waste beyond the pasture, keeping to it until she is opposite the cottage of Dickon the waggoner. A child has been born, three days back, to Dickon and Meg his wife. It is not yet baptised, for the priest lives four miles away, beyond the downs, and Dickon has been too pressed with work to go for him. To-morrow will be time enough, for it is the healthiest child, not to say the most beautiful, the gossips have ever set eyes upon. Perhaps, if Meg had not forgotten in her newfound happiness how, just after her wedding, when old Mother Hackett passed her door, she made the sign of the cross and cried out upon the old dame for a foul witch, she might not be sleeping so easily now with her first-born on her bosom.

The black cat creeps on under the shadow of a hedge. Old Trusty, the shepherd's dog, left to guard the flock during the night, sees where she goes, and, taking her for a lurking fox, charges fiercely towards the hedge, too eager to give tongue. But at the first flash of the green eyes as she turns her head, he knows with what he has to deal, and flies whimpering for shelter in the gorse, his tail between his legs. For a dog can tell a witch more readily than can his master—and fears her as greatly.

The black cat being come to Dickon's cottage, waits for a moment to be sure that all is quiet, then leaps upon the low roof, gains the summit, and so descends by way of the chimney to the room where lie the sleeping family. Again it waits, listening to their regular breathing, its tail whipping to and fro in suppressed excitement. It rises upon its hinder legs and makes certain passes in the air, North and South and East and West. It approaches the bed, and softly, softly draws the child from its sleeping mother's arms. It makes again for the chimney, and in two bounds is in the open air, carrying the child nestled against its warm black fur. Scarcely has it gained the shadow of the hedge when the mother, her sleep disturbed, it may be, by some vague presentiment of danger, opens her eyes. But the warm weight is still upon her breast, and she drops off to sleep again in security. Did you peep into the witch's cottage now, you would find that the black shapeless Thing is gone. For the Devil's imps can take what shape they will in their master's service.

The black cat, with its sleeping charge, hastens back towards the dingle. Reaching the cottage, it places the child upon the bed, turns twice, and in that moment the witch, clad only in her shift, stands where the cat has been. She is awaiting something, and grows anxious and uneasy, hobbling hither and thither about the room, mumbling below her breath, and once, when the child wakes and wails, taking it in her arms and hushing it, almost as might a woman. It is close upon midnight, yet the sign has not come. For the Evil One, being above all things inconstant, never lets his servants know time or place until the last moment, and that in some unlooked-for way.

At last, when she is quite tormented with anxiety lest she have unwittingly angered her master, comes a stealthy clattering of wings upon the thatch, and down through the hole that serves for chimney rustles a black raven with fiery eyes. It flutters straight for the witch's shoulder and there settles, whispering hoarsely in her ear, while the light from its eyes throws her lean features, with their twitching muscles, into pale relief against the darkness. Nodding eager assent to the message, Mother Hackett hobbles to her bed, and, from a safe hiding-place among the rustling pine-needles, draws out a phial. Next she makes for the corner beside the hearth, and picks up the broomstick leaning against the wall. The raven quits her shoulder for the pillow, thence to watch her with its head at an approving angle. She opens the phial and smears the contents on the broomstick, head and handle. It is an ointment, and it shines with the phosphorescent light that is born of corruption. Well it may, for it is compounded of black millet and the dried powdered liver of an unbaptised child, just such a one as now lies upon the witch's bed, with the grim raven gazing down on it. The witch—deluded wretch—believes the ointment to have magic powers; that, smeared upon her broomstick, it gives the senseless wood volition and the power to carry her sky-high; or, if she swallows it, that it will render her insensible to pain, so that the worst efforts of the torturer and the executioner shall force her to confess nothing. The Devil, her master, knows—none better—that no such potency is in any ointment, but that his own hellish magic supports his minions in the air and comes, an he so will, to their aid in time of trial. But this he hides from them, so that in their folly they may be led to murder babes—the sacrifice he loves above all other.

The witch takes a broken eggshell and smears it also with the ointment. She goes to the bed and picks up the child, the broomstick hopping after her across the floor. Being now ready to set out, she steps astride the broom-handle, that holds itself aslant for her easier mounting. She waves her hand to the attendant raven, and with a rush that sends a spirtle of bright sparks up from the embers, she is away—up the chimney, through the overhanging branches, through the ragged clouds, and far on her journey under the stars. Yet, if any should enter the witch's hut then or thereafter till the dawn, they would find her sleeping peacefully upon the bed. The raven, having carried their master's message, has this further duty: to take upon himself the witch's shape until her return, lest any, finding her from home, should scent out her errand.

The wind is from the East. The witch must steer across it, for the Sabbath-General, as the corvine messenger has told her, is to be held on a lonely peak of the Cevennes, in mid-France. Her task is not of the easiest, for the gusts come fierce and sudden, and the broomstick dips and leaps before them like a cockle-boat on a rough sea. The witch's scanty locks _ and scantier clothing stream out almost at a right angle, and once the baby in her arms raises its voice in a tiny wail that would soften the heart of any but a servant of the Devil. Up here the moonlight wells down unchecked, turning the clouds below into the shifting semblance of snow mountains and lakes of silver. They open out now and again at the wind's bidding to allow glimpses of the dark, silent earth far down beneath.

So for a time—a little time, for Devil's messengers fly fast—the witch drives onward in midair. At last the broomstick slackens speed, seems to hesitate, circles twice or thrice, and then dives earthwards. The hag alights upon the seashore, upon a pebbly beach whereon the waves fling themselves in white fury at the lashings of the wind, now grown so high that Mother Hackett can scarcely stand against it. Whether because he foresees some chance of evil-doing, or from mere inconstancy, for he works without method and against reason, the Devil has ordered that she shall not cross the Channel on her broomstick. She seizes the interval between two waves to launch the eggshell she has brought with her, steps into it, raises the broomstick aloft as sail or ensign, and puts out to sea in the teeth of the gale. The great waves roar far above her head, in foaming whirlpools that might sink a war-fleet, but the eggshell rides triumphantly among them, dancing upon their crests and shipping never a drop of water on its passage. Nor can the best efforts of the wind stay its speed. Only once does it deviate from its course, when a straining ship, its spars and sails all splintered and riven, drives through the mist to leeward. As she nears it, the witch rises to her feet, throws out one skinny hand towards it, and shrieks an incantation down the wind. A flicker of lightning shows itself in the East, and a cloud drives over the face of the moon. When its shadow is past, there is no more sign of the ship or its toiling crew upon the lonely face of the waters. Mother Hackett mews gleefully as she speeds Francewards.

Coming to where the low grey coast rises from the waves, she once more sets herself astride the broomstick. As she speeds on, sky-high, towards the meeting-place, she falls in with company bent on the same errand. From all sides they come, converging to the goal, old, lean hags like herself, women in the prime of life, young girls not yet out of their teens. Some bear with them unweaned babes, others children of a larger growth, yet others youths or grown men, as offerings to Satan. These they carry pillion-wise before them, for in the Devil's kingdom all is awry, imperfect, contrariwise to the ways of Christian folk. Some of them are mounted on goats, some upon great toads, or flying snakes, or reptiles of uncertain shape, or simple broomsticks, as fancy has directed their imperious despot. One—a man—rides side-seated upon a great fiery dragon, that in the distance glows like a newly-risen star. He is a mighty sorcerer, one who commands Satan instead of serving him, coming to the Sabbath for some reason of his own, and mounted on a steed of his own providing.

The meeting-place of the Sabbath-General, as Satan, in mockery of Christian ritual, chooses to call this foregathering of his servants, is a bare peak in the loneliest part of the Cevennes. It stands a little removed from the centre of a great mountain amphitheatre, and just below the summit is a mountain tarn, crystal-pure and casting back the starlight as peacefully as though there were no such things as witch or warlock beneath God's Heaven. Yet it is not the first time the same meeting-place has been chosen, for not a blade of grass, not the humblest creeping plant, grows upon the sterile rocks. Every growing thing withered away, root and branch, when last the forces of Hell gathered here. So must the place remain, desert and bare, mute witness of its desecration, until the Judgment Day.

The witches come skirling down from the sky like a flight of unclean birds, circling above the crags, hovering to choose a settling-place where no sharp-pointed rock shall gash their naked feet, chattering shrilly the while. Those already arrived are seated in a wide circle on a flat rock-ledge jutting from the mountain side. They are mostly witches of the neighbourhood, who have come afoot and have set out betimes lest they be detained upon the way. As more and more join the circle you may find proof that they lie who declare the Devil's servants mostly women. It is true that woman, by reason of the frailty of her nature, seeks more often to pry into forbidden things, to her own destruction, and thus there are many more witches than warlocks or magicians. Yet of those gathered for this Sabbath-General, for every witch there is one mortal man, to say nothing of demons; for while some, as Mother Hackett, have come alone, others, being the younger and fairer of the witches, have brought with them two or even three youths or young men, ready to take service with the Evil One and cast away their hope of salvation, as did our Father Adam, at the bidding of these Delilahs. Thus it is that, in the unholy dances which are to follow, every witch will have a man for her partner, save the most favoured who dance with the superior demons, for thus the Devil will have it.

Mother Hackett, when she dismounts from her broomstick, takes her place beside one Luckie, a gossip of former Sabbaths, ill-favoured as herself, who comes from the kingdom of Fife, where she is much feared for the sudden tempests she raises when the fishing-fleets are sailing homeward with full catches. Next to her is a younger witch, fair and well-born, Sidonia by name, of a noble house in Mecklenburg. She is a tall, pale girl, with hair the colour of ripe wheat, and grey-blue eyes. She is held in high esteem by Satan, both for her beauty and for the number of well-born youths she has delivered into his hands. Next to her is a witch of Spain, beautiful also, though brown and with black, beady eyes. Between these two there is little love lost, seeing that they are women no less than witches, and either would do the other a mischief could she compass it.

Though all those bidden have joined the circle, there is yet no sign of the Devil's coming. The witches cease their clacking and scan the sky impatiently, muttering curses against their master. Can it be that he means to play them false, having bidden them merely for a jest and to make a mock of them? It would not be for the first time—for his mind is so crafty and so uncertain, his purpose so errant, that not the most favoured of his ministers has any inkling of it.

Suddenly there is an eager rustling around the expectant circle. A figure has appeared in the centre. But their relief fades into angry disappointment. It is not the Devil himself. It is a small, mean, inconsiderable devil, so inferior in the infernal hierarchy that he has not even horns upon his head. The circle grows smaller as the witches press towards him, buzzing with angry questions. They have no fear, no respect for him; he is a servant like themselves. If he have been deputed to represent his master, he must expect to pay dearly for the honour. He scans the lowering faces anxiously and mutters apologies. No doubt their Master is upon the way and will soon arrive. He himself is but a poor devil, a little devil; they may be sure that he would not think of putting a slight on witches of such eminence. But fair words will not placate them. Already hands are raised to strike him, already some of them are preparing to scratch him with the nails of their little fingers, always worn long and sharp by witches, such being one of the signs you may know them by. Already he has been tweaked and buffeted as earnest of what he is to look for. But now another, more dreadful shape looms up in the very centre of the circle, and the angry witches fall back before it in grovelling terror. At first, seen in the dim light of the waning moon, it is shapeless, inchoate. Slowly it takes form before their eyes into the trunk of a great tree, with tangled limbs stretching out from it. It has about it the suggestion of a face, leering and horrible, with set features that half emerge and half conceal themselves in the gnarling of the bark—such a face as a man may see peering after him out of the darkness when he passes, tip-toe, through the depths of an ancient forest at midnight. Before it the witches make obeisance, turning their backs upon it and bowing to the ground, in mockery of Christian reverence. When they turn again the tree has changed into a goat, its eyes aflame with obscene passion, and, even as they look, the goat fades into a lion with bloody jaws. The lion fades in turn into a man, a comely man in all but his expression, and his eyes, which, whatever his shape, are always those of a goat, bestial and foul. He is dressed all in black, but his face and hands are dull red—for his vitals are consuming in the flames of Hell—and when he raises his hand, his wrist and forearm glow within his cuff as though they were made of molten iron. On his left hand the fingers are all grown together into one misshapen claw, for however fair the human seeming into which the Devil moulds himself, you may always know him for what he is, in that some part of him, an ear, a foot, or a hand, is horribly misshapen.

Now at last, all being prepared, attendant imps pass round the circle, checking the numbers of those present and who bears the Devil's mark and who must still receive it, and who has carried out her appointed task and who has failed. Returning, they whisper the tale into their master's ear, who gibbers with delight and leaps into the air and cracks his heels together, for there is nothing noble or of dignity about him, being in all things mean and petty, a thing of low vices rather than of heroic crimes. Thereafter he sits upon a throne, seemingly of gold, that rises from the earth to receive him, while his attendants hold aloft candles made of the fat of drowned mariners, burning with a pale blue light. One by one he calls the witches before him, calling them by nicknames, as "Old Toothless," or "Wag-in-the-wind," or "Cozling," but never by the names given them in Holy Baptism. And they, making obscene obeisance before his throne, speak to him thuswise also, calling him "Monsieur," or "Grizzleguts," or other fouler names. Next, standing with her back towards the throne, each in turn makes recital of her foul deeds since their last meeting: how many of God's children she has ruined and undone, what evil spells she has cast upon crops and bestial, what tempests she has raised, how she has fared in furthering her master's kingdom. Those who have done well Satan fondles and caresses, promising them great reward, but the others he hands over to his imps for present punishment. Thus there is one, plump and well-favoured, being a witch of Sweden, who, having been given for her task that she shall bring a neighbour's son —a rich young farmer—to her master's allegiance, has failed therein, and that although granted extension of time for the emprise. Her the Devil, losing all further patience, of which he has but little at the best of times, marks out for punishment, and his demons, casting her straightway to the ground, beat her with whips of living snakes and scorpions, and bite and otherwise torment her with tooth and claw, so ,that the blood runs from her in streams. And while she yells and screams for mercy, flapping here and there upon the ground like a fish upon a line, the whole assembly shakes with hideous laughter at the grotesqueness of her agony.

Mother Hackett, her turn being come, rises eagerly, knowing that she has done evil full measure since the last Sabbath. The waggoner's child she hands to Gossip Luckie, the time for its presentation being not yet come, and hobbles her fastest to her place before the throne, puckering her old eyes beneath the glare from the surrounding corpse-candles. It is for this that she has borne the hardships, the hatred and persecution of her Christian neighbours, the starvation of hunger and cold during the long winter months since the last Sabbath. Her tale is of murrains cast upon a rich farmer's cattle, of a crop of barley that has withered away beneath her spell, of a tempest raised by her to unroof the priest's tithe-barn three parishes away, of the digging up of bodies from the churchyard to grace the Sabbath banquet, of three boys who, having stoned her, have ever since gone cross-eyed, vomiting needles incessantly, and of the ship sunk in mid-Channel upon her late crossing. Also there is the unbaptised child she has brought with her, to be devoted to the Devil's service for all time. When her tale is told she waits yet a long moment, expectant of praise and reward. Praise indeed her master lavishes upon her, though he chides her also for having brought him but a waggoner's brat in place of a child well-born, for in them he delights most—and of future reward great promise. But he speaks as one whose thoughts are elsewhere, and his eyes—which are always the eyes of a lustful goat—wander to where the beauteous Sidonia waits smiling for her turn. So Mother Hackett must hobble back to her place in the circle, her heart full of bitterness and disappointment, feeling that she has been tricked out of her deserts, knowing that she must labour in ill-doing yet another year before she can hope for the rich rewards promised her so many weary years ago, yet still to look for. And she curses under her breath as Sidonia passes in all the pride of her unholy beauty, going to where the Evil One leans forward in his chair, his eyes glowing like hot coals, and motions to her to come yet nearer as she tells with trills of silvery laughter, that yet is altogether horrible, of three youths she has bewitched, and how one has hanged himself, cursing the name of God, and how another has murdered his own brother, and now lies in durance awaiting death, and the third she has brought with her to the Sabbath, to enter himself among the Devil's servants, abandoning his hope of Heaven for her sake. Of her tale Satan loses no word, and when she is done he clips her in his arms and fondles her and keeps her beside him throughout what follows.

When all the witches have rendered account, it is the turn of the victims they have brought with them, the unbaptised children first and they of tender years. They are led or carried before the Devil's throne, and stand there, curious and open-eyed, understanding nothing of what is going forward, clustering together in a group, the elder girls holding the infants in their arms and hushing them awkwardly when they cry. The Evil One speaks to them, suiting his words to their condition, his voice purring like a cat. He draws bright pictures of the reward they may expect for absolute obedience—if they renounce their kindred and, those of them who are baptised, their godfathers and godmothers, and with them God and the Child Jesus. Some of the elder among them demur at this, whereupon he reasons with them, his voice still soft and cruel as a cat's, telling them that what they have learned of Holy Writ is but an old wife's tale, and that there is no God but he who speaks, being master of both worlds. Then his eyes blaze brighter and his voice grows fierce and menacing, and he leads them to the side of the mountain and shows them, far below, a dreadful chasm with fierce flames leaping about it and grim fire-monsters lifting up their open jaws from its centre. It is but a lying vision, conjured up by his hellish arts; but how should such poor babes know false from true? The witches gather round them and cozen and threaten, telling them that if they refuse they will be surely cast into the flames, but if they obey they shall have all that a child best loves, full measure. So at last they do as they are bidden, and swear away their young souls and their hope of salvation for ever and ever, and make obeisance to Satan with obscene ceremonies of which they understand nothing, doing all for fear of the witches who instruct them. When all, even to the unweaned babes, are bound for ever to Satan's allegiance, they are led away to the shore of the mountain tarn, whither come great toads swimming up from its clear depths and clambering to the shore. These the children are set to mind, being given little white switches for that end—Satan promising that next year, if they have deserved well, they shall be granted the full privileges of servants of Hell. Childlike, when they have overcome their first horror of the hideous toads, they make playthings of them, seeking to make them gallop with the white switches, and, especially the boys, forgetting all that has passed in the gleefulness of the moment.

Meanwhile the more mature recruits to Satan's army are called in turn before him, to be examined in their love of evil, to make obeisance and to receive his mark—invented by him in impious mockery of our Saviour's wounds and the stigmata borne on their bodies by many of His saints. All this to the accompaniment of rites so foul and bestial that they may not be written down. And next, the present business being disposed of, the whole crew falls a-dancing, men, women, and imps together. Back to back the couples dance, for the most part stark-naked, and some with black cats hanging from their necks or waists, spitting and scratching, and some with hideous toads and serpents pressed to their bosoms, and all capering and gesturing with such lewd and obscene antics that the mind of man can scarcely follow them. The imps who are of the number hold aloft their corpse-candles, to light their paces, and in the middle of all sits the Devil blowing upon a bagpipe, sometimes in one form and sometimes in another, as the whim takes him. Higher and higher they leap, and faster and faster grow their steps, whirling hither and thither under the blue light of the candles, spurred on by the droning of the infernal pipes, until they fall a-gasping. When the last couple has ceased its pirouettings, the Devil—being now again in the form of a man—lays aside his instrument and leads them to where a banquet is prepared for them. The tables are heaped high with all the delicacies of the earth, the rarest fruits, the choicest meats, and the most costly wines, heaped upon golden dishes that might ransom all the kings of Christendom. For attendants there are demons of inferior rank, who have tricked themselves out into the strangest shapes they can devise. Thus, one has a monstrous nose, shaped like a flute, upon which he plays with his hands. Another has sparks shooting from horns and tail, the which, as they fall upon the table, turn into great beetles. Another, having neither arms nor legs nor head, rolls like a wheel upon his belly, in the centre of which blazes one great eye. Another is nought but a huge mouth, and hops underneath the tables biting the ankles of the witches. While yet another takes the shape of a beaker, whence pours sparkling wine into the goblets of the guests. If they seek to drink, it turns to burnings pitch. Thus it is indeed with all the viands, for though they seem all that the heart or belly of man can desire and of all things plenty—saving only salt, for that Satan cannot abide, as recalling the Last Supper upon earth of the Lord Christ—yet being tested they are proved a mockery. For when the guests stretch out their hands for what they most covet it vanishes from their eyes, and in its place is corruption and rottenness, the reeking flesh of murderers and heretics or of cattle that have died of a murrain, the entrails of reptiles or the scrapings of middens, with, for drink, water in which drowned suicides have rotted, and such-like. Some of those but newly entered draw back in horror from such fare, whereat the more hardened mock at them, falling upon it themselves with horrid zest.

Grown merry after such feasting, they fall a-rioting, jesting, and playing after such wise as may not be told, until the time is come for their next enterprise, what time the Devil toys with the most well-favoured wantons among them. When at last the signal is given, the whole hellish crew rise into the air again, their master leading them, shrilling and squawking like a flight of wild geese across the darkling sky. The Devil leads them to an old cathedral town, a place of ancient towers and crumbling walls and tall, high-shouldered houses that lean out over narrow lanes as if a-gossiping. Before the great cathedral is a wide market-place, very busy in the day, but silent now as a graveyard, with only now and then the creaking of some wind-harried sign to tell of human energies. Four roads meet in the centre of the market-place, and there the Evil One alights, his ministers behind him, and there his throne is set up facing the portal of the cathedral—for it is thus that Satan loves best to carry on his mockery of Christian ritual. First is gone through a blasphemous parody of Holy Baptism, toads taking the place of children. Each is tricked out in a velvet suit of black or scarlet, with a bell tied to each paw and one hung round its neck. An unfrocked priest, who has been a miracle of shamelessness and is now sold to Satan, performs the blasphemy, and the oldest and foulest witches stand as sponsors, vying with each other in the lewdness of their responses. While this is going forward a brace of night-rovers, intent upon a deed of sacrilege, come creeping through the shadows round the cathedral walls, seeking to force an entrance into the holy place. Their eyes and ears are at their keenest, lest they be apprehended, but though they look right through the crowd of demons and witches thronging the open market-place, they yet see nothing of them—for, evil-doers though they be, they have not yet lost their chance of salvation, and none but those irrevocably sworn of Satan's following can see what befalls upon a Witches' Sabbath.

The christening of the toads being gone through, follows the yet more blasphemous celebration of the Black Mass. The foresworn priest again officiates, the imps, witches, and demons acting as deacons, acolytes, or worshippers, all impiously mimicking the servants of God. In place of the Host is exalted a black wafer, cut in the form of a triangle, and the whole service of the Mass is gone through backwards from end to beginning. The onlookers also make their obeisances backwards, with lewd gesture not forgotten, towards where the father of all evil sits grinning and mowing upon his throne over against the cathedral door. Yet are they not permitted to finish their blasphemies, for even as the false priest makes to administer the wafer to an imp, who receives it, for the greater mockery, standing upon his head, the first pale shadow of the dawn creeps up the eastern sky. Seeing it, a lusty cock, roosting in some farmyard beyond the city walls, welcomes it with shrill crowings. The Devil's brood break off and listen fearfully, for Chanticleer is a servant of God, and held in awe by all demons, witches, and sorcerers as the herald of God's daylight. A rival bird takes up the challenge, and it is echoed far and wide over the countryside. The Evil One waits no longer, but sinks at once, with his throne, downwards through the cobble-stones to his abiding-place, followed by his attendant demons. The witches and sorcerers of the company tarry not, but cast themselves afloat upon the air, wasting no time or breath upon their farewells lest daylight surprise them ere they can reach their homes and all their wickedness be made clear.

Mother Hackett, among the rest, throws herself astride her broom-handle and sails off down the wind. On this her return she wastes no time at the sea-coast, but shoots onward high in the air, through the increasing pallor of the morning. Over sea and down she flies, and, dropping like a stone into the dingle, enters her cottage by the chimney, unseen even by the earliest ploughman. At her coming the expectant demon in her shape rises from the bed and takes again the semblance of a raven. A few words of greeting and inquiry, and it makes its exit by the road it came, flying off heavily across the fields, regardless of the daylight, for who, seeing a raven fly towards the sea, would think of sorcery or witchcraft? Who, again, entering her humble cot and seeing there a poor old woman sleeping on a bed of poverty would recognise in her a foul witch, forward in all wickedness and a most potent agent of her master Satan. For so cunningly do these devilish hags, aided by their master's arts, conceal their exits and their entrances, their spells and incantations, that there be many ignorant men who, openly flouting Holy Writ, declare, even in these enlightened days, that there is no such thing as witchcraft or sorcery, and that they who seek out witches and slay them are no better than cruel murderers of poor helpless old women. Such are the craft and malice of Satan and the folly of mankind.

III. THE ORIGINS OF THE WITCH

The witch, in the broader sense of the word, may be said to have existed ever since mankind first evolved an imagination, and may be expected to expire only with the death of the last woman. Given the supernatural, and sorcery must follow in some shape or other as its corollary. Whence also the witch is as ubiquitous as she is enduring. Under some form or other she exists, and has existed, in every quarter of the globe; she is as familiar to the English peasant as to the West African, in South America as in Japan. Her attributes vary, and have varied, with the racial temperament and the religious conceptions of her worshippers and persecutors, as widely as do, and have done, their gods. But it was left for mediæval Christianity to give her the definite shape in which she is now most universally recognised, and it is to the Christian ideal of celibacy that she owes, if indirectly, the more obscene, and latterly the more grotesque, of her attributes, lifting her at first to an evil equality with the horned Devil of the Middle Ages, degrading her ultimately to the "horrid old witch" of nursery legend.

It is a far cry from this same "horrid old witch" to the pagan divinity, but there is no break in the long pedigree. It may be traced still further through the mists of antiquity—to the earliest days of human motherhood. Only, as between goddess and witch, we are confronted with a Darwinian problem. Is the witch indeed daughter of the goddess, or are both descended from a common ancestress? To my mind, the latter is the more correct line of descent, with the pagan priestess as connecting link.

"To one wizard, ten thousand witches," quotes Michelet from a forgotten writer of the days of Louis Treize; and throughout all the history of sorcery women have formed the majority of its practitioners. Our forefathers attributed this to the weakness of womankind, always curious to probe the mysteries of the Unknown, always prone to fall into the snare of evil. A more charitable—and correcter—explanation would be found in the greater quickness of her perceptions. If Eve first gave the apple to Adam, she gave with it the future of civilised humanity. The first mother gave birth to twin-daughters, the goddess and the witch, and from one or other of them came the impetus which has carried mankind to its present stage of progress, and will carry it yet nearer towards Heaven.

The primitive father was an animal, with potentialities—among animals without them. His intellect was concentrated in his activities, in providing for the material needs of himself and his family. His position towards his wife was very much what satirists would have us believe is that of the American business man to-day. His laborious days were spent in tracking his prey through the forest, his leisure in sleeping, eating, and digesting. The mother, on the other hand, was bound to the home by reason of her motherhood. Less active, she was more contemplative, noting in the order of events the best means of preservation for the small pink thing that could not live without her care, her mind always alert to the exigencies of the moment. Thus she acquired knowledge of things beneficent or harmful, of the food most apt for its nourishment, of the herbs growing around the clearing best fitted to cure its infantile complaints. She experimented, cautiously but continuously, and with each recurrent need she added a little to her small stock of wisdom. Small in itself, but vast in proportion to that of men or childless women. Little by little she "walked her hospital"; little by little she learnt the relative value of her simple potions, to whom they should be given, and how, and when. To the primitive mind this was cause for wonder, as indeed it is, almost as wonderful as the first smile of the first baby. Pain can no longer run riot unchecked. If it have not yet found its mistress, at least a protest has been entered against it—reason not only for joy and wonder, but for respect and gratitude—even perhaps for worship.

Whatever his divinity, Man worships himself. In every form of religion the worshipped tends to become confused with the worshipper. Man cannot escape his own environment. The thunderstorm frightens him; there must be a storm-demon. What is that demon but another man like himself,- though uglier and wickeder and very much more powerful? Such a demon must be flattered and propitiated as an angry man of might must be. But a Primitive with his living to make cannot spare the time necessary to propitiate a worldful of demons. He deputes the duty to a weaker neighbour, one who sits at home, engaging for his own part to find food for both. Whence the first priestess—from whom later descends the first priest. For who so apt at propitiation as she who can cajole that most domesticated of demons, the ever-present Pain. So, later, when the propitiation of Evil gives place to the invocation of good, who so worthy of honour, which is to say of worship, as she who, in the dawning of the race, first relieved poor humanity of its bodily ills? Goddess, priestess, White Witch and Black—all are but variations on that oldest and most beautiful of themes, Motherhood.

To return to the first house-wife. Throughout her life she adds always a little to her store of natural knowledge, and when she dies she bequeaths it to her daughters. They in turn add to it until the time comes when to the cure of bodies is added that of minds. For Man's nascent mind begins to trouble him almost as much as does his body. Already the eternal problem of why and wherefore raises its head; already he begins his age-long struggle with the inevitable. That "all that is, is good" does not commend itself to Prehistoric Man. He knows so much better. He must often go hungry, his cattle die, drought destroys his meagre crops, his neighbour robs him of his warspoil. He appeals to the woman, who thinks so much, for a way out. Cannot she, who with her potions drove the pain out of his body, help him in this also? Can she not cure his cattle? Can she not reason with the delinquent rain-demon, or, by making a little rain herself, move him to emulation? Best of all, can she not, out of the plenitude of her wisdom, suggest some means of outwitting that treacherous neighbour? He will reward her handsomely, especially for this last.

It is at this point that the priestess and the witch come to the crossing of the ways, henceforward to follow divergent paths. The one sister, from whom is to be born the devout priestess, is ready to do all that she can. She invokes the cattle-demon, the rain-demon; she, no more than the man, has any doubt of their invocability, but if they refuse to answer it must be because they are angry. She cannot make it rain if the demon gainsay her prayer. She is honest, acknowledging her inferiority to the supernatural. Only she claims to understand more than most the best way to approach it.

Consider the other woman—the ancestress of the witch, in the opprobrious sense. She knows very well that she cannot make rain. Probably she has made the experiment already. But—such faith in her power is tempting—so are the gifts thus easy to be earned. The man believes in her—almost she begins to believe in herself. Perhaps she tries to persuade herself that she may succeed this time. She is weatherwise, and she reads in natural signs the probability that rain may shortly be expected. If it should not—well, she must take precautions against incurring blame. She must impose conditions, and any failure must be set down to their non-fulfilment. There is a very pleasant sense of power in gulling the overgrown baby who is so ready to be gulled. She accepts the trust, commands the rain-demon to let down his showers. Her reading of the signs is justified—the expected rain comes. Her reputation is assured—until belief in the supernatural shall be no more. Her daughter and her granddaughters inherit her claims. They also command the storm, using the same form of words. Possibly they are themselves deceived—believing that there is some virtue in the form of their mother's words, now become an incantation. From the first claim to power over the elements, to the finished sorceress, and thence to the "horrid old witch" of fairy legend, is but a matter of regular evolution.

Just as the priestess was the mother of the priest, so the wizard is born of the witch. Man, though he start later—very much as the boy is slower in development than is his sister—is not content always to remain second in the race for knowledge. For a time—perhaps for long centuries—he has been content to leave things intellectual to his womenfolk. But when he starts he is not content to stay upon the threshold of knowledge, as woman, who has approached it only from necessity, has done. One day a male iconoclast rebels, pitting his awakening intellect against the woman's inherited reputation. Victorious, he yet trembles at his victory, while all Palseolithia awaits the angry fire from Heaven. But nothing happens. No lightning strikes him; no swift disease destroys him, or his children, or his cattle. A new era has begun—the wizard places himself beside the witch, slowly but surely to elbow her into the second place.

As the slow centuries pass society has been gradually forming and shaping itself. In his search for a civilisation Man has left the secluded cave wherein he wrung the empire of the world from the jaws of the cave-bear and the scythe-toothed tiger. He has built himself homes and collected them into villages; from the scattered family he has evolved the tribe, and from the tribe the nation. Having learned his own power when buttressed upon that of his neighbours, he is slowly broadening and extending it until it is little inferior to that of the divinities before whom it pleases him to tremble. He—or Nature for him—chooses out rulers, who become his gods in all but divinity; and his respect for them, if less absolute, is more immediate than for his gods. Government, making all things possible, becomes an accomplished fact.

Government, once instituted, loses no time in measuring itself against Heaven. In one form or other the conflict between Church and State—disguise it as men may—has lasted from the beginning, and must last as long as both survive. That ideal which reached the point nearest of attainment in the theoretic constitution of the Holy Roman Empire, of two rulers, co-existent and co-equal, governing one the spiritual and one the material empire of the world, was in the very nature of things doomed to remain an ideal. Either God or Man must be first. With their struggles for the mastery the fortunes of the witch, as of all exponents of the supernatural, were intimately bound up.

At first sheltering itself beneath the wings of the spiritual power, the material flourished—at its protector's expense. The realm of Nature seemed at first so inconsiderable compared to that of the supernatural, that he were a bold iconoclast who dared compare them. Only, the King was always in the midst of his people; the god, century by century, retreated further into the unscaleable skies. Slowly the civil power emancipated itself from the tutelage of the spiritual—as it is still doing in our own time—slowly and with many falterings and many backward glances, asserting itself in prosperity, appealing for help in adversity, retreating often, but never so far as it advanced.

With the first introduction of civil government the witch and the priestess finally part company, to range themselves henceforward upon opposite sides. It is true that as religion follows religion the priestess of the former era often becomes the witch of its successor, thereby only accentuating the distinction. For, in the unceasing efforts to arrange a *modus vivendi* between the human and the supernatural worlds, the priestess accommodates herself to circumstances—the witch defies them. The priestess, acknowledging her own humanity, claims only to interpret the wishes of the god, to intercede with him on behalf of her fellow-men. The witch, staunch Tory of the old breed, claims to be divine, in so far as she exercises divine power unamenable to human governance, and thus singles herself out as one apart, independent of civil and ecclesiastical powers alike—and as such an object of fear and of suspicion. Even so she is still respectable, suspect indeed, but not condemned. The public attitude towards her is variable; she is alternately encouraged and suppressed, venerated and persecuted—and through all she flourishes, now seductive as Circe, now hag-like as was Hecate.

Ages pass, empires flourish and decay, and slowly a great change is coming over society. Unrest is in the air; old systems and old creeds are dying of inertia, and men look eagerly for something to take their place. The spirit of individual liberty steals round the world, whispering in all men's ears. The slave, toiling at the oar, hears them, though he dare not listen, and hugs them in his heart—and a heresy, threatening the very foundations of society, spreads far and wide. Is it just possible that men are not born slave or master by divine decree?

The First Socialist is born in the East. He and His disciples preach a creed so blasphemous, so incompatible with the rights of property, that it becomes a sacred duty, if vested interests are to be preserved, to crucify Him as an encouragement to others. He proclaims, in a word, that all men are equal. It is well for Christianity that He adds the qualification, "In the sight of God," or how could either slave or master believe in anything so contrary to the senses evidence? Vested interests notwithstanding, the new creed spreads, as any creed so comforting to the great majority, the downtrodden and oppressed, is bound to spread. But, though it preached the acceptable doctrines of liberty, equality, and fraternity, Christianity introduced with them sin into the world. All men might be equal in the sight of God, but they were all equally sinners. Humility and self-abasement were to take the place of the old pagan joyousness. To the Christian—to the Early Christian, at any rate—the world ceased to be man's inheritance, as Heaven was that of a congerie of shifting divinities—an inheritance the enjoyment of which was as blameless as it was natural. It was become a place of discipline and education, a hard school designed to prepare him for a glorious future, and one in which only the elect were to share. Everything that did not actively help towards that end was evil; all who did not work towards that end were evil-doers. The pagan and his easy-going paganism were alike accursed and tolerance a sin.

The contest between two such schools of thought—however long drawn out—could have but one conclusion. Capricious persecutions, on civil rather than religious grounds, gave the iconoclasts the one remaining impetus needed to snatch the sceptre of the world. Successful, they persecuted in their turn, systematically and with the thoroughness born of conscious virtue. In spite—

or because of—such attempts to stamp out pagan and paganism together, the old order still survived in secret long after the known world was officially Christianised. Naturally enough, the Christian could only suppose that such criminal persistence was the direct work of that Evil One whom he first had exploited. Pagan rites were nothing more nor less to him than Devil worship, those who practised them the direct representatives of Satan. Some of the pagan gods had been pressed into the service of Christianity as saints, their festivals as saints' days. Those that remained were classed together, with their ministers and attributes, under the generic heading of Magic, shunned and feared at first, but as the Church more and more stepped into the shoes of the civil power, warred upon without mercy.

Faced by such forcible arguments for conversion, the Pagan witch was not long in adopting the Christian Devil as a more potent protector than the old, easy-going gods who had formerly peopled the supernatural world. Pagan or nominal Christian, she was equally anathema to the Church, if only that she was consistently Protestant, claiming to hold direct communication with the Unseen quite regardless of the proper ecclesiastical channels. And by this very independence her hold upon the imagination of her neighbours continued to increase as Christianity progressed towards universal empire. The very definite pronouncements of the Church against witches, witchcraft, and all kinds of magic served to foster the general belief in their powers. What was so forcibly condemned must of necessity exist. There was, moreover, a certain satisfaction in this same tangibility. It simplified, smoothed out the path of virtue. With witchcraft about, your duty was plain and your task easy. You had but to mention a holy name, to make a sacred sign, to sprinkle a little holy water, and victory was assured. If all assaults of the devil were so straightforward and so vincible, the path to Heaven were broad and smooth indeed.

It was, perhaps, the popular sense of victorious ability against her spells which protected the witch, *per se*, against over-severe persecution until towards the twelfth and thirteenth centuries. Absolute confidence in the power to suppress an evil diminishes the urgency for its suppression. Here and there a witch was executed, local persecutions of inconsiderable extent occurred, but for general holocausts we must wait until the more enlightened times of a James I. or a Louis XIV. The witch of the Dark Ages might count upon a life of comparative security, sweetened by the offerings of those who, pining for present joys, acted upon the advice of Omar Khayyam rather than following that of their ghostly advisers. Meanwhile, however, a mass of tradition and precedent was growing up, to be put to deadly purpose in the animadversions of learned sixteenth and seventeenth century writers upon the vile and damnable sin of witchcraft.

By the eleventh century the witch was firmly identified, in the popular as well as the ecclesiastical mind, as a woman who had entered upon a compact with Satan for the overthrowing of Christ's kingdom. The popular conception of her personality had also undergone a change. By the twelfth century there was no more question of her as a fair enchantress—she was grown older and uglier, poorer and meaner, showing none of the advantages her compact with the Evil One might have been expected to bring in its train.

The increasing tendency towards dabbling in things forbidden brought about greater severity in its repression, but it was not until the days of Innocent VIII., when witchcraft was officially identified with heresy, that the period of cruel persecution may be said really to have begun. Sorcery in itself was bad enough; associated with heresy no crime was so pernicious and no punishment too condign, especially when inflicted by the Holy Inquisition. The inquisitorial power was frequently misused; the fact that the possessions of the accused became forfeit to her judges when tried in an ecclesiastical court may seem to the sceptic to provide ample reason why the ecclesiastical authorities undertook so many more prosecutions than did the civil. But of the absolute sincerity with which all classes set themselves to stamp out so dreadful a crime, the portentous and voluminous writings of the period leave no doubt whatever. Catholic and, after the Reformation, Protestant, rich and poor, patriot and philanthropist alike, vied with each other in the enthusiasm with which they scented out their prey, and the pious satisfaction with which they tortured helpless old women to the last extremity in the name of the All-Merciful.

From the fourteenth century onwards the type of recognised witch varies only in detail. Though not invariably she is commonly the conventional hag. If young, she has been led astray by a senior, or taken to the Sabbath in childhood under constraint—which was not, however, regarded as a valid defence in time of trial. Many such were executed in the sixteenth and seventeenth centuries, in many cases mere children. But it was the toothless hag whose mumblings held the public ear and became acknowledged as the truest type. Even when men ceased to fear her she lost nothing of her grotesque hideousness to the childish mind, and as such has become finally enshrined in the nursery lore of Europe. As such, also, I have endeavoured to reconstruct her in her habit as she lived in the eyes of her mediæval contemporaries elsewhere in this volume.

IV. THE HALF-WAY WORLDS

Having decided, very early in his earthly career, to acknowledge a supernatural world, Man promptly set to work to people it after his own image. One not providing scope for his quickening imagination, he added another to it, supplementing the heavenly by the infernal, good by evil—if, indeed, as is more probable, he did not rather deduce good out of evil. But just as there are many stages between high noon and midnight, so to the world he saw and those he imagined he added yet others which should act as their connecting links. Between the divine and the human he placed the semi-divine, between the human and the infernal the half-human. He mated God with Man and both with Devil, and dowered them with a numerous family, God-Man, Man-Devil, God-Devil, and so on, until the possibilities of his earlier imagination were exhausted. Each has his own world—and the stars cannot rival them in number; each world has its cities and its nations, differing in all things save one—that all alike feel, act, think, after the manner of mankind. So is it, again, with the other universe of half-way worlds, filling the space between the human and the bestial—centaur, satyr, were-wolf, or mermaid, all alike reflect the human imagination that has evolved them—to nondescript bodies they unite the reflected mind of man.

Conforming to the general rule, the witch is but one dweller in a half-way world that is thickly populated and in itself forms one of an intricate star-group. Externally at least, its orbit nearly coincides with that of our human world, in that its inhabitants are for the most part of human origins acquiring those attributes which raise them above —or degrade them below—the commonalty subsequently to their birth. This not invariably—nothing is invariable to the imagination. Thus the fairies, although not human beings, may yet be witches—demons also, unless many grave and reverend authorities lie. Under certain conditions they may even become human beings, as mermaids may—many a man has married a fairy wife

—and it is an open question whether they have altogether lost their hope of Heaven, as witches invariably have. As witches, they must be regarded as belonging to the White, or beneficent, type; for although, as Mercutio has told us, they may sometimes play unkind pranks upon the idle or undeserving, they have always a kindly eye for the virtuous, and frequently devote themselves altogether to good works, as in the case of Lob-lie-by-the-Fire, and others equally difficult to catalogue. For the more we investigate the various orbits of the half-way worlds, the more do we find them inextricably interwoven. The Western Fairy or Oriental Djinn may partake of half-a-hundred different natures—may pervade half the imaginative universe—and as does the Fairy, so does the Witch. Hecate, a goddess, was yet no less notorious a witch than was Mother Shipton, a human being of no elevated rank. The werewolf, though usually of human parentage, might yet have been born a wolf and obtained the power of taking human shape from some subsequent external cause. The Beast in the fairy story, though at heart a youthful Prince of considerable attractions, once transmogrified might have remained a Beast for good and all but for his fortunate encounter with Beauty's father. Who shall say exactly in which world to place, how to class beyond possibility of confusion, Circe—witch, goddess, and woman, and the men she turned to swine—or the fairies and mermaids who have, usually for love, divested themselves of their extra-human attributes and become more or less permanently women—or those human children who, stolen by the fairies, have become fairies for good and all—or how distinguish between all of these and the ladies with romantic names and uncertain aspirates who deal out destinies in modern Bond Street.

Even if we agree to confine the witch to the narrowest limits, to regard her, that is to say, as primarily a human being and only incidentally possessed of superhuman powers and attributes, there still remain many difficulties in the way of exact classification. Her powers are varied, and by no means always common to every individual. Or, again, she has the power to turn herself corporeally into a wolf or a cat—which brings her into line with the were-wolf, just as the cat or wolf may under certain circumstances transform themselves, permanently or otherwise, into a human witch. She may acquire the mind of a wolf without its body; on the other hand, many a beautiful princess has been transformed into a white doe by witchcraft. So with her male colleagues—sorcerer, magician, wizard, warlock, male-witch, diviner, and the rest of the great family. *We* may reach firm ground by agreeing to recognise only such as are of human origin, though by so doing we rule out many of the most eminent—the great Merlin himself among them. But even so, it is impossible to dogmatise as to where the one begins, the other ends. There have been many male-witches—more particularly in Scotland—as distinguished from wizards. Wizard and warlock again, if it be safe to regard them as distinct species, though differing from magician and sorcerer, are yet very difficult of disentanglement. The position is complicated by the fact that, just as a man may be clerk, singer, cricketer, forger, philanthropist, and stamp-collector at one and the same time, so might one professor of the Black Art take half a dozen shapes at the same time or spread over his career.

There is indeed but one pinnacle of solid rock jutting out from the great quagmire of shifting uncertainty—witch, wizard, were-wolf, or whatsoever their sub-division—one and all unite in one great certainty: that of inevitable damnation. Whatever their form, however divergent their powers, to that one conclusion they must come at last. And thus, and only thus, we may know them—posthumously.

It is true that certain arbitrary lines may be

drawn to localise the witch proper, even though the rules be chiefly made up of exceptions. Thus she is, for the most part, feminine. The Scots male-witch, and those elsewhere occurrent in the sixteenth and seventeenth centuries, might as correctly be termed wizards or warlocks, for any absolute proof to the contrary. The witch, again, has seldom risen to such heights in the profession as have her male competitors. The magician belongs, as we have seen, to a later stage of human development than does the witch, but, once evolved, he soon left her far behind; it is true that he was able to avail himself of the store of knowledge by her so slowly and painfully acquired. With its aid he soon raised himself to the highest rank in the profession—approaching it from the scientific standpoint, and leaving her to muddle along empirically and by rule of thumb. Nor was he content until he had made himself master of the Devil—using Satan and all his imps for his own private ends—while the less enterprising witch never rose to be more than the Devil's servant, or at best his humble partner in ill-doing.

The Magician, whatsoever his own private failings, has certainly deserved well of posterity. Just as the quack and the Bond Street sybil are representatives of the witch in the direct line, so, from the alchemist and the sorcerer are descended the great scientists of our own day—an impious brood indeed, who deny that their own father was aught but an impostor and a charlatan. The proprietor of, let us say, "Dr. Parabole's Pellets," is own brother—illegitimate though he be—to the discoverer of the Rontgen ray. The researches of the old-time sorcerer into the Forbidden, whatever their immediate profit, at least pointed out the direction for more profitable researches. Merlin, Cornelius Agrippa, or Albertus Magnus, had they been born in our day, would certainly have achieved the Fellowship of the Royal Society—and with good reason. It is to the search after the philosopher's stone and the elixir vitæ that we owe the discovery of radium. It was only by calling in the aid of the Devil that mankind acquired the prescience of a God.

The witch proper, on the other hand, did not trouble herself with research work. Having attained that dominion over her fellows dear to the heart of woman, she was content to rest upon her laurels. Certain incantations or charms, learned by rote, the understanding of the effect and cure of certain poisons—these were sufficient stock-in-trade to convince her neighbours, and perhaps herself. Doubtless Dr. Parabole, however aware in the beginning of the worthlessness of his own pills, comes after years of strenuous advertising to believe in them. He may stop short of taking them himself—at least he will prescribe them to his dearest friend in absolute good faith. So with the witch, his grandmother. Many, no doubt, of the millions offered up as sacrifice to the All-Merciful, were guiltless even in intention; many more allowed themselves to be convinced of their own sinfulness by the suspicions of their neighbours or the strenuous arguments of their judge-persecutors; many were hysterical, epileptic, or insane. But the larger proportion, it is scarcely too much to say, only lacked the power while cherishing the intention—witches they were in everything but witchcraft.

We thus may briefly state the difference between the witch and the magician as that the one professed powers in which she might herself believe or not believe, inherited or received by her, and by her passed on to her successors without any attempt to augment them. The magician, on the other hand, was actually a student of the mysteries he professed, and thus, if we leave aside his professional hocus-pocus devilry, cannot be considered as altogether an impostor. With the alchemist and the astrologer, more often than not combining the three characters in his one person, he stands at the head of the profession of which the witch—male or female—brings up the rear.

Another distinction is drawn by sixteenth-century authorities between witches and conjurers on the one side, and sorcerers and enchanters on the other—in that while the two first-mentioned have personal relations with the Devil, their colleagues deal only in medicines and charms, without, of necessity, calling up apparitions at all. It is to be noted in this connection that the sorcerer often leads Devil and devilkin by the nose, in more senses than one—devils having extremely delicate noses, and being thus easily soothed and enticed by fumigations, a peculiarity of which every competent sorcerer avails himself. Thus, Saint Dunstan, and those other saints of whom it is recorded that they literally led the Devil by the nose, using red-hot pincers for the purpose, were but following the path pointed out for them by professors of the Art Magical.

Between the witch and the conjurer a wide gulf is fixed. The conjurer coerces the Devil, against his infernal will, by prayers and the invocation of God's Holy Name; the witch concludes with him a business agreement, bartering her body, soul, and obedience for certain more or less illusory promises. The conjurer is almost invariably beneficent, the witch usually malignant, though the White Witch exercises her powers only for good, if sometimes with a certain mischievousness, while the Grey Witch does good or evil as the fancy takes her, with a certain bias towards evil. The wizard, again, though often confused with the male-witch, is in reality a practitioner of great distinction, possessing supernatural powers of his own attaining, and, like the magician, constraining the Devil rather than serving him. He also is capable of useful public service, so much so indeed that Melton, in his "Astrologastra," published in 1620, includes what may pass as a Post Office Directory of the wizards of London. He enumerates six of importance, some by name, as Dr. Forman or "Young Master Olive in Turnbull Street," others by vaguer designations, as "the cunning man of the Bankside" or "the chirurgeon with the bag-pipe cheek." He includes one woman in the list, probably a White Witch.

The Diviners, or peerers into the future, form yet another sub-section of dabblers in the supernatural—and one which numbers very many practitioners even in our own day. Naturally enough, seeing that the desire to influence the future is the obvious corollary to that of knowing it, the part of diviner was more often than not doubled with that of witch or sorcerer. Divination is an art of the most complicated, boasting almost as many branches as medicine itself, each with its select band of practitioners. Different nations, again, favoured different methods of divining—thus the Hebrews placed most confidence in Urim and Thummim; the Greeks were famous for axinomancy, the machinery for which consisted of an axe poised upon a slate or otherwise handled. This method was as apt for present as for future needs, being especially potent in the discovery of criminals. Crime detection by divination has been—and remains—greatly favoured in the East. The Hindus, in particular, place greater reliance upon it than upon the more usual methods of our Occidental police, and many stories are told of the successes achieved by their practitioners. Nor is this surprising in cases where the diviner shows such shrewd knowledge of human nature as in that, oft-quoted, whereby all those under suspicion of a theft are ranged in a row and presented with mouthfuls of grain, with the assurance that the guilty man alone will be unable to swallow it—a phenomenon which nearly always does occur if the thief be among those present—and not infrequently when he is not! This and similar stories, though scarcely falling under the heading of divination proper, are so far pertinent to the subject that they suggest the explanation of many of its more remarkable successes. Tell a nervous man that he is destined to commit suicide upon a certain day, and, granted that he has any faith in your prophetic powers, the odds are that he will prove the correctness of your prophecy. We may compare with this the powerful influence of "tapu" upon the South Sea Island mind. Many natives have died—as has been vouched for by hundreds of credit-worthy witnesses—for no more tangible reason than fear at having incurred the curse of desecrating something placed under its protection. It may be added that the Islanders, observing that white men do not suffer the same fate, account for it by declaring that the White Man's Gods, being of a different persuasion from their own, protect their own votaries.

Divination proper takes almost innumerable forms. Without entering too closely upon a wide subject, a few examples may be profitably quoted. Among the best known are Belomancy, or divination by the flight of arrows, a form much favoured by the Arabs; Bibliomancy (of which the "Sortes Virgilianæ" is the most familiar example); Oneiromancy (or divination by dreams, honoured by Archbishop Laud and Lord Bacon among others); Rhabdomancy (by rods or wands. The "dowser," or water-finder, whose exploits have aroused so much attention of recent years, is obviously akin to the Rhabdomancist). Crystallomancy, or crystal-gazing, was first popularised in this country by the notorious Dr. Dee, and still finds many votaries in Bond Street and elsewhere. Hydromancy, or divination by water, is another variety much favoured by the Bond Street sybil, a pool of ink sometimes taking the place of the water. Cheiromancy, or Palmistry, most popular of any, may possess some claim to respect in its least ambitious form as a means towards character reading. Divination by playing-cards, another popular method, is, needless to say, of later, mediæval origin. The Roman augurs, who, as every schoolboy knows, deduced the future from the flight of birds, provide yet another example of this universal pastime, perhaps the least harmful sub-section of the Black Arts.

Among the most brilliant luminaries of the half-way worlds are those twin-stars inhabited by the Alchemist and the Astrologer. The pseudo-science of star-reading may be supposed to date from the first nightfall—and may thus claim a pedigree even older, if only by a few months or years, than that of Magic proper. Alchemy, despite its Moorish name, has a scarcely less extended history. It owes its birth—traditionally, at any rate—to the same Egyptian Man-God who first introduced witchcraft and magic in their regularised forms to an expectant world. Its principles having been by him engraved in Punic characters upon an emerald, were discovered in his tomb by no less a person than Alexander the Great. It should perhaps be added that doubts have been cast upon this resurrection. However that may be, it was much practised by the later Greeks in Constantinople from the fifth century A.D. until the Moslem conquest of the city. From them the Arabs adopted it, gave it the name by which it has ever since been known, and became the most successful of its practitioners.

To attempt any close study of the great alchemists were foreign to my present purpose, and would entail more space than is at my disposal. At the same time, so close was their connection, in the eyes of the vulgar, so intimate their actual relationship with witchcraft, that it is impossible altogether to ignore them. What is more, they lend to the witch a reflected respectability such as she can by no means afford to forgo. They held, in fact, in their own day, much the same position as do the great inventors and scientists of to-day. Mr. Edison and Mr. Marconi, had they been born ten centuries since, would certainly have taken exalted rank as alchemists or magicians. As it is, in ten centuries a whole world of magical romance will have been very likely woven about their names, even if they have not been actually exalted to divinity or inextricably confused with Lucifer and Prometheus. While some of their predecessors may have actually claimed power over the supernatural—either in self-deception or for self-aggrandisement—the great majority undoubtedly had such claims thrust upon them, either by their contemporaries or by posterity, and would have themselves claimed nothing higher than to be considered students of the unknown. The Philosopher's Stone and the Elixir Vitæ may have served indeed as the ideal goal of their researches, much as they do under their modern form of the Secret of Life in our own time; but their actual discoveries, accidental and incidental though they may have been, were none the less valuable. After such a lapse of time it is as difficult to draw the line between the alchemist-scientist and the charlatan as it will be a century hence to distinguish the false from the true among the "inventors" and "scientists" of to-day, so absolutely do the mists of tradition obscure the face of history. Leaving out of the question such purely legendary figures as Merlin, we may class them under three headings, and briefly consider one example under each. In the first may be placed the more or less mythical figures of Gebir and Albertus Magnus, both of whom, so far as it is now possible to judge, owe their ambiguous reputations entirely to the superstitions of their posterity.

Such a personage as the great Arabian physician Gebir, otherwise Abou Moussah Djafar, surnamed Al Sofi, or the Wise, living in the eighth century, was certain to gain the reputation of possessing supernatural power, even had he not busied himself in the discovery of the Philosopher's Stone and the Elixir. Though he found neither, he yet in seeking them made other discoveries little less valuable, and it is scarcely too much to say, made their discovery possible in later centuries. Thus, in default of the means of making gold, he gave us such useful chemicals as nitric acid, nitrate of silver, and oxide of copper. Incidentally he wrote several hundred treatises on his two "subjects," an English translation of one, the "Summæ Perfectionis," having been published in 1686 by Richard Russell, himself an alchemist of respectable attainments.

Albertus Magnus, again, gave every excuse to the vulgar for regarding him as infernally inspired. That is to say, he was a scholar of great attainments in a day when scholars were chiefly remarkable for their dense ignorance, and fully deserved some less ambiguous sobriquet than that bestowed upon him by some writers of "Founder of the Schoolmen." A Dominican, he held the chair of Theology at Padua in 1222 while still a young man. Grown weary of a sedentary life, he resigned his professorship and taught in many of the chief European cities, and more particularly in Paris, where he lived for three years in company with his illustrious pupil, Thomas Aquinas. He was at one time appointed Bishop of Regensburg, but very soon resigned, finding his episcopal duties interfere with his studies. Of the twenty-five folios from his pen, one is devoted to alchemy, and he was a magician of the first class—so, at least, succeeding generations averred, though he himself very likely had no suspicions thereof. Among other of his possessions was a brazen statue with the gift of speech, a gift exercised with such assiduity as to exhaust the patience even of the saintly Thomas Aquinas himself, so that he was constrained to shatter it to pieces.

Roger Bacon, inventor and owner of an even more famous brazen head, was no less illustrious a scholar, and as fully deserved his admiring nickname "The Admirable Doctor," even though he were not in actual fact the inventor of gunpowder and the telescope, as asserted by his admirers. A native of Somerset, and born, traditionally, the year before the signing of Magna Charta, he might have ranked among the greatest Englishmen had not his reputation as a magician given him the suggestion of being a myth altogether. Something of a heretic he was, although in orders, and his writings brought down upon him the suspicions of the General of the Franciscan Order, to which he belonged. Pope Clement IV. extended protection to him for a time, even to the extent of studying his works, and more particularly his "Magnum Opus," but later the Franciscan General condemned his writings, and he spent fourteen years in prison, being released only two years before his death. But his historical achievements were as nothing to his legendary possession, in partnership with Friar Bungay, of the Talking Head. Less garrulous than Albertus' statue, it emitted only three sentences: "Time is. Time was. Time is past." Its last dictum, having unfortunately for all audience a foolish servant, and being by him held up to ridicule, it fell to the ground and was smashed to pieces, thus depriving its inventor of his cherished scheme—by its help to surround England with a brazen rampart no whit less efficacious against the assaults of the King's enemies than are our present-day ironclads.

Friar Bacon was not undeserving of the posthumous popularity he achieved in song and story, for he it was who made magic and alchemy really popular pursuits in this country. So numerous were his imitators that rather more than a century after his death—in 1434—the alchemical manufacture of gold and silver was declared a felony.

Twenty-one years later Henry VI., being, as he usually was, in urgent need of ready money, saw reason to modify the Governmental attitude, and granted a number of patents—to ecclesiastics as well as laymen—for seeking after the Philosopher's Stone, with the declared purpose of paying the Royal debts out of the proceeds. In which design he was, it is to be feared, disappointed.

Dr. Dee, the friend and gossip of Queen Elizabeth, may be taken as marking the point at which the alchemist ceases to be an inhabitant of any half-way world and becomes altogether human. A Londoner by birth, he was born in 1527, became a B.A. of Cambridge University and Rector of Upton-upon-Severn. His ecclesiastical duties could not contain his energies, and so well versed did he become in arts magical that, upon a waxen effigy of Queen Elizabeth being found in Lincoln's Inn Fields—and a waxen effigy had only one meaning in Elizabeth's time—he was employed to counteract the evil spells contained in it, which he did with such conspicuous success that the Royal Person suffered no ill-effects whatever. Unfortunately for himself, Dr. Dee acquired in course of time a disciple, one Edward Kelly. Kelly proved an apt daunter of demons, but he was totally lacking in the innocent credulity so noticeable in the character of his reverend mentor. At his prompting Dr. Dee undertook a Continental tour, which resulted in disaster of the most overwhelming and the total loss of Dr. Dee's good name. It is true that he may be considered to have deserved his fate, for so absolute was his belief in his disciple that when that *chevalier d'industrie* received a message from a demoniacal familiar that it was essential for the success of their alchemical enterprises that they should exchange wives—Mrs. Dee being as well-favoured as Mrs. Kelly was the reverse—the doctor accepted the situation with implicit faith, and agreed to all that the spirits desired.

Among other seekers after the Philosopher's Stone and the Elixir Vitse who may be briefly referred to were Alain de l'Isle, otherwise Alanus de Insulis, notable in that he actually discovered the elixir, if his contemporaries may be believed, and who so far lived up to his reputation as to defer his death, which occurred in 1298, until his 110th year; Raymond Lully, who, visiting England in or about 1312, was provided with a laboratory within the precincts of Westminster Abbey, where many years later a supply of gold-dust was found; Nicholas Flamel, who died in 1419, and who gained most of his occult knowledge from a volume written in Latin by the Patriarch Abraham; and, to come to later years, William Lilly, a famous English practitioner of the seventeenth century, and an adept in the use of the divining rod, with which he sought for hidden treasures in Westminster Abbey, possibly those left behind him by Raymond Lully.

Perhaps no symptom of civilisation is more disquieting than the increasing tendency to compress the half-way worlds—built up by our forefathers with such lavish expenditure of imagination—into the narrow limits of that in which we are doomed to spend our working days—not too joyously. We have seen how the alchemist and the magician from semi-divine beings, vested with power over gods and men, have by degrees come to be confounded with the cheap-jack of a country fair. So it has been with many another denizen of the Unseeable. Consider, for example, the once formidable giant. Originally gods, or but little inferior to them, so that Olympus must exercise all its might to prevail against them; at one time a nation in themselves, located somewhere in Cornwall, with kings of their own, Corcoran, Blunderbore, and the rest, aloof from man except when, for their pastime or appetite, they raided his preserves, vulnerable, indeed, though only to a superhuman Jack; where are your giants now? Goliath, though defeated by David, was yet not dishonoured, in that he was warring not against a puny, sling-armed shepherd, but against the whole might of the Jewish Jehovah. There were giants on the earth in those days, the Scriptures tell us, and that in terms giving us to understand that a giant was to be regarded with respect, if not with admiration. Polyphemus, again, though outwitted by a mortal, was none the less a figure almost divine, god-like in his passions and his agony. The whole ancient world teems with anecdotes, all proving the respectability of the old-time giant. And to-day? I saw a giant myself some few years back. He was in a show—and he was known as Goliath. A poor, lean, knock-kneed wavering creature, half-idiotic, too, with a sickly, apologetic smile, as though seeking to disarm the inevitable criticism his very existence must provoke. Yet he was not to blame, poor, anachronistic wretch. Rather it was the spirit of the age, that preferred to see him, set up for every fool to jeer at, at sixpence a time, in a showman's booth, rather than to watch him afar off, his terror magnified by distance, walking across a lonely heath in the twilight, bearing a princess or a captive knight along with him as his natural prey. The same spirit that has made the giant shrink to an absurdity can see only the charlatan beneath the flowing robes of the astrologer; and has argued the witch even out of existence.

So it is with the mermaid. They showed one at the same booth wherein the degenerate giant was mewed. A poor, shrunken, grotesque creature enough, yet even so it might have passed for a symbol, if no more, had they been content to leave it to our imagination. Instead they must explain, even while they pocketed our sixpences, that the whole thing was a dreary sham, concocted out of the forequarters of a monkey and the tail end of a codfish, the whole welded together by the ingenious fingers of some Japanese trickmonger. Yet there are those who would uphold such cruel candour, who would prefer to pay sixpence in order to see an ape-codfish rather than to remain in blissful ignorance, rather than imagine that every wave may have its lovely tenant, a sea-maiden of more than earthly tenderness and beauty. Civilisation prates to us of dugongs and of manatees, and other fish-beasts that, it says, rising upon the crest of a wave, sufficiently resemble the human form to be mistaken for it by credulous, susceptible mariners. But is not our faith in that tender story of the little mermaid who, for love of a man, sought the earth in human shape even though she knew that every step must cause her agony, every footmark be outlined with her blood—is not it better for us to believe that fairy-tale than to cram our weary brains with all the cynical truths of all the dime-museums or schools of science between London and San Francisco?

Even those who smile at Neptune and his daughters cannot refuse the tribute of a shudder to the Man-Beast. For however it be with the mermaid, the were-wolf is no figment of the imagination. Not the fanciful alone are convinced that many human beings partake of the nature of certain beasts. You may pass them by the hundred in every city street—men and women showing in their faces their kinship with the horse, the dog, cat, monkey, lion, sparrow. And not in their faces alone—for their features do but reflect the minds within them—the man with the sharp, rat-like face nine times out of ten has all the selfish cunning of the rat. We have no need to seek for further explanation of the centaur myth—to argue that some horseless nation, seeing horsemen for the first time, accepted the man and his mount as one and indivisible; there are plenty of men who have as much of the equine as of the human in their composition. So it is with the wolf-man—the were-wolf. He exists, and to this day, despite all your civilising influences. Not among savages alone—or chiefly. He roams the streets of our great cities, seeking his prey. Perhaps he lives in the next street to you—a prosperous, respected citizen, with a shop in Cheapside, a wife and family, and the regard of all his neighbours. The wolf in him has never been aroused—may never be. Only, let Fate or chance so will it, and—well, who can tell us Jack the Ripper's antecedents? And where in all the annals of lycanthropy can you find a grimmer instance of the man-wolf than Jack the Ripper?

With the were-wolf we return to closer contact with witchcraft proper. It is true that the werewolf was not always bewitched. Sometimes the tendency was inborn—the man or woman was transformed into the wolf at each recurrent full moon. In France—and more particularly in the South, where lycanthropy has always had one of its strongholds—the liability of certain individuals, especially if they be born illegitimate, to this inconvenience is still firmly credited by the popular mind. The were-wolf may be recognised for that matter, even when in his human form, usually by the shape of his broad, short-fingered hands and his hairy palm. It is even possible to effect a permanent cure should the opportunity occur, and that by the simple means of stabbing him three times in the forehead with a knife while in his lupine shape. Again, in Scandinavia and elsewhere certain men could transform themselves into wolves at will—a superstition arising naturally enough out of traditions of the Berserkers and the fits of wolfish madness into which they threw themselves. Yet again, as Herodotus tells us, lycanthropy was sometimes a national observance. The Neuri, if the Scythians were to be believed, were in the habit of changing themselves into wolves once a year and remaining in that shape for several days. But more frequently the change was attributable to some evil spell cast by a witch. It is true that the wolf was only one of many animals into whose shape she might condemn a human soul to enter. Circe is, of course, a classical example; Saint Augustine, in his "De Civitate Dei," relates how an old lady of his acquaintance used to turn men into asses by means of enchantments—an example which has been followed by younger ladies ever since, by the way—while Apuleius' "Golden Ass" gives us an autobiographical testimony to the efficacy of certain drugs towards the same end.

Doubtless because the wolf was extirpated in this country at a comparatively early date English were-wolf legends are few and far between. They could indeed only become universally current in a country mainly pastoral and infested by wolves, as, for instance, in ancient Arcadia, where indeed the were-wolf came into his highest estate, or in many parts of Eastern and South-Eastern Europe to-day. In certain Balkan districts the were-wolf shares the attributes of the vampire, another allied superstition which is by no means without its foundations of fact. Most people must have, indeed, been acquainted at some time or other with the modern form of vampire, individuals who unconsciously feed upon the vitality of those with whom they come into contact. Many stories have been written, many legends founded upon this phenomenon, to the truth of which many people have testified from their own experience. At which point I leave the subject to those with more scientific knowledge than myself.

In case there should be any who desire to transform themselves into a wolf without the trouble and expense of resorting to a witch, I will close this chapter with a spell warranted to produce the desired effect without any further outlay than the price of a small copper knife. It is of Russian origin, and is quoted from Sacharow by Mr. Baring Gould. "He who desires to become an oborot" (oborot = "one transformed" = werewolf) let him seek in the forest a hewn-down tree; let him stab it with a small copper knife and walk round the tree, repeating the following incantation:

> *On the sea, on the ocean, on the island,*
>   *on Bujan,*

*On the empty pasture gleams the moon,
   on an ash-stock lying
In a greenwood, in a gloomy vale.
Towards the stock wandereth a shaggy
   wolf,
Horned cattle seeking for his sharp
   white fangs;
But the wolf enters not the forest,
But the wolf dives not into the shadowy
   vale.
Moon, moon, gold-horned moon
Check the flight of bullets, blunt the
   hunters' knives,
Break the shepherds' cudgels,
Cast wild fear upon all cattle,
On men, on all creeping things,
That they may not catch the grey wolf,
That they may not rend his warm skin!
My word is binding, more binding than
   sleep,
More binding than the promise of a
   hero!*

"Then he springs thrice over the tree and runs into the forest, transformed into a wolf."

V. THE WITCH'S ATTRIBUTES

In his very learned and exhaustive treatise, "De la Démonomanie des Sorciers," the worthy Bodin, with enterprise worthy of a modern serial-story writer, keeps his reader's curiosity whetted to its fullest by darkly hinting his knowledge of awesome spells and charms commonly employed by Satan's servants. Unlike the modern writer, however, he refrains from detailing them at length in his last chapter, fearing to impart knowledge which may easily be put to the worst account. However valuable a testimony to his good faith and discretion, this would certainly have brought down upon him the strictures of modern critics, and might indeed have entailed serious loss to the world had not other less conscientious writers more than rectified the omission.

It were, of course, impossible to include within the limits of such a volume as is this—or of a hundred like it—one tithe of the great store of spells, charms, and miscellaneous means towards enchantment gathered together in the long centuries since the birth of the first witch. So also it is impossible to select any particular stage in her long evolution as the most characteristic, as regards her manners and customs, of all that we imply by the word "witch." On the other hand, she has definitely crystallised in the minds of those of us who have ever been children, in the shape of the "horrid old witch" of fairy lore; and just as, in a preceding chapter, I have endeavoured to reproduce one of her working days—as imaged in the popular mind—so the witch of the Middle Ages may best be chosen when we would reconstruct her more human aspect.

Of her actual appearance, divested of her infernal attributes, no better description could be desired than that given by Reginald Scot in "The Discoverie of Witchcraft":—"Witches be commonly old, lame, bleare-eied, pale, fowle, and full of wrinkles; poore, sullen, superstitious, and papists"—(it is perhaps unnecessary to point out that Scot was of the Reformed Faith)—"or such as know no religion; in whose drousie minds the devill hath goten a fine seat; so as, what mischiefe, mischance, calamitie or slaughter is brought to passe, they are easilie persuaded the same is doone by themselves, imprinting in their minds an earnest and constant imagination hereof. They are leane and deformed, showing melancholie in their faces to the horror of all that see them. They are doting, scolds, mad, divilish."

Endowed with so unfortunate a personality, it is not surprising that, as Scot goes on to inform us, the witch should have found it difficult to make a living. It is indeed an interesting example of the law of supply and demand that such woeful figures being needed for the proper propagation of the witch-mania, the conditions of mediæval life, by their harsh pressure upon the poor and needy among women, should have provided them by the score in every village. You may find the conventional witch-figure to-day in the lonely hamlet or in the city workhouse, but, thanks to our better conditions of life, she has become almost as rare as have accusations of witchcraft against her.

The only means of subsistence open to her, Scot goes on, is to beg from house to house. In time it comes about that people grow weary of her importunities. Perhaps they show their impatience too openly. "Then," says Scot, "she curses one or the other, from the master of the house to the little pig that lieth in the stie." Someone in the wide range between those two extremes will be certain to suffer some kind of mischance before long—on much the same principle as that which gives life to one of our most popular present-day superstitions, the ill-luck attending a gathering of "thirteen at table." Any such disaster is naturally attributed to the old beggar-woman—who is thus at once elevated to the dangerous eminence of witch-hood. Nor did the sufferer always wait for her curse. Edward Fairfax, for example, the learned seventeenth century translator of Tasso, upon an epidemic sickness attacking his children, sought out their symptoms in a "book of medicine." Not finding any mention of "such agonies" as those exhibited by his children, he determined that some unholy agency must be at work. His thoughts turned, naturally enough, to the gloomy forest of Knaresborough, within convenient distance of his abode. Nothing could be more suspicious than the mere fact of living in such a suggestive locality, yet Margaret White, widow of a man executed for theft, her daughter, and Jennie Dibble, an old widow coming of a family suspected of witchcraft for generations past, were imprudent, or unfortunate, enough to live within its borders. The natural result attended their rashness—and so earnest was the worthy Fairfax that he set the whole proceedings down in a book, adding a minute account of the symptoms and delusions of the invalids.

As the King has his orb and sceptre, the astrologer his spheres and quadrant, so the witch has her insignia of office. And it is a strong indication of her descent from the first house-wife that most of them are domestic or familiar objects.

The imp or "familiar" who attends her may have the form of a bird or dog, but is far more often the most domestic animal of all, the cat. Frequently it is malformed or monstrous, in common with Satan himself and all the beings who owe him allegiance. It may have any number of legs, several tails, or none at all; its mewing is diabolic; it may be far above the usual stature of its kind. Usually it is black, but is equally eligible if white or yellow. As is a common incident of all religions, the symbol is sometimes confused with the office, the witch and her cat exchanging identities. Thus witches have confessed under torture to have formerly been cats, and to owe their human shape to Satan's interference with natural laws. A piebald cat is said to become a witch if it live for nine years, and the witch, when upon a nefarious errand, frequently assumes a feline shape.

A characteristic of the witch, in common with demons and imps in general, is that she does everything contrary to the tastes and customs of good Christians. With the one steady exception of the cat, she most esteems animals repellent to the ordinary person, to women in particular, and her imps may appear as rats or mice, usually tailless, spiders, fleas, nits, flies, toads, hares, crows, hornets, moles, frogs, or, curiously enough, domestic poultry. An important item in her outfit is her broomstick—as homely an insignia as the cat. Its feminine connection is obvious, though possibly its power of flight may be derived from the magic wand. Smeared with a Satanic ointment, it acts as her chariot, or is prepared to serve her as a weapon of offence or defence—and woe to him who suffers a beating from the witch's broom-handle.

The spindle, emblem of domesticity, becomes in the witch's hands a maleficial instrument, and may be applied by her to a number of evil uses. The idea of the thread of life enters into many mythologies, and it, from some confusion of ideas, may well have been instrumental in transforming the natural occupation of an old woman into one of the dangerous tricks of witchcraft.

Just as "loathly" reptiles, the snake, the lizard, and the toad, stand in close relation to the witch, so plants growing in suggestive places or notoriously poison-bearing are especially connected with her. Hemlock, mandrake, henbane, deadly nightshade—or moonshade, as it was sometimes called—saffron, poplar-leaves, all avoided by the common folk, are held in high esteem by Satan's servants for their use in the concoction of love-philtres and other noxious brews.

For the brewing of potions a cauldron is a matter of course, and the mixtures popularly supposed to have been brewed in it were enough to have given it an evil reputation for all time.

The enumeration of their ingredients is unpleasantly suggestive, even to the unbeliever, and the credulous may well have shuddered at such a mixture as:

> *Eye of newt and toe of frog,*
> *Wool of bat and tongue of dog,*
> *Adder's fork and blindworm's sting,*
> *Lizard's leg and howlet's wing,*
> . . . .
> *Liver of blaspheming Jew,*
> *Gall of goat and slips of yew,*
> . . . .
> *Finger of birth-strangled babe, &c., &c.*

It is true that a Macbeth was not to be catered for every day, and simpler effects could have been obtained by less complicated, though perhaps not less unappetising means.

Of all these insignia and attributes of her office the most important, as the most characteristic, were her "familiars" or imps. In mediæval real life, just as in modern fairy-lore, the witch's possession of a cat—or other animal, however harmless it might seem—was proof positive of her guilt. Without her familiar, indeed, she could scarcely have claimed the powers attributed to her, for, whatever its form, it was the ever-present reminder of her contract with their common master, and in many cases the channel through which his commands and the means for their carrying out were communicated to her. The infinite variations of form and kind of these same "imps" as set out in the proceedings at the trials, bear strong testimony of the wild imaginations possessed by our forefathers for the Devil, as we may prefer to believe. Thus Margaret White, in the Fairfax case just referred to, had for familiar a deformed creature with many feet, sooty in hue and rough-haired, being of name unknown. Her daughter, who resembled her in all things, with the addition of "impudency and lewd behaviour," had a white cat spotted with black. Jennie Dibble had a black cat called Gibbe, "who hath attended her above 40 yeares." All these imps, whatever their shape, obtained their nourishment by sucking their mistress's blood, leaving marks upon her body, which formed deadly evidence against her at her trial. Nor was there any hope of cheating justice by giving these devil's marks commonplace forms, for they were recognised even when made, by the Devil's cunning, to appear like moles, birthmarks, or even flea-bites!

There is some slight confusion about the provenance of this same witch-mark, unless it varied in individual cases—whether, that is to say, the marks were the result of suckling the imps, or whether, being already imprinted on the witch's body, they were selected for that reason. Certainly there is frequent reference to the ceremony of its imprinting immediately after the signature of the contract with Satan, and at the same time that her nickname and familiars were assigned to his new servant. Its object is ingeniously explained by the unctuous Pierre de Lancre, no mean authority. Satan, he tells us, wishing to ape God in all things, has instituted this marking of his servants in imitation of the stigmata and also of the circumcision. A more practical explanation, given by some writers, is that the Devil's mark, having the quality of itching at certain seasons, is conferred upon witches that they may never oversleep themselves and thus be late for the Sabbath ceremonies. The root of the whole matter, however, as the worthy Pierre is half-inclined to believe—and as some of us may be half-inclined to agree with him in thinking—is that the mark (he compares it to a toad's foot) has merely been instituted by Satan out of his love of importance and display, and with no further motive.

Although in earlier ages this formality may have been dispensed with, by the sixteenth century the witch invariably signed a definite contract with Satan. As was only too probable, seeing that they dispensed with an attorney, while the other person to the bargain, himself of no mean intelligence, might chose among an infinity of legal advisers, the contract was of a very one-sided nature. Nothing, at least, was ever outwardly visible of those advantages for which she bartered away body and soul. Even such satisfaction as may have come from attending the Sabbaths was dearly bought, for not only did her earthly neighbours show their resentment in the most forcible manner, but her reception by Satan, unless she had carried out his instructions to the furthest limit, was apt to be unamiable in the extreme. Of any more material satisfaction—save, of course, that, and it is perhaps as substantial as human happiness can be—of paying off old scores, there is no sign at all. It is perhaps this lack of business instinct which most markedly differentiates the witch from the sorcerer. He almost invariably gained whatever worldly advantages he desired during the term of his agreement, and not infrequently tricked Satan out of his share of the bargain at the end of it.

Of the preliminaries leading up to the bargain we are given an illuminating glimpse by Edward Fairfax in his already quoted book. His daughter Helen, being in a trance, saw the wife of one Thorp, and, with the impertinent enthusiasm of youth—as it now seems to us—urged her to pray "with such vehemence that Thorp's wife wept bitterly a long time. Then she asked her how she became a witch, and the woman answered that a man like to a man of this world came unto her upon the moor and offered her money, which at first she refused, but at the second time of his coming he did overcome her in such sort that she gave him her body and soul, and he made her a lease back again of her life for 40 years, which was now ended upon Shrove Tuesday last. The man did write their lease with their blood, and they likewise with their blood set their hands to them. That her lease was in his keeping, and every 7th year he showed it unto them, and now it was 3 years since she saw hers, and that each 7th year they renewed it. She said further that she knew 40 witches, but there were only 7 of her company." From other accounts we learn that in the act of signing the contract the witch frequently put one hand to the sole of her foot and the other to the crown of her head—a gymnastic exercise that can scarcely have been coincident—with the affixing of her signature, however. Anyone who, despite his cozening of witches, may urge the number of times when Satan was over-reached by sorcerers, as a proof that his intelligence is over-rated, may find evidence that he is occasionally gifted with business acumen in the confession of one M. Guillaume de Livre, Doctor of Theology, who was so unlucky as to be condemned for witchcraft in 1453. By the terms of his bargain with Satan he was bound to preach whenever possible that there was no such thing as real sorcery. "Such," as Bodin very acutely remarks, "are the wiles and lures of the Evil One."

Her contract once signed, the witch naturally became as soon as possible proficient in the "Devil's rudiments" which James I. describes as "unlawful charms without natural causes. Such kinde of charms as commonlie dafte wives use, for healing of forspoken goodes, for preserving them from evil eyes, by knitting roun trees or sundriest kinde of hearbes, to the haire or tailes of the goodes; by curing the worme, by stemming of bloode; by healing of Horse-crookes, by turning of the riddle, or doing of such-like innumerable things by words without applying anie-thing meete to the part offended, as Mediciners doe." "Children cannot smile upon a witch without the hazard of a perpetual wry smile," writes Stephens in 1615. "Her prayers and amens be a charm and a curse . . . her highest adoration hie yew trees, dampest churchyards, and a fayre moonlight; her best preservatives odde numbers and mightie Tetragrammaton."

Her crimes were many and varied enough to provide contemporary writers with long pages of delectable matter. Thus, Holland declares, in "A Treatise Against Witchcraft" (1590), that:—

> *They renounce God and all true religion.*
> *They blaspheme and provoke His Divine Majesty with unspeakable contempt.*
> *They believe in the Devill, adore him, and sacrifice unto him.*
> *They offer their children unto devills.*
> *They sweare unto Satan, and promise to*

> *bring as many as they can unto his service and profession.*
> *They invocate Satan in their praiers, and sweare by his name."*

Besides preaching gross immorality:—

> *They commit horrible murders, and kill young infants.*
> *All Sorcerers for the most part exercise poison, and to kill with poison is far more heinous than simple murder.*
> *They kill men's cattle.*
> *And, lastly, the witches (as they themselves confesse) commit many abominations and filthenes.*

Other accounts follow similar lines or add further indictments; as Jean Bodin, who also details the crimes of eating human flesh and drinking blood, destroying fruit and causing famine and sterility. Generally speaking, then, the crimes of witchcraft fall under the headings of offences against religion and the Church; of those against the community in general, such as causing epidemics or bad weather; and of those against individuals, including murder, especially of young children, causing disease, and injury to property.

Such catholic appreciation in wrong-doing could not fail to arouse the disapproval of all right-thinking people, and as the mere charge of witchcraft, supported by any one accusation, implied the perpetration of all these various misdeeds, it is scarcely wonderful that the witch, once apprehended, had small chance of escape.

Although less generally harmful in its effects, the witch's passion for aviation was as reprehensible as the rest of her proceedings. For one thing, it was generally considered an offensive parody of the angels mode of progression. Pierre de Lancre, indeed, who is unusually well informed, states this as a fact. He points out further that the good angels can fly much faster, being able to use their wings, while the witch has to make use of some artificial means of support, as, for example, a broomstick. It is characteristic of the cross-grained eccentricity of witches that whereas a good angel, like a good Christian, enters or leaves the room by the door, the witch prefers the less convenient egress of the chimney. This was the more aggravating that it rendered useless any attempts by beleaguering the house to catch her in the act, seeing that she only flies by night; and Satan further provides against discovery by allowing her to leave her imp in her own shape behind her, and thus, if need be, provide a satisfactory alibi. The only way of getting at the real fact of the matter was then by obtaining a confession from the witch herself—which could, however, usually be arranged for by the authorities. The broomstick, be it noted, was not an essential to the witch's aerial journeys; asses and horses, if properly anointed with witch-ointment, could be used at a pinch, as could a straw, an eggshell, or a barndoor fowl—to mention three out of many-possible mounts. Satan has been known to take upon himself the shape of a goat, and thus to provide a steed for those he most delights to honour. This is, however, attended by one grave and dangerous disadvantage. Satan hates the sound of churchbells, and should he hear the sound of the Ave Maria while carrying a witch through the air, will very likely drop her at once—as actually happened to a witch named Lucrece in 1524.

The ever-helpful De Lancre details four ways of getting to the Sabbath:

- (1) By thought or meditation, as in the vision of Ezekiel.
- (2) On foot.
- (3) By being carried through the air by Satan.
- (4) By going in dreams or illusions, which leave the witch uncertain

whether she has really been present in the flesh or only had a nightmare. But De Lancre is assured that the transport is real, seeing that they have actually been seen descending from the clouds, naked and often wounded, while they are often so exhausted thereafter as to be obliged to keep their beds for several days.

The ointment used by witches for such purposes are by many considered to have been but another instance of Satan's cunning and lack of good faith. As a tangible token of her service, they flatter the witch's sense of importance—though in themselves quite useless—while the obtaining of these ingredients necessitates a good deal of mischief being done to good Christians. Holland, who tells us that "Witches make oyntements of the fatte of young children" adds that Satan has no great opinion of the said "oyntements," but loves the bloodshed it entails. Wierus provides us with a more detailed gruesome recipe. By their spells witches cause young children to die in the cradle or by their mother's side. When they are dead, of suffocation or other causes, and have been buried, the witches take them out of the grave and boil them in a cauldron until the flesh leaves the bones, and the rest is as easy to drink as melted wax. Of the thicker portions the ointment is made; while whoever drinks the liquid will become mistress of the whole art of witchcraft. Bacon speaks of several other ingredients. To the customary fat of children "digged out of their graves," he adds the juices of smallage, wolf-bane, and cinque-foil, mingled with the meal of fine wheat, and, he says, "I suppose the soporiferous medicines are likest to do it, which are hen-bane, hemlock, mandrake, moon-shade, tobacco, opium, saffron, and poplar-leaves." Some are of opinion that such soporific elements are introduced into the ointment by the Devil in order to dull the senses of his servants, that he may the more easily do as he likes with them—but as those who have gone so far in procuring the *pièce de resistance* of the mixture are not likely to be over-scrupulous, such a precaution seems almost unnecessary.

The poisons, "charms" and baleful powders needed by the witches in their ordinary business-routine may be made either in their own domestic cauldron or at the Sabbath. They include such ingredients as the heads of toads, spiders, or the bark and pith of the "Arbre Maudit." The semi-solids are the most poisonous to human beings, while the liquid varieties are used to destroy crops and orchards. For doing damage on the sea or among the mountains, powders are well considered—made of toads' flesh, roasted, dried, and pulverised, and subsequently cast into the air or scattered on the ground, according to the circumstances of the case. Another and very baleful poison may be made of "green water"; so potent is it that even to touch it causes instant death. A paste entirely efficacious against confession under torture may be made with black millet mixed with the dried liver of an unbaptised child. A skinned cat, a toad, a lizard or an asp, roasted, dried, pulverised, and burned until required, may be put to excellent purposes of offence. Cast in the air or on the ground, with the words "This is for corn, this for apples," and so forth, such a powder, if used in sufficient quantities, will turn a smiling countryside into a desert. There is, indeed, one plant which resists all such spells—the common onion. Thus De Lancre tells us of a certain garden so injured by these powders that everything died except the onions—for which, he adds, the Devil has a particular respect. If this respect comes from dislike of its smell—and Satan is known to have a very delicate nose—our modern prejudice against the onion-eater immediately after dinner would seem to be only another proof of man's natural tendency to evil.

In deference to the unceasing demand, the

witch has ever been a prominent exponent of prophecy and divination—nor have any of her practices given more offence to Holy Church. At the late period of her history we are now considering, she had acquired a sufficiently varied repertoire of methods to satisfy the most exacting. To quote from a long list supplied us by Holland, the witch of his times could divine:—"By fire, by the ayer, by water, by the earth, by the dead, by a sive, by a cocke, by a twibble or an axe, by a ring, by Ise, by meale, by a stone, by a lawrell, by an asse's head, by smoake, by a rodde, by pieces of wood, by a basin of water, by certain round vessels of glasse full of water, by rubbing of the nayles." All of which go to show that she had lost little of the skill possessed before her by Egyptian necromancers and mediæval magicians.

But the most fantastic, as it became the most famous, incident of the witch's life, as viewed by her contemporaries, was certainly the Sabbath. In a previous chapter I have endeavoured to provide some narrative account of such a gathering as being the simplest and directest method of reconstruction. It was, however, obviously impossible to include one tithe of the various incidents at one or other period attached thereto by writers, Inquisitors or witches themselves—and this quite apart from the obvious limitations entailed, in matters of detail, upon one who writes for the general public.

These same Sabbaths might be described in modern terms of commerce as Satan's stocktakings, whereon he might check the number and loyalty of his subjects. They were of two kinds—the more important, or "Sabbaths-General," to which flocked witches from all parts of the world, and the more localised and frequent "Sabbaths" simple. Their place and time varied, though most frequently held after midnight on Friday—an arrangement agreeable to the Church view of the Jews and their Sabbath, and not impossibly arising therefrom. In earlier days—or so De Lancre informs us—the Devil chose Monday, the first day of the week, as most suitable, but, with his usual inconstancy, has varied it several times since then. Darkness was not essential, Sabbaths having been occasionally held at high noon. In Southern countries, indeed, the hours between midday and 3 p.m. were considered the most dangerous to mortals, the terrestrial demons having then most power. The pleasures of the midday meal might have a fatal influence in putting the intended victim off his guard, his sleepy content making him peculiarly susceptible to the attacks of Satan's agents. Some authorities give from 11 p.m. to 2 a.m. as the hours, seeing that, as in more legitimate assemblies, everybody could not arrive at once, and there was much business to be gone through. The Sabbaths-General, in mockery of the Church, were usually held on the four great annual festivals. They might take place anywhere, though certain spots were especially favoured. Marketplaces, especially if beside an important church, were among them. The mountain of Dome, in Perigord, again, was among the most famous meeting-places in France, as were the Wrekin in England, the Blocksburg in Germany, and the Blockula in Sweden. Attendance was not a mere matter of pleasure, witches who failed being severely punished by demons sent in search of them or on their next appearance.

Satan himself usually presided in person, though he was occasionally represented by an underling, to the great anger of the witches. Thus, on one occasion, he deprecated their wrath by the explanation that in view of a strenuous persecution then on foot he had been pleading the cause of his followers with Janicot—an impious name for Jesus—that he had won his case, and that they would not be burnt. As a reward, he added, they must bring him eighty children, to be given to a certain priest present at the Sabbath, and later tried for sorcery. He appeared in many forms, that of a goat being perhaps his favourite. Anyone who has ever studied a goat's face, and more particularly the expression of its eyes, can testify to Satan's sense of the fitness of things in so doing, as also to that of the old Flemish painters, and more particularly Jerome Bosch, who, in the paintings of devils for which he is so justly famous, has made copious use of the goat's head as a model for his most demoniacal demons. As a goat Satan was usually of monstrous size, having one face in the usual position and another between his haunches. Marie d'Aguerre, who attended a Sabbath at the mature age of thirteen, and afterwards paid the penalty with her life, testified that in the middle of the assembly was a huge pitcher of water, out of which Satan emerged as a goat, grew to enormous size, and, on his departure, returned again into the pitcher. Sometimes he had two pairs of horns, in front and behind, more usually only three in all, that in the centre supporting a light, to serve the double purpose of illuminating the proceedings and of lighting the candles carried by the witches in mockery of Christian ceremonies. Above his horns he sometimes wore a species of cap, and sometimes he had a long tail, in the usual place, with a human face above it. This was saluted by his guests, but he was unable to speak with it.

He might also appear in the form of a tree-trunk, without arms or feet, but with the indistinct suggestion of a face, seated on a throne; sometimes like a giant, clad in dark clothes, as he does not wish his disciples to realise that he is himself suffering the proverbial torture of hell. Some attendants at the Sabbath—as, for instance, poor little Corneille Brolic, aged twelve—saw him as a four-horned man; others, Janette d'Abadie among them, vouch for his having two faces; others saw him as a black greyhound or a huge brass bull lying on the ground. The constant uncertainty as to the form likely to be taken by the host must have been an added interest to the proceedings—and it has been supposed by some that his powerful imagination led him occasionally to appear in a different shape to each several guest, and to change from one to another at frequent intervals during the proceedings.

The actual ceremonies, festivities, and ritual of the Sabbath varied greatly at different times and places, but having already given a typical example in an earlier chapter, it is unnecessary to dwell further on so unsavoury a subject. The various accounts, evolved from the imaginations of overwilling witnesses or tortured witch, however much they may suffer in detail, unite in being the expression of the foulest and most obscene images of a disordered brain, and as such we may leave them. So again the Devil's Mass was conducted in such a manner as might most impiously parody the Christian ritual. The Devil, however, as an old writer astutely points out, in thinking to imitate Christ by sitting on a great golden throne during the ceremony, only shows his exceeding folly, forgetting that, although Christ often spoke while sitting, He yet gained His greatest triumph on the Cross. With the aforesaid throne Satan conjures up all the paraphernalia of worship—temples, altars, music, bells—though only little ones, for he hates and fears church-bells—and even crosses. Four priests, one serving the Mass, a deacon, and a sub-deacon usually officiate. Candles, holy water, incense, the offertory, sermons, and the elevation of the Host all find place in the Devil's Mass. The sign of the cross is made with the left hand, and in further mockery they chant:—

> *In nomine Patricia Aragueaco*
> *Petrica, agora, agora!*
> *Valentia Jouanda goure gaitz goustia.*

Which is to say:—

> *Au nom de Patrique, Petrique d'Arragon, à cette heure. Valence, tout nostre mal est passé.*

Three languages, according to French authorities, Latin, Spanish and Basque, are employed in mockery of the Trinity. The priest usually elevates the Host—which is black and triangular—standing upon his head. At the elevation of the cup—often black—the whole assembly cry "Black crow!" but not even Satan dare say this at the elevation of the Host. The ceremony of baptism is performed upon toads; while even martyrs are not forgotten—this part being played by sorcerers so bemused that torture has become a mockery to them.

One Jehannes du Hard, in her confession, gives us an account of the method of compounding poisons and witch-ointments at the Sabbaths. On her second attendance she saw a great man dressed in black. At attendant produced an earthenware pot, in which were many great spiders and a white slug, along with two toads. These latter Jehannes skinned, while a companion pounded the spiders and the slug with a pestle. To this mixture the skinned toads were added later, having first been beaten with switches to render them more poisonous. The resultant mixture was used with entire success to poison cattle. There is some uncertainty whether this, and similar poisons, was identical with the ointment used by witches to anoint their broomsticks. In any case, it is intended by Satan in mockery of the sacrament of baptism and Holy Unction.

Were there any room for doubting that Satan habitually breaks faith with his servants, it would be dispelled by the testimony given before the oft-quoted authority, Pierre de Lancre, when that learned gentleman was holding an inquisition in the hag-ridden district of Labourt by command of the Parliament of Bordeaux. That of one witness, Legier Riuasseau, was the more dependable in that, although an eye-witness at the Sabbath, he was yet under no sort of obligation to Satan, having bought the privilege from him for the moderate price of two fingers and two and a half toes. His object was worthier than the mere gratifying of curiosity, for he wished to disenchant a certain Jeanne Perrin, who was among those present. That he might be present without danger, two friends shut him in a dark room, wherein he remained for eight days. There the Devil appeared to him, and explained that if he wished to see the Sabbath and also acquire the power of healing he could do it for two toes and half a foot, to which bargain he agreed. His friends afterwards released him from his voluntary captivity, but he could not escape the dark man, who eight days later took the flesh from the great and second toes and half the third of his left foot, without, however, hurting him in the least. Had he desired the power of doing evil as well, he might have bought it for the remainder of his toes and half the foot, but being as good as he was prudent he refrained. From his further evidence we learn that the Sabbath takes place in the market-square towards midnight on Wednesday or Friday—Satan preferring stormy weather, that the wind may scatter poisons over a wider area. That witnessed by Riuasseau was presided over by a large and a small devil, and all present—the witness presumably excepted—adored Satan by kissing his posterior face. Thereafter sixty witches danced before him, each with a cat tied to the tail of her shift. Marie de la Ralde, another witness, deposed that she often saw Satan approach the children present with a hot iron, but could not say definitely whether or not he branded them. She asserted that all enjoyed the Sabbath to the utmost, the Devil having absolute command over their hearts and wills. Witches, she added, hear heavenly music and really believe themselves to be in Paradise. The Devil persuades them that there is no such place as Hell, and further, by rendering them momentarily immune, that fire has no power over them. As a further proof of Satanic astuteness, she declared that witches see so many priests, pastors, confessors, and other persons of quality attending the Sabbath as to be perfectly convinced of the entire correctness of the proceedings. She herself, even when she saw that the Host was black instead of white, did not at the time realise that anything was wrong.

VI. SOME REPRESENTATIVE ENGLISH WITCHES

Having seen how the witch in general lived and went about her evil business, it may be well to consider the personality of individual members of the craft. There have been, needless to say, many women famous in other directions, who have been incidentally regarded by their contemporaries as possessing superhuman powers. Indeed, to be condemned as a witch was but to have an official seal set upon the highest compliment payable to a woman in more than one period of the earth's history, seeing that it marked her out from the dead level of mediocrity to which her sex was legally and socially condemned. It is as unnecessary as it is unfair to believe that the English and French worthies who burnt Joan of Arc were hypocrites. That a woman could do as she had done was to them capable only of two explanations. Either she must be inspired from above or from below, according to the point of view. As it was too much to expect that those whom she had defeated should regard her victories as divine, it followed that they could seem nothing but infernal. From Cleopatra or the Witch of Endor onwards, the exceptional woman has had the choice of effacing her individuality or of being regarded as an agent of the devil. It is true that in our own more squeamish days, we prefer to regard her as either eccentric or improper, according to her social position and other attendant circumstances.

We may then disregard such historical characters as have other claims to fame, and confine our attention to those whose activities were concentrated upon witchcraft pure and simple. Nor have we to go far afield for noteworthy examples, seeing that they abound, not only in England, but even in London itself. Perhaps the most generally respected of English witches, alike by her contemporaries and succeeding generations is Mother Shipton, who flourished in the reign of Henry VII. More fortunate than the majority of her colleagues, she died a natural death, and it is scarcely too much to say that her memory is green even to-day—among certain classes of society, at any rate.

In common with the Marquess of Granby, Lord Nelson, and other popular idols, Mother Shipton has acted as sponsor for more than one public house in different English counties; the most familiar to Londoners being perhaps that at the corner of Malden Road, Camden Town, a stopping-place on the tram and omnibus route to Hampstead Heath. I have not been able to trace any definite connection between the witch and the hostelry—probably the choice of a sign was made in order to rival another inn named after Mother Redcap—herself a witch of some eminence—in the same district. Mother Shipton was a native of the gloomy forest of Knaresborough, in Yorkshire, a famous forcing-ground of Black Magic, and, although few details of her life have been preserved, we know, so far as tradition may be trusted, that despite her evil reputation and the certainty that she had sold herself to the devil, she was granted Christian burial in the churchyard at Clifton, in Yorkshire, where she died. Whether this implies that she repented, and cheated the devil of his bargain, before her death, or only that the local authorities were lax in their supervision of the parish cemetery, is an open question. At least, a tombstone is said to have been there erected to her memory with the following inscription:—

Here lies she who never lied,
Whose skill often has been tried.
Her prophecies shall still survive
And ever keep her name alive.

No doubt Mother Shipton was as gifted as her fellows in the customary arts of witchcraft, but tradition draws a merciful veil over her exploits as poisoner or spell-caster. Her fame rests upon her prophecies, and whether she actually uttered them herself or they were attributed to her after the event, by admiring biographers, they have ever since been accepted as worthy of all respect even when not attended by the result she anticipated. Thus, although she is said to have foretold the coming of the Stuarts in the person of James I. with the uncomplimentary comment that with him:—

From the cold North
Every evil shall come forth.

the British Solon yet placed the greatest reliance upon her prognostications, as did Elizabeth before him. It is even said that his attempts by various pronunciamentos to stay the increase in the size of London were prompted by Mother Shipton's well-known prophecy that:—

*When Highgate Hill stands in the midst
   of London,
Then shall the folk of England be
   undone.*

If it be argued by the sceptical that, although the London boundaries are now considerably beyond Highgate Hill, the country has so far prospered, it is to be remembered that the prophetess gave no date for the undoing of the English people, and that, if we may believe the mournful views taken of our national future by the leaders of whichever political party happens to be out of office, Mother Shipton's reliability is in a fair way of being vindicated within a very few years.

Yet another of her predictions—perhaps the most famous, indeed—may have been verified already in the days of Marlborough, Nelson, or any of several eminent commanders, or may be still in process of fulfilment. It runs as follows:

*The time shall come when seas of blood
Shall mingle with a greater flood;
Great noise shall then be heard;
Great shouts and cries
And seas shall thunder louder than the
   skies;*

> *Then shall three lions fight with three, and bring*
> *Joy to a people, honour to a king.*
> *That fiery year as soon as o'er*
> *Peace shall then be as before;*
> *Plenty shall everywhere be found,*
> *And men with swords shall plough the ground.*

The vagueness of this and other prophecies by Mother Shipton, however much they may exasperate the stickler for exactitude, bear witness to her direct descent from the ancient sibyls and pythons, few, if any, of whom ever vouchsafed anything more definite.

Passing by Young Nixon, the dwarf, who, although a prophet scarcely less inferior in fame to Mother Shipton, scarcely falls within the limit of this volume—though it may be noted that one of his best-known prophecies, that he would starve to death, did actually come true—we may next consider the life-history of a witch less legendary than Mother Shipton—the Mother Redcap referred to above as having provided a sign for a Camden Town public house. Her career is detailed with such care in Palmer's "St. Pancras and its History" and at the same time provides so vivid a sketch of the probable career of many another witch, that I may be excused for quoting the extract at length:—

"This singular character, known as Mother Damnable, is also called Mother Redcap and sometimes the Shrew of Kentish Town. Her father's name was Jacob Bingham, by trade a brickmaker, in the neighbourhood of Kentish Town. He enlisted in the army, and went with it to Scotland, where he married a Scotch pedlar's daughter. They had one daughter, this Mother Damnable. This daughter they named Jinney. Her father, on leaving the army, took again to his old trade of brick-making, occasionally travelling with his wife and child as a pedlar. When the girl had reached her sixteenth year, she had a child by one Coulter, who was better known as Gipsy George. This man lived no one knew how, but he was a great trouble to the magistrates. Jinney and Coulter after this lived together, but being brought into trouble for stealing sheep from some lands near Holloway, Coulter was sent to Newgate, tried at the Old Bailey, and hung at Tyburn. Jinney then associated with one Darby, but this union produced a cat and dog life, for Darby was constantly drunk; so Jinney and her mother consulted together; Darby was suddenly missed, and no one knew whither he went. About this time, her parents were carried before the justices for practising the black art, and therewith causing the death of a maiden, for which they were both hung. Jinney then associated herself with one Pitcher, though who or what he was never was known; but after a time his body was found crouched up in the oven, burnt to a cinder. Jinney was tried for the murder, but acquitted because one of her associates proved he had "often got into the oven to hide himself from her tongue." Jinney was now a lone woman, for her former companions were afraid of her. She was scarcely ever seen, or if she were it was at nightfall, under the hedges or in the lane; but how she subsisted was a miracle to her neighbours. It happened during the troubles of the Commonwealth that a man, sorely pressed by his pursuers, got into her house by the back-door, and begged on his knees for a night's lodging. He was haggard in his countenance and full of trouble. He offered Jinney money, of which he had plenty, and she gave him a lodging. This man, it is said, lived with her many years, during which time she wanted for nothing, though hard words and sometimes blows were heard from her cottage. The man at length died, and an inquest was held on the body, but, though everyone thought him poisoned, no proof could be found, and so she again escaped harmless. After this Jinney never wanted money, as the cottage she lived in was her own, built on waste land by her father. Years thus passed, Jinney using her foul tongue against everyone, and the rabble in return baiting her as if she were a wild beast. The occasion of this arose principally from Jinney being reputed a practiser of the black art—a very witch. She was resorted to by numbers, as a fortune-teller and healer of strange diseases; and when any mishap occurred, then the old crone was set upon by the mob, and hooted without mercy. The old, ill-favoured creature would at such times lean out of her hatch door, with a grotesque red cap on her head. She had a large broad nose, heavy shaggy eyebrows, sunken eyes, and lank and leathern cheeks; her forehead wrinkled, her mouth wide, and her look sullen and unmoved. On her shoulders was thrown a dark grey striped frieze with black patches, which looked at a distance like flying bats. Suddenly she would let her huge black cat jump upon the hatch by her side, when the mob instantly retreated from a superstitious dread of the double foe.

"The extraordinary death of this singular character is given in an old pamphlet." Hundreds of men, women, and children were witnesses of the devil entering her house, in his very appearance and state, and that although his return was narrowly watched for, he was not seen again; and that Mother Damnable was found dead on the following morning, sitting before the fireplace holding a crutch over it with a teapot full of herbs, drugs, and liquid, part of which being given to the cat, the hair fell off in two hours and the cat soon after died; that the body was stiff when found and that the undertaker was obliged to break her limbs before he could place them in the coffin, and that the justices have put men in possession of the house to examine its contents." "Such is the history of this strange being whose name will ever be associated with Camden Town, and whose reminiscence will ever be revived by the old wayside house which, built on the site of the old beldame's cottage, wears her head as the sign of the tavern."

Mother Redcap who, to judge from the above account, would have had little cause of complaint had she suffered at the hands of the executioner instead of those of the devil, was more fortunate than many other London witches. Wapping, nowadays, is a sufficiently prosaic spot. In the seventeenth century it was the abode of one Joan Peterson, widely famous as the witch of Wapping. She was hanged at Tyburn in 1652 on evidence such as it must be confessed would nowadays scarcely satisfy even a country J.P. trying a poacher. A black cat had alarmed a woman by entering a house near Joan's abode. The woman consulted a local baker, who replied that "on his conscience he thought it was old Mother Peterson, for he had met her going towards the island a little while before." He clenched the matter when giving evidence at the trial by declaring that although he had never before been frightened by a cat, the sight of this one had terrified him exceedingly. After which no reasonable jury could entertain a doubt of Mother Peterson's guilt. Fifty years before, as recorded in Sinclair's "Satan's Invisible World Displayed," another notorious witch, Mother Jackson by name, was hanged for having bewitched Mary Glover, of Thames Street, and similar cases are common enough to show that the seventeenth-century Londoner was as open to this form of the devil's assaults as he now is to others more subtle. It is true that some professed victims of the black art were proved to be impostors. Thus in 1574, as we learn from Stow, Rachel Pinder and Agnes Briggs did penance at Paul's Cross for having pretended to be diabolically possessed, vomiting pins and so forth, much, no doubt, to the relief of the witch accused of besetting them.

The earliest English witch to attain any individual immortality was she of Berkeley, who differed from most of her successors by being extremely well off. Possibly because of this—for even in the ninth century money had its value—

she was accorded Christian burial, and the prayers of the church thereafter. They were not, however, sufficient to ensure her salvation, for under the very nose of the priest the devil carried her body away from where it lay at the foot of the high altar. Although sufficiently historical to have inspired one of Southey's ballads, the Witch of Berkeley is a shadowy figure enough. Another who, seeing that she was acquitted, does not perhaps deserve to be here considered was Gideon, accused of sorcery by Agnes, wife of the merchant Odo, in the tenth year of King John's reign. Although less popular as a legendary figure, Gideon has a definite claim to regard in that her trial is the first to be found in English legal records—the "Abbrevatio Placitorum," quoted by Thomas Wright in his narrative of sorcery and magic. It is satisfactory to know that Gideon, having passed through the ordeal by red-hot iron, was acquitted in due course.

A famous witch was Margery Jourdemain, better known as the Witch of Eye, who gains a reflected halo of respectability in that she was burnt at Smithfield in 1441 as an accomplice of Eleanor of Gloucester, elsewhere referred to. The Duchess of Bedford, charged in 1478 with having bewitched Edward IV. by means of a leaden image "made lyke a man of arms, conteyning the lengthy of a mannes finger, and broken in the myddes and made fast with the wyre," as well as the unhappy Jane Shore, come under the heading of political offenders against whom witchcraft was alleged only as a side issue. More apt to our purpose, in that she was charged with the offence of witchcraft only, and for it condemned to death by Henry VIII., and executed at Tyburn in 1534, was Elizabeth Barton of Aldington, better known as the Fair Maid of Kent. It is true that she was a crazed enthusiast, suffering from a religious mania, rather than a witch, and that she was, further, a pawn in a political intrigue whereby the Catholic party endeavoured to influence the King's matrimonial schemes.

Mother Demdyke, of Pendle Forest, in Lancashire, immortalised by Harrison Ainsworth in "The Lancashire Witches," is elsewhere referred to.

Elizabeth Sawyer, the Witch of Edmonton, though during her life gaining only local fame, yet achieved the posthumous glory of providing Ford and Dekker with the material for a play. In this, indeed, she did but plagiarise Mr. Peter Fabell of the same town, otherwise known as the Merry Devil of Edmonton, who there lived and died in Henry VIII's reign, and upon whose pranks was founded the play called after him, and long attributed to no less an author than Shakespeare. But whereas Mr. Fabell was a sorcerer of no mean power, in that he successfully cheated the devil and died in his bed, poor Elizabeth was no more than a common witch, and as such came to the usual end. The manner of her death in 1621 may be found in the chap-book published in that year and entitled, "The Wonderfull Discoverie of Elizabeth Sawyer, A Witch late of Edmonton: Her Conviction, Condemnation and Death: Together with the relation of the Devil's Accesse to her and their Conference together. Written by Henry Goodcole, Minister of the Word of God, and her Continual Visitor in the Gaol of Newgate."

VII. THE WITCH OF ANTIQUITY

Such zealous sixteenth and seventeenth century dogmatists as King James I., the Inquisitor Sprenger, Jean Bodin, or Pierre de Lancre might have found it difficult to put forward satisfactory proof for the cause in which they were briefed had it not been for the fortunate existence of one quite unimpeachable witness—the direct command in the book of Exodus, "Thou shalt not suffer a witch to live." Probably no other sentence ever penned has been so destructive to human life or so provocative of human misery; certainly it has provided Saladin with the excuse for his bitter indictment of Christianity as being *par excellence*, as based upon the Old Testament, the religion of witchcraft. To which he adds that Christianity, now grown ashamed of its former belief, seeks to explain it away by the suggestion that the Hebrew word "chasaph" should be translated, not as "witch," but as "poisoner."

It is, of course, as true as it was natural that Christian writers on witchcraft seized eagerly upon definite Biblical authority for the sin they were condemning. Origen, who protests against literal interpretation of the Bible, is inclined to ascribe Biblical witchcraft altogether to the Devil, basing his theory upon the tribulations of Job. But St. Augustine needs no more definite proof for this variety of sin than the Bible denunciation, while Luther and Calvin, in a later age, are equally definite. At the same time, it is to be remembered that the cult of witchcraft would certainly have existed had there been no mention of it in the Bible at all. It is as universal, as ubiquitous, and as enduring as the religious instinct itself; Christianity did not invent the witch, it did but improve upon her. A Biblical text was perhaps the most convincing evidence; failing it, early Christian Fathers or late Inquisitors would have found little difficulty in adducing a substitute. Even as it was, although they quoted the Bible—and in both Old and New Testaments, from Genesis to Revelations, witchcraft is recognised and condemned—they also referred with equal zest to the great edifice of tradition and superstition founded upon the struggles after celibacy of the early fathers and their relegation of all pagan rites to the realms of Black Magic.

The Christians, in adopting to their own uses certain pagan rites and beliefs, and regarding all the rest as witchcraft and an abominable sin, were but following the example of their predecessors, the Jews. Throughout the Old Testament Jehovah is proclaimed as the one and only God, despite the backslidings to which the constant reiterations of "Thou shalt have none other gods but Me" would, in the absence of other record, be sufficient witness. The deities of other nations were "false gods" and idols, being regarded by the Jew very much as were witches and sorcerers by the Christian. Again and again he turned from the one and only God to the gods of the heathen, just as the early Christian was wont to help himself out with pagan rites when his new faith failed him, a course of action which of late years shows signs of a reviving popularity. Such being the case, it was as natural that the great Jewish rulers should denounce to the furthest limits of their vocabulary those who, religiously and politically, were undermining a theocratic government, as that a modern Pope should hail the Italian King accursed who seized upon the Patrimony.

The Jews had no national system of magic or witchcraft. Though Abraham migrated to Canaan from Ur of the Chaldees, the God of Abraham was sternly opposed to those beliefs and rites for which the Chaldeans have ever since been famous. These they partly inherited from that earlier Shumiro-Accadian people inhabiting the region between the lower courses of the Tigris and the Euphrates, whose country they invaded some forty centuries B.C.

Besides peopling the universe with good and evil spirits, and having knowledge of the arts of writing and of metalworking, the Shumiro-Accadians practised sorcery and magic wherewith to conjure evil spirits, reserving prayers in the more ordinary sense of the word for the beneficent gods. At the coming of the Chaldeans, the old religion was superseded by the worship of the Sun-god Bel, whose priests were the first practising astrologers. Astrology, divination, conjuration, and incantation thus all had their part in the magico-religious practices of the Chaldeans. An elaborate system of demonology provided constant menace to the happiness of the poor Chaldeo-Babylonian, and, very naturally, by degrees he established a counter influence by whose aid to obtain relief from his tormentors. Most potent were the regular magicians, who, with elaborate ritual and ceremony, were able to drive out the demons possessing the worshipper. Such demons were controlled by the use of potions, by the tying of knots wherewith to strangle them, or by such incantations as the following:—

> *They have used all kinds of charms to entwine me as with ropes, . . .*
> *But I, by command of Marduk, the lord of charms,*
> *By Marduk the master of bewitchment,*
> *Both the male and the female witch,*
> *As with ropes I will entwine,*
> *As in a cage I will catch,*
> *As with cords I will tie,*
> *As in a net I will overpower,*
> *As in a sling I will twist,*
> *As a fabric I will tear,*
> *With dirty water as from a well I will fill,*
> *As a wall throw them down.*

Side by side with the regular magicians was a vast host of sorcerers practising without elaborate ritual, amongst whom witches were greatly in the ascendant. These same Babylonian and Assyrian witches were as efficient as they were unamiable. In contradistinction to the magician, the witch was in league with the demons, and ably assisted them in the infliction of bad dreams, misfortune, disease and death itself. With enthusiasm worthy of a better cause, she tore her victims' hair and clothes, brought about delusions or lasting insanity, destroyed family concord, and aroused hatred between lovers. She was past-mistress in the use of the evil eye, the evil mouth, and the evil tongue, of effigies and magic knots, while her imprecations were the most dreaded of all her practices. Of the witches of Babylon we are told that they haunted the streets and public places, beset wayfarers, and forced their way into houses. Their tongues brought bewitchment, their lips breathed poison, death attended their footsteps. Whether as originators or adaptors they were extremely proficient in that method of enchantment by means of clay, wood, or dough figures, which has continued as among the most familiar of witch-arts until our own times, and they were adepts in the tying of witch-knots. Naturally enough, such practices gained for them the unfriendly attention of the government, but it is perhaps significant of the dread inspired by them that although the law provided for their execution by fire, there is no definite proof that anything other than their effigies was ever actually burnt.

Considering the superstitions amid which

their great forefather had been brought up, it was scarcely surprising that the monotheistic ideal peculiar to the Jews should have suffered occasional eclipses. Nor were Chaldean magic and Persian Zoroastrianism alone responsible for the Jewish conception of witchcraft. In time of famine Abraham and his wife went down into Egypt, just as did his descendants, and the Egyptian magician has earned for himself a fame no less enduring than has the Chaldean. Thot, who revealed himself to man as the first magician, was their divine patron—and it is significant that he also first taught mankind the arts of writing and of music, to say nothing of arithmetic, geometry, medicine, and surgery. This divine schoolmaster pointed out in advance days of ill-omen, and, his magical arts making him master of the other gods, provided counteracting remedies. The Egyptian magician interpreted dreams, cured demoniacal possession, and was skilled in casting nativities. In less amiable mood, he could send nightmares, harass with spectres, constrain the wills of men, and cause women to fall victims to infatuations. For the composition of an irresistible charm he required no more than a drop of his subject's blood, some nail-parings, hair, or a scrap of linen from his raiment—to be incorporated in the wax of a doll modelled and clothed to resemble him or her. As with the Babylonian witch and her mediæval successors, anything done to the effigy was suffered by the original. Thot also taught the magicians how to divide the waters, and a pleasant story has been preserved of a fair maiden who dropped a new turquoise ornament from a boat into the river, and, appealing in her distress to an amiable magician, was consoled by finding it, he having divided the waters for her, safe and sound on a potsherd. It is not difficult to trace to a similar origin the Jewish legend of the Red Sea passage.

Isis, another prominent protector of witchcraft, was, in fact, more witch than goddess. An Egyptian formula against disease, dating from about 1700 B.C., commences, "O Isis, mistress of sorceries, deliver me, set me free from all bad, evil (red) things." Red, it may be noted, was the colour of Set, and thus of evil. Woman was, indeed, supposed to possess more completely than man the qualities necessary for the exercise of magic, legitimate or otherwise. She saw and heard that which the eyes and ears of man could not perceive; her voice, being more flexible and piercing, was heard at greater distances. She was by nature mistress of the art of summoning or banishing invisible beings. The "great spouse" or Queen, of Pharaoh attained, upon her accession to such rank, magical powers above the ordinary. In this connection we find another conception of the witch in the sequel to the loss of Pharaoh's army in the Red Sea. The women and slaves of the drowned warriors, fearing aggressions from the Kings of Syria and the West, elected as their queen one Dalukah, a woman wise, prudent, and skilled in magic. She collected all the secrets of Nature in the temples and performed her sorceries at the moment when the celestial bodies were most likely to be amenable to a higher power. Whenever an army set out from Arabia or Assyria for the invasion of Egypt, the Witch-Queen made effigies of soldiers and animals corresponding in numbers to its strength, as ascertained by her spies. These she caused to disappear beneath the ground—a fate which thereupon befell the invaders also.

The Egyptians were very learned in the concoction of love-charms, spells, and philtres, a branch of their profession which we may suppose to have appealed more to the witch than to the magician. On at least one occasion a witch gained a notable victory over a male competitor in this direction, for it is recorded that Prince Setnau, familiar from his birth with all the magical arts, was yet bewitched by a very beautiful woman named Tabubu—an occurrence which, if not altogether unique in history, vouches for the potency of the lady's charms.

The use of love-philtres was common among the Jewish women, and it is probable that, with other magical operations, they borrowed it from the Egyptians. Nevertheless, Jewish references to Egyptian magic are somewhat scornful. Thus, in the divination of Pharaoh's dreams, a Jew triumphs over the best efforts of the Court magicians. When the Egyptian sorcerers cast down their rods in emulation of the magic powers exercised by Aaron, their rods changed into serpents as readily as did his. But his superiority was made manifest by the fact that his serpent devoured all the rest. So, too, Nebuchadnezzar, in his own realm, found Daniel and his three friends more than able to hold their own against the local magicians and astrologers.

The Jew, then, was no less apt in magic than were his contemporaries. Where it differed was that it was only legitimate when practised in the name and for the service of the God of Abraham, any attempt towards making use of alien rites or deities being sternly repressed.

The Babylonian captivity served to strengthen and extend the full-blooded belief in a comprehensive system of demons already inherited by the Hebrews. They recognised two varieties of evil spirits—the fallen angels and those who were but semi-supernatural. These latter were again divided into the offspring of Eve by certain male spirits and those descended from Adam by Lilith, the first really Jewish witch. Nor were the Jews slow to test the benevolence of such beings whenever the severity of Jehovah proved irksome. Saul banished from the land all wizards and those who had familiar spirits. Nevertheless, being on one occasion afraid of the Philistines, and unable to obtain favourable assurances from Jehovah either by dreams, by Urim, or by the prophets, he disguised himself and came by night to the witch of Endor. The apparition of Samuel has given rise to much speculation. Wierus, an enlightened sixteenth century writer, though a firm believer in witchcraft withal, holds that the Devil himself took the form of Samuel for the occasion. But Wierus is essentially humane, and his contemporaries held much less charitable views of the women they regarded as servants of Satan.

Although the idea of a personal Devil was familiar to the Jews—as, for instance, in his trial of strength with Jehovah for the allegiance of Job—we find no mention of his having entered into compacts with witches as in later times. On the other hand, they had dealings with familiar spirits, and, as was natural in a nation distinguished by its genius for prophecy, they excelled in divination. The early law is very severe on the subject.

The law-abiding Jew might, indeed, attempt to unravel the future so long as he confined his investigations to legitimate channels. These included dreams, prophecies, and Urim and Thummim, two stones carried in the pocket of the High Priest's ephod, engraved with an affirmative and a negative respectively, one of which being taken out, the message upon the other represented the Divine will. All these, being in connection with the service of Jehovah, were permissible. On the other hand, we read in Leviticus that "a man also or a woman that hath a familiar spirit or that is a wizard shall surely be put to death. They shall stone them with stones." And again, "Regard not them that have familiar spirits, neither seek after wizards to be defiled by them." Saul died not only for transgressing "against the word of the Lord, which he kept not," but also for asking counsel of "one that had a familiar spirit, to enquire of it." His further sin would seem to have been that in his perplexity "he enquired not of the Lord."

Manasseh (about the eighth century) incurred condemnation because "he made his children to pass through the fire," practised augury and sorcery, used enchantments, "and dealt with them that had familiar spirits and with wizards." Nor was it until the Lord punished him by causing him to be carried captive to Babylon that he humbled himself and "knew that the Lord He was God." Regarded as a preventative, this form of punishment is curious enough, seeing that the daughters of Babylon are vehemently accused of the very crime for which Manasseh was sent among them. Isaiah says, in no doubtful terms, that "the daughters of Babylon are to be punished for the multitude of sorceries and enchantments with which they have laboured from their youth." And throughout Jewish history the influence of these Babylonian witches is noticeable.

Love-magic was practised in Israel almost entirely by women, and many of the Jewish feminine ornaments were amatorial charms. Indeed, the demand for charms of all kinds was as great among the monotheistic Hebrews as their neighbours. To quote one example out of many, a charm very popular with Jewish mothers against Lilith, the witch of darkness, much feared by women in travail as having an evil propensity for stealing new-born babes, was to write upon the walls the names of three angels, Senoi, Sensenoi, and Semangelof.

Despite the wide sway of the evil and the severity of the laws against it, spasmodically enforced by several of the kings, as Saul and Hezekiah, there are no definite records of witch-persecutions comparable to those of mediæval

Christianity until the reign of King Alexander Jannai, in the first century B.C. Between 79 and 70 B.C. Simon ben Schetach caused eighty witches to be hanged. After the birth of Christ but a few instances are recorded, although the Apostle of the Gentiles waged war against witchcraft with considerable energy. Thus by virtue of his superior powers he brought about the blindness of Elymas, the sorcerer who practised in the island of Paphos. At this early date a distinction was made between the witch active and those involuntarily possessed of evil spirits, a distinction too fine to be regarded by the mediæval Inquisitor. Thus the maid "having a spirit of divination" was not held criminally responsible for her powers. Her soothsaying brought her little or no personal gain, and, far from committing voluntarily "the abominable sinne of witchcraft," she was dominated by a spirit, subsequently cast out by Saint Paul by means less drastic than might have been the case fifteen centuries later.

It is, at first sight, surprising that the Chaldean, Egyptian, or Jewish witch should have conformed so closely to the type familiarised by the witch-mania of the Middle Ages. If we remember, however, how great a proportion of Christian superstitions are directly descended from Hebrew practices, and how eagerly those who made it their life-work to harry old women in the name of the Lord sought Biblical precedent, this persistence in type becomes natural enough, unique though it be. The conception of the Power who guides the universe must vary according to human conceptions of what composes that universe, but so long as we are afraid of the dark the foundations upon which we build our manifestations of evil need vary little.

VIII. THE WITCH IN GREECE AND ROME

Although the Christian witch was the direct descendant of the Jewish, there were yet other branches of her family tree not without their influence upon her final development. Chief among them were the great witch families of Greece and Rome, the one being in some sense a development of the other and through it inheriting more than a trace of Persian blood.

It is a natural feature of anthropomorphic religion that from a few representatives of the more important phases of human existence the gods and goddesses tend to increase, until there is hardly a department of human activity without its presiding deity. As there are kings and queens among men, so there will be sovereigns among the gods. The divine king will have his officers, servants and warriors just as do those earthly kings who worship him. The personal appearance of the god differs from that of the man only in degree, his connection with his worshippers is almost undignified in the closeness of his intimacy. He suffers the same passions, commits the same crimes, occasionally aspires to the same virtues; he is, in a word, man in all but name and divine only in his humanity.

Among no people was this tendency more highly and minutely developed than among the Greeks. Not only did their deities adapt themselves to every phase of human life; the famous altar to "the Unknown God," attests the limitless potentialities of the Greek Pantheon. Were all other records destroyed we could exactly reconstruct Grecian life and feeling from the doings of the Grecian gods; we may expect to find accordingly such a phase of belief as witchcraft accurately mirrored in Grecian mythology. And, accordingly, the witch proves to have her definite niche in the Greek Pantheon. Naturally also, she did not rank among the greater goddesses. On the one hand she may be looked for as the degenerate form of a goddess; on the other she corresponds nearly enough to the heroic demigods in whose veins royal blood mingled with divine ichor.

To the first category belongs the dire and dreadful form of Hecate. Originally an ancient Thracian divinity, she by degrees assumed the attributes of many, Atis, Cybele, Isis, and others. As the personification of the moon, whose rays serve but to increase the mystery of night, she was the patroness of all witches, and was invoked on all their most baleful undertakings. Gradually she grew into the spectral originator of all those horrors with which darkness affects the imagination. Hecate it was who first cast spells and became learned in enchantments; Hecate who at the approach of night loosed demons and phantoms from the lower shades. Did you, hastening through the twilight, meet with a formless monster, hoofed like an ass and radiating a stench incomparably foul, you might recognise the handiwork of Hecate—designed, perhaps, to punish you for having neglected to offer on her altars your accustomed sacrifice of dogs, or honey, or black lambs, or to set out her monthly offering of food—perhaps only in wanton exercise of her mysterious power. Did the mournful baying of your kennelled hounds lend point to the gloomy solitude of night, you might know that Hecate was abroad upon the earth somewhere at hand, with dead souls to form her retinue. Must you pass the cross-roads, or visit the place of tombs, hasten, and especially beware the spot where the blood of murdered persons has been spilt, for all such places are Hecate's chosen haunts. In the gloom and darkness she did her grisly work, now brewing philtres, now potions, with reptiles, human flesh or blood of man or beast that had died dreadful deaths for her ingredients.

The rites of Hecate worship varied in different parts of Greece; she plays a leading part in the Orphic poems, and when the old religion began to be submerged beneath foreign elements, she yet held her own and was even invoked by strangers. Her statues were erected before the houses and at the cross-roads in Athens, and such Hecatea were consulted as oracles. Her personal appearance was the reverse of attractive. She had either three bodies or three heads, according to time and circumstance, one being of a horse, the second of a dog, the third of a lion. Although usual, this habit of body was not constant, her magic arts allowing her to take whatever form she chose as freely as could her fellow divinities. But however she appeared she was invariably hideous. Nevertheless, there seem to have been those among her votaries bold enough to desire personal interviews with her, and for their benefit she provided a formula of her own composition and of such power that she was constrained to obey the citation of those availing themselves of it. It may be quoted for the benefit of those readers who desire her closer acquaintance. Make a wooden statue of the root of the wild rue, well-polished, and anoint it with the bodies of little common lizards crushed into a paste with myrrh, storax, and incense. Leave it in the open air during the waxing of the moon, and then (presumably at full moon) speak as follows: —'Come, infernal, terrestrial and celestial Bombo, goddess of the highways and the cross-ways, enemy of the light who walkest abroad at night, friend and companion of the night, thou who delightest in the barking of dogs and in the shedding of blood, who wanderest amongst the shades and about the tombs, thou who desirest blood and who bringest terror unto mortals—Gorgo, Mormo, moon of a thousand forms, cast a propitious eye upon our sacrifices." Then take as many lizards as Hecate has forms and fail not to make a grove of laurel boughs, the laurels having grown wild. Then, having addressed fervent prayers to the image, you will see her.

Hecate, who became the mother of Scylla, and, according to some accounts also of Medea and of Circe, was arch-mistress of the knowledge of herbs and simples, more especially of poisons. She is almost more typical of the later developments of the witch than of those of her own times. Hag-like and horrible, she worked only for evil, inspiring her votaries with that terror which she herself personified. Goddess though she be, she provides a poignant illustration of one characteristic of the Greek Pantheon which it shares with no other. Its gods and goddesses are always a little more human than their votaries, more prone to human weaknesses if not to human virtues. Thus Hecate shows herself more horrible and terror-breeding than any of those who did their best to model themselves upon her. Just as Mars represented the soldier, carried to his logical conclusion, so Hecate represents the witch conception carried to its furthest limits—the concentrated essence of witchcraft.

To the class of semi-divine witches belong those of Thessaly, as well as Medea and Circe, the putative daughters of Hecate, from whom they learned their magic arts. Circe was assisted by four attendant witches, who gathered for her the herbs wherewith she might brew such potions as turned the companions of Ulysses into swine. The influence of Medea was, on the whole, more benign. She cured Hercules of madness, and taught the Marubians the decidedly useful accomplishment of fascinating and subduing venomous serpents. Not that her knowledge of ointments, poisonous and otherwise, was in any way inferior to that of her sister. Euripides represents her as invoked in terms almost identical with those already quoted in connection with Hecate. The lovesick maiden, Simaetha, in the second Idyll of Theocritus, appeals to Hecate to "make this medicine of mine no less potent than the spells of Circe, or of Medea, or of Perimede of the golden hair."

Equally skilled in poison were the witches of Thessaly, who could, moreover, draw down the moon out of the sky by their magic songs and philtres. If less awful than Hecate, their proceedings inspired equally little confidence. They were addicted, for example, to such practices as tearing off with their teeth flesh from the faces of the dead, for the concoction of their spells. To prevent this early variant of body snatching, dead bodies had to be watched by night. To circumvent the watchers, the witches, as we learn from Apuleius, took the form of dogs, mice, or flies, so that the guardians of the dead must look neither to the right nor to the left, nor even wink while on duty.

Nor were such grisly exploits confined to Thessaly, for in Syria, as Marcassus tells us, troops of witches haunted the battlefield during the night, devouring the bodies of the slain. During the day they took the shape of wolves or hyenas, thus providing a link with the more common phases of lycanthropy. These same witches were definitely human beings, as distinct from spirits, and it was comparatively easy for anyone who so wished, and could obtain the necessary recipe, to follow their example. Such magic salves were usually composed of narcotics, among them being aconite, belladonna, opium, and hyoscyamus, boiled down with the fat of a little child, murdered for the purpose, and with the blood of a bat added. They needed careful and expert usage, however, lest such a mischance might befall as occurred to "the Golden Ass," who, seeking to become an owl, found himself to be no more than a donkey.

While the Thessalian witches paid more attention to the toxicological aspect of Hecate's teaching, the pythons exploited one no less important —the prediction of events to come. Every prudent Greek consulted the oracle at Delphi, before undertaking anything of importance—the oracle displaying equal prudence in the non-committal vagueness of her replies. Theseus, who, on the death of his father, wished to introduce a new form of Government in Athens, sought advice thereon, and received as his answer:—

> *Son of the Pitthean maid,*
> *To your town the terms and fates*
> *My father gives of many states.*

> *Be not anxious or afraid,*
> *The bladder will not fail to swim*
> *On the waves that compass him.*

To Philip of Macedon, again, the utterance of the Pythian priestess ran:—

> *The Battle on Thermodon that shall be*
> *Safe at a distance I desire to see.*
> *Far like an eagle watching in the air,*
> *Conquered shall weep, and conqueror*
> > *perish there.*

That even oracles were—and perhaps are—open to human influence may be deduced from Demosthenes' irreverent suggestion that the prophetess had been tampered with in Philip's favour.

The manner of delivering an oracle doubtless gave a ritualistic example to the witches of later ages, and, as such, may be quoted. After the offering of certain sacrifices, the priestess took her seat on a tripod placed over a fissure in the ground at the centre of the temple. From this came forth an intoxicating gas which, when she breathed it, caused her to utter wild, whirling words. These were interpreted by the attendant priest and by him handed to the applicant, having been first written down in hexameters by an official poet. Divination in Greece thus owed as much to the witch as to the goddess, and it should be noted that, in the case of the Delphic oracle at any rate, the priest acted as go-between, the Pythia being only an item of the oracular machinery.

The Persian wars brought new influences to bear upon Greek religion in general and witchcraft in particular. With Darius and Xerxes came the magic practised by the followers of Zoroaster. Pliny has it that Xerxes was accompanied by Osthanes, a writer on magic, and this statement, whether or no correct in itself, expresses a general truth. Later, after the Greek irruptions into Persia and Assyria, the Chaldeans effected a peaceful occupation of Greece to such effect that "Chaldean" came to be synonymous with doctor, magician, or sorcerer. Like those of their descendants whose advertisements make the fortunes of our newspaper proprietors today, they cured sufferers from incurable diseases, provided, for a small fee, infallible recipes for making money quickly, and acted as mediators between heaven and such offenders as could not approach it through the regular channels with any hope of success. Naturally, also, they did not neglect such a popular "line" as prophecy, sometimes for distinguished clients, as, for example, the father of

Euripides, who is said to have consulted a Chaldean as to his son's destiny. In a word, they took the place of quack-doctors, palmists, "get-rich-quickly" colleges, and the various other practitioners in allied branches of swindling, whose operations to-day are generally hailed as remarkable instances of American "cuteness" and originality.

That the Greek witch of the older school should be powerfully influenced by such innovators was natural enough, the more so that in Chaldea women took a foremost part in practising the more evil kinds of magic. Accordingly, we may accept the date of the Persian Wars as that in which commenced a change in the whole character of Grecian witchcraft. The witch became less terrible in that she was less spiritual, but more pernicious in that she dabbled more with material evil. Hecate was a sufficiently awesome figure, but her terrors were more or less impartial in their scope, and might affect one man as well as another, did he happen to come into contact with them. The witch of later times concentrated her malignancy upon a particular object, and thus became the apt instrument of private vengeance and a force definitely detrimental to social weal.

Yet another powerful influence upon Greek magic was exerted by Egypt. Witchcraft and astrology after the Egyptian method were held in as high respect as were those of the Chaldean convention, and Nectanebus, the last native King of Egypt (about 350 B.C.), was acknowledged in Hellas as the most redoubtable of the magicians. He was an adept in the use of waxen images, and among those to whom he sent dreams was Philip of Macedon.

Thus with the gradual rise of astrology in Greece and the decay of the old religion a state of things arose very similar to what is even now taking place—the nations of the East coming under the influence of Grecian culture, and in return providing her with new cults and crazes, one more fantastic than the other, but all seized upon with equal avidity by the hungry Hellenic intellect, craving always for some new thing. From comparatively simple beginnings Greek witchcraft added always to its complexity until it included everything popularly associated with the name, including a full understanding of hallucinations, dreams, demoniacal possession, exorcism, and divination, the use of wax images and useful poisons, mostly from Eastern sources, and with them a very nice understanding of philtres. A good example of a love charm is to be found in Theocritus, writing in the first decades of the third century B.C. Among the charms of which the heroine of his idyll avails herself to bring about the return of her faithless lover are laurel-leaves, bright red wool, and witch-knots—this last a distinctively Babylonian practice. The charm has a recurrent refrain of "My magic wheel, bring back to me the man I love." Barley grains must then be scattered in the fire while the following spell is intoned:—

> *'Tis the bones of Delphis (or another) I am scattering.*
> *Delphis troubled me, and I against Delphis am burning this laurel. Even as it crackles loudly, when it has caught the flame, and suddenly is burned up, and we see not even the dust thereof, lo! even thus may the flesh of Delphis waste in the burning.*
> *Even as I melt this wax, with the god to aid, so speedily may he by love be molten.*
> *Three times do I pour libations, and thrice my Lady Moon, I speak this spell. Be it with a friend he lingers, be it with a leman that he lies, may he as clean forget them as Theseus of*

> old did utterly forget the fair-tressed Ariadne.
> Coltsfoot is an Arcadian weed that maddens on the hills the young stallions and fleet-footed mares: Ah, even as these may I see Delphis.
> This fringe from his cloak Delphis has lost, that now I shred and cast into the flame...
> Lo, I will crush an eft, and a venomous draught tomorrow I will bring thee.
> But now, Thestylis, take these magic herbs and secretly smear the juice on the jambs of his gate—and spit and whisper, 'Tis the bones of Delphis that I smear.
> When first I saw Delphis I fell sick of love, and consulted every wizard and every crone, &c., &c.

Here, then, we have a detailed account of practices identical with those such as subsequently became the object of fierce persecutions—the use of effigies, of magic herbs, the burning of some substance while calling the name of the person to be influenced, the using of a fragment of his personal belongings to his detriment, the consulting with "crones" for the satisfaction of love-cravings. It was, however, too closely related to religion for there to be any continuous expression of unfavourable public opinion. At the same time, laws existed against it, subsequently to find an echo in Roman legislation. Theoris, "the Lemnian woman," as Demosthenes calls her, was publicly tried in Athens and burned as a witch. Demoniacal possession and exorcism were believed in at least as early as 330 B.C., in which year Demosthenes refers to them in an oration. His feeling towards the practice of exorcism may be deduced from his reproaching Eschinus as being the son of a woman who gained her living as an exorcist. Plato, in the Laws, decrees: —"If any by bindings-down or allurements or incantations or any such-like poisonings whatever appear to be like one doing an injury, if he be a diviner or interpreter of miracles, let him be put to death."

But despite such minor inconveniences, the Greek witch had little to fear in the way of persecutions, so that her mediæval successors might well have looked back to the days of ancient Hellas as their Golden Age, alike spiritually and materially.

If the Greeks, who recognised no predecessors in the possession of their country, yet imported so much of their witchcraft from abroad, it is little to be wondered at that the Romans, by their own account foreign settlers in Italy, should have done so. Unlike those of Greece, Roman legends provide a definite beginning for Rome itself. The. city was founded by a foreigner. What more likely than that he should bring with him the customs, cults, and superstitions of his own country.

Granting that the pious Æneas ever existed, we may also suppose that he was responsible for the Roman tendency in things magical. Of Greek magic he would have learned enough—and to spare—in the long ten years warring on the plains of Ilium. From Dido also he might well have learned something. Virgil himself was by popular report familiar with all the laws of witchcraft, and Virgil tells us of Didos acquaintance, if not with witchcraft, at least with a witch of unquestioned eminence. Half-priestess, half-enchantress, she could cause rivers to run backwards, to say nothing of knowing the most secret thoughts of men. Certainly if Æneas wished to introduce a reliable system of witchcraft into his adopted country, he could have gone to no better instructress.

As in Greece, so in Rome, the personal character of the witch was identical in some respects with that of the goddess, so as to be frequently indistinguishable. Egeria, the friend and counsellor of Numa, was the first witch altogether worthy of the name. The Vestal Virgins were also possessed of certain magical powers. An old French authority disposes of them summarily as thorough-going servants of Satan, his zeal outrunning his sense of chronological fitness. He adds that when Tuscia was accused of having broken her vow of chastity, Satan assisted her to prove her innocence by carrying water in a sieve—an expedient which would have certainly caused her to be burnt two thousand years later.

Like the pythoness of Greece, the Roman sibyl was priestess as well as witch. The existence of the famous Sibylline books presupposes culture above the ordinary; she was also a student of medicine, and, in later times, more particularly of poisons. This latter art became in time a fashionable craze, as we may gather from the many laws enacted against poisoners, and Livy, in common with many other male writers, believes that poisoning and superstition alike originated with women. He also, descending to particulars, relates how Publicia and Licinia divorced their husbands expeditiously by poison, two instances out of many quoted by Latin writers.

In the comprehensive provisions of the Laws of the Twelve Tables drawn up by the Duumvirs in the fifth century B.C., witchcraft is not overlooked.

> *He shall be punished who enchants the corn;*
> *Do not charm the corn of others;*
> *Do not enchant,*

are among some of its injunctions.

Roman morality being enforced upon social rather than religious grounds, witchcraft was forbidden only in so far as it was considered a pernicious influence within the State. Even in later times, when various kinds of magic were prohibited, magical rites for curing diseases and protecting the harvest from hail, snow, or tempest were not only allowed, but even encouraged. The Lex Cornelia de Sicariis et Veneficis provided against offering sacrifice in order to injure a neighbour. The maleficent sorcerer could be burned alive, and those who consulted him or her were liable to crucifixion. The possession of magical books was made criminal, and the administration of love-philtres was punishable by labour in the mines, or, in the case of persons of rank, by a fine. This contrasts with the earlier laws, which were interpreted in a far more liberal spirit and only enforced in extreme cases.

Already in the early days of the Laws of the Twelve Tables, Greek influence on Roman witchcraft was noticeable—it increased in proportion as

Greek thought extended its sway over the Roman mind. By way of Greece also, as well as through independent channels, Oriental magic found its way to Rome, where the wisdom of the Egyptians was held in as high regard as in Greece itself. By the time of Marius, when the Romans had come into direct relations with the East, Chaldeans, sacrificers and interpreters of the Sibylline books positively swarmed in the city, while the use of love-philtres and waxen images was become among the commonplaces of everyday life.

How early Diana, whose close connection with the moon places her on a par with Hecate, came to be regarded as queen of the witches may be doubted; later Italian legends and customs are unanimous in according her that questionable honour. That must at least be a late conception which regards her as a constant visitor to the Witches Sabbath, along with her daughter Herodias! Many such legends are still current in Tuscany, where, in common with other parts of Italy and Europe, Diana was worshipped long after Christianity was nominally supreme. The Italian "strege" are the direct descendants of the Latin "striges," who took their name from a bird of ill-omen that flies by night, the screech-owl, and witchcraft is still known to its votaries as "la vecchia religione," while actual belief in the old gods still survives in one form or other in many parts of the Peninsula.

It may here be noted that Herodias father is sometimes said to have been no other than Lucifer. She also appears under the name of Aradia. Diana sends her to sojourn for a time on earth:—

> *Thou must go to earth below*
> *To be a teacher unto women and men*
> *Who would fain study witchcraft.*
> *And thou shalt be the first of witches,*
> *And thou shalt teach the art of poisoning,*
> *And thou shalt teach how to ruin the crops of a rich peasant.*
> *How to be revenged upon a priest.*
> *Double the harm and do it in the name of Diana,*
> *Queen of Witches all.*

And Aradia taught mortals:—

> *To bless or curse with power friends or foes,*
> *To converse with spirits,*
> *To find hidden treasure in ancient ruins,*
> *To conjure the spirits of priests who died leaving treasure,*

> *To understand the voice of the wind,*
> *To change water into wine,*
> *To divine with cards,*
> *To show the secrets of the hand,*
> *To cure diseases,*
> *To make the ugly beautiful,*
> *To tame wild beasts.*

Little cakes of meal, salt, honey and water are still made in the shape of Diana's horned moon, and are baked after an incantation to the goddess.

There are, of course, earlier indications than these of Diana's patronage of witchcraft. Thus Horace, in his Ode to Canidia, written in the first century B.C., puts these words into the mouth of Canidia, the witch:—

> *Oh, night and Dian who with true*
> *And friendly eyes my purpose view,*
> *And guardian silence keep whilst I*
> *My secret orgies safely ply,*
> *Assist me now, now on my foes*
> *With all your wrath celestial close.*

In the same ode Horace details many witch-customs, which serve to mirror the witch superstitions of the time:—

> *Canidia with dishevelled hair,*
> *And short crisp vipers coiling there*
> *Beside a fire of Colchos stands*
> *And her attendant hags commands.*

For her fire, she makes use of fig-trees torn from dead men's sepulchres, cypress, eggs rubbed over with the envenomed gore of "filthy toads," screech-owl's plumes, evil herbs, and fleshless bones snatched by a witch from the jaws of starving dogs. The smell from such cookery must have been deadly enough in itself to kill any number of victims, even though it does not altogether explain why she bites her long, sharp, unpared thumbnail while brewing her deadly potion.

However universal in its appeal, love was by no means the only disease for which witchcraft provided its remedy. According to Cato, for example, dislocation of a joint could be cured by the utterance of the following charm:—

> *Motas, danata, daries, dardaries, astataries.*

To which Pliny adds that it must be used in conjunction with split reeds, a prudent suggestion enough. From him also we may learn particulars of other charms in common use. Love-philtres were composed of wild parsnip or mandrake, while the external application of asses' fat mixed with gander grease was a means of making certainty more sure. Amateur gardeners with a taste for early rising may be interested to know of a cure for the caterpillar pest:—A woman (presumably the gardener's wife) is to walk at a particular season round the tree affected before sunrise, ungirt and barefoot. And so on, a remedy being provided for all the ills that flesh is heir to.

The Emperors held widely divergent views on the matter of witchcraft. Augustus, realising its hold upon the popular imagination, collected the verses of the sibyls from Samos, Troy, Africa, and elsewhere, and ordered them to be submitted to the prefects of the city, there to be judged and reported on by fifteen very learned men. During the latter days of Pagan Rome there was a marked revival of witchcraft, Marcus Aurelius and Julian setting the example by their patronage. The earlier Christian Emperors revived the old laws against it, but diverted them to attack the old religion. The secret magic condemned by the Duumvirs was by them extended to cover the whole system of paganism. Almost immediately after his conversion Constantine decreed that any haruspex (diviner) entering a citizen's house with the intention of celebrating his rites should be burned alive, while the property of his employer should be confiscated and his accuser rewarded. The Emperor showed that he was in earnest by ordering the execution of one of his favourites for having caused bad weather and prevented his corn-traffic with Constantinople. It was, nevertheless, declared some two years later that the Emperor had no desire to prohibit such magical rites as cured disease or prevented bad weather. In the reign of his successor, Constantius, any person accused of witchcraft was liable to be put to torture. Proven sorcerers were ordered to be thrown to wild beasts or crucified, while, if they persisted in denying their offence, their flesh was to be torn from their bones with iron hooks. This edict also differentiated between Black and White Magic; magic charms being permitted as remedies for drought, disease, storms, and the like.

Julian the Apostate, perhaps not unnaturally, regarded sorcery with a more favourable eye, but later emperors showed themselves always more inimical. Valentian added impious prayers and midnight sacrifices to the list of things forbidden; under Theodosius every detail of pagan worship was included under the heading of magic, and as such rigorously forbidden. In the reign of Honorius, the Sibylline verses collected by Augustus were suppressed. The Codex Justinianus devotes a whole title to witchcraft.

The history of the Roman witch is thus prophetic of that of her Christian successor. So long as she was subject to the civil power alone she suffered little interference from the State, but as soon as she aroused the jealous attention of the more orthodox interpreters of the supernatural, her doom was sealed. We are apt to boast great things of the increase of knowledge in our time, and to instance the decay of superstition in evidence, but, were a sudden religious revival to take place at all comparable to the birth-throes of early Christianity or the Reformation, it is doubtful whether we should not find a belief in the wicked prowess of the witch revive along with it, and possibly our spiritual pastors and masters among the first to attack it with temporal weapons. It is difficult to see how they could logically refrain.

IX. FROM PAGANISM TO CHRISTIANITY

Seeing that it affects ourselves so considerably, we are in the habit of proclaiming the introduction of Christianity as the greatest revolution in history—a claim which will be more capable of demonstration when a few more thousand years have passed, and a few more religions have waxed and waned. At least, the mind of the cultured "Christian" of to-day varies little in its outlook—save in so far as it is affected by modern material discoveries—from that of the cultured "Pagan" of Imperial Rome, much less, indeed, than do either of them from the earnest Early Christian. The ovine tendency of human nature makes it inevitable that a few sincere believers—

whatever their belief—will always attain a comet-like tail of followers, hypnotised by their earnestness, and themselves understanding very little about it. However it may have been with the small band of early Christians—whose belief was given reality by their sufferings in its cause—one may be sure that the ideas of the sixth century Christian in the village street upon Heaven, Hell, and their denizens, differed only in the change of a few names, and the addition of some intolerance from those of his pagan ancestor six centuries before. His spiritual advisers bade him worship the names of Christ, St. John, and St. Peter, in place of Apollo, Mercury, or Mars, and he, troubling his head about very little but his means of daily livelihood, accepted the change without demur. Meanwhile his mind—such as it was—worked along its old lines. As in all great religious movements, we find no sudden or violent change—except, of course, in individual cases—the older ideas were abandoned, in name, though only very slowly, and the change from Diana to Christ, so far as it affected the great bulk of worshippers, was mentally imperceptible.

There were many Christians before Christ, just as there were many pagans after the death of Paganism. For centuries the new ideas, afterwards called Christian, had been fermenting in the minds of thoughtful pagans. The spirit of the age called for their crystallisation in a leader and the call of the West again received its answer from the East. But just as Naaman, a believer in the God of Israel, was yet permitted to bow down in the house of Rimmon—or as the theory and practice of modern Socialism are time after time directly contrary—so, save for martyrs and enthusiasts— the Tolstoys of their age—the general public accepted Christianity as filling up awkward gaps in their earlier beliefs rather than as superseding them altogether.

Roman witchcraft—continually reinforced from the Orient—grew in importance as faith in the greater gods decreased. Frowned upon by the police, as being contrary to public order, it was thus liable to be confounded with Christianity— which was forbidden on similar grounds—both alike being practised in secret and penalised if brought too prominently into public notice. Christianity, as being the more aggressive, was more severely repressed—and was accordingly destined to more success. And it was reserved for the successful Christian to prove upon his former companions in misfortune the utter uselessness of persecution. Just as we may thank the pagan persecutor that we now live in the Christian era, so the mediæval—and modern—witch owed much of her existence to the persevering efforts of the early Christian towards the suppression of witchcraft and the witch. It was natural—and indeed praiseworthy—that the prominent features of paganism should be relegated to the realms of darkness by the successors to the pagan empire—the god of one religion inevitably becomes the devil of its supplanter. But whereas it was easy enough to lump together satyr, faun, centaur and siren, as varieties of demon, the witch was on a different footing. She really existed, for one thing—in so far as that she was of flesh and blood at any rate—and she exercised more personal functions than any number of divinities. Everyone was ready to acclaim reforms which did not interfere with his own comfort—and the witch was a fireside necessity. She was family doctor, lawyer, and spiritual director—and payer-off of your old scores to boot—a factor in your life the loss of which could be compensated by no amount of religion. Also she stood for tradition, "the good old times," the respectability of unchanging conservatism. Christianity—novel and iconoclastic—might make head among the inconstant townsfolk, always ready for some new thing; the provinces, the village, the lonely farmhouse or the fishing hamlet clung tenaciously to what had been good enough for their grandfathers—as, indeed, they have been doing ever since.

Nevertheless, from the great cities the creed of Christ spread slowly to the villages—suffering many modifications before it reached them. Delivered straight from the lips of a Church father, Christian doctrine might be rigid and direct enough. Passed from mouth to mouth, ignorant, or understanding, they might reach the distant flock so diluted as to have opportunity for compromise with time-honoured precedent—and what more so than witchcraft. You might—if you were an open-minded husbandman—conceive that you had been mistaken in seeing fauns dancing where the sunlight glinted down through tossing leaves, or in hearing the voices of nymphs in the chattering of a brook; but a witch—whom you could see, touch, hear, who had cured your toothache and revenged you on your dishonest neighbour—she took a great deal of explaining away. Wicked she might be, getting her power from unholy compact with the Evil One—burn, slay, persecute her by all means—if it would please Heaven—but to disbelieve in her altogether, that were asking too much of a plain man. How, indeed, could you expect it of him when the very Emperors proved by their edicts the openness of their minds. A Marcus Aurelius not only studied magic, but persecuted Christians—slaying, among others, the venerable Polycarp. An Augustus might feel called upon to take police measures against witches; an Aurelian rebuked the Senate for not consulting the Sibylline books when the barbarians threatened the gates of Rome. "One might imagine" he said, "that we were assembled in a Christian church, rather than in the temple of all the gods." Where an Elagabalus renewed old superstitions and introduced yet others, a Constantine executed his favourite for seeking to influence the weather.

The personal predilections of the Emperors did but reflect the many and involved influences at work during the first four centuries after Christ.

Apart from the enduring influx of Eastern practices and superstitions, Neo-Platonism was responsible for the revival of belief in the supernatural as apart from the divine. The Alexandrian school, discarding the old systems of philosophy, converted its study into that of magic. The barbarians, again, were everywhere astir. The long warrings between Rome and the Germans culminated in the 9th year of the new era when the German Herman by his great victory over Varus brought about the eventual liberation of his country. In 259 A.D. the Emperor Gallienus married a barbarian princess and before the close of the third century A.D. the Empire had become largely "barbarised" by the Goths and Vandals who did it military service, and who, incidentally, served to bolster up paganism and to introduce new features into it. The Teutonic witch met her Roman sister, and introduced her to darker, grimmer, and more vigorous conceptions of her art. The dreadful pestilence which, in the third century, ravaged the Empire gave a new popularity to the black arts, and the Roman witch was never more sought after than in the years preceding the last and most violent persecution of the Christians at the hands of Diocletian.

Persecuted or petted, the witch was never able to progress in the good opinion of the Christian, whose protest against her existence was steady and constant whatever his own fate or condition.

As soon as the last of his own persecutors had laid aside the sword, he at once seized it and set to harassing the witch with a deserving vigour which has never altogether relaxed.

Whereas the pagan had chastised the witch with rods for injuring man, the Christian set about her with scorpions as an enemy of God. Nor was the exalted testimony of the Fathers lacking to inspire his energies. Tertullian, in the second century, declared the world to be over-run with evil spirits, including among them all heathen gods, whether amiable or the reverse, from Hebe to Hecate. Origen, in his third book on Job, mentions that enchantments are sometimes of the devil. Saint Augustine, in "De Civitate Dei," has no doubt that demons and evil spirits have connection with women. The earliest ecclesiastical decree bearing on the subject is that of Ancyra, in 315 A.D., by which soothsayers are condemned to five years' penance. In 525 the Council of Auxerre prohibited all resort to soothsayers. Witchcraft, which thus took upon its shoulders all the enormities of paganism, attained an importance it had never before possessed. The plain man began to realise that his family witch was a more important person than he had hitherto believed. If not herself of semi-infernal birth, he had it on Saint Augustine's authority, as aforesaid, that she was in all probability the mistress of a sylvan, faun, or other variety of devil, and that her offspring were themselves no less diabolical. Naturally enough they increased and multiplied, so that between corporeal and spiritual devils the world was overpopulated. The Messalians, indeed, went so far as to make spitting a religious exercise—in the hope of casting out the devils inhaled at every breath; and the common superstition concerning sneezing has the same origin. It might almost be said, indeed, that in those early days devils filled, and to admiration, the part now played by the microbe in every-day life.

It is to be feared that, except by those who seriously studied the question, the existence of so many devils of one kind or another did not cause such general uneasiness as the clergy might desire —very much as now happens when the medical world is appalled by the discovery of some new microbe in strawberry, telephone receiver, or shirt-cuff. The plain man accepted them, and having after some centuries discovered that they made little practical difference to his life, ceased to feel more than a languid interest in even the most appalling new varieties discovered by saintly specialists. Their constant insistence upon the inherent wickedness of humanity and the almost insuperable dangers which assail the Christian on all sides lost something of their freshness in time, one may suppose, and were succeeded by a certain weariness. Granted that Christianity was the one sure road to salvation in the next world, it was so difficult to follow without stumbling that few, if any, could hope to arrive at the goal, save by some such lucky accident as a martyrdom. Christianity was thus bound, in practice, if not in theory, to come to some working agreement with the old, comfortable pagan customs it had superseded. Certain of the more popular pagan customs and festivals found their way into Christian observance, certain popular deities were baptised and became Christian saints. A familiar instance of this occurs in the case of Saint Walpurg. In Christian hagiology she occurs as a virgin saint, and as having accompanied Saint Boniface upon his missionary travels—all of which would seem to show that pious scandal-mongering was less rife in contemporary religious circles than is the case to-day. In folklore we find many wells and springs associated with her and thus acquiring valuable medicinal qualities. The oil exuded from her bones upon Walpurgisnacht was valued as relieving the pangs of toothache and of childbirth. Potent in the cure of hydrophobia, the dog is included among her pictorial attributes, while she is also represented as bearing in her hand either oil or ears of corn—the symbols of agricultural fertility. The festivals and rejoicings which took place upon Walpurgisnacht, with their special connection with witchcraft, would further seem to show that Walpurg before she became a Christian saint had a long history as a mother-goddess. In the same manner in the cult of the Virgin may be found traces of that worship of Diana which for 600 years persisted side by side with Christianity, and is far from being altogether extinct in Italy even to-day.

As may readily be understood, these paganising tendencies were not favourably regarded by the fathers. In the year 600 A.D., St. Eligius felt called upon to forbid dancing, capering, carols, and diabolical songs upon the festival of Saint John. A statute of Saint Boniface forbids choruses of laymen and maidens to sing and feast in the churches. As the Church increased in power, many such practices—as, for example, the dancing of women round sacred trees and wells, with torches or candles in their hands, the common meal, the choral song and sacrifice—were roundly forbidden as witchcraft, the uprooting of which the Church at last felt capable of taking seriously in hand. This was indeed become a matter almost of life and death, for the Church found itself in many ways in acute competition with the witch, the one attaining by lawful means similar results to those achieved by the other through the assistance of Satan. And just as Adam, upon learning that the apple was forbidden to him, immediately hungered after it to the exclusion of all other fare, so the public showed itself more eager to obtain the forbidden services of the witch than those of the legitimate practitioner. So much was this the case that the

Church was sometimes forced to resort to other means than persecution to show itself capable of competing against the witch with her own weapons. Occasionally, it must be confessed, these methods suggested rather the American Trust magnate than the fair competitor, as, for instance, the case of the Blocksberg. This hill was a place of considerable importance to witches, providing a large choice of magical herbs as the raw material for their trade in weather-charms. These could, however, be gathered only upon the eve of Saint John and during the ringing of the neighbouring church bells. The ecclesiastical authorities, becoming aware of this, gave orders that the bells should be rung only for the shortest possible period on that date—a proceeding the unfairness of which could only have been exceeded by not ringing the bells at all.

Another story of the kind, quoted by Mr. Lecky, shows that, even in fair and open competition, holy water could hold its own against the most powerful of black magic. A certain Christian, Italicus by name, was addicted to horse-racing at Gaza. One of his most dangerous and constant competitors was a pagan Duumvir. This latter, being versed in the black arts, therewith doped his horses so successfully that he invariably won. Italicus, being prohibited from following his example, at last appealed to Saint Hilarion, exhorting him to uphold the honour of the Church by some signal display of supernatural power. The saint, after some hesitation, complied, and presented Italicus with a bowl of specially consecrated holy-water. At the start of the next race Italicus liberally besprinkled his team, whereupon they drew his chariot to the winning-post with supernatural rapidity. The Duumvir's horses, on the other hand, faltered and staggered, as though belaboured by an unseen hand—and, needless to say, lost the race. Whether the Duumvir appealed to the contemporary Jockey Club to disqualify the winning team, and, if so, with what result, we are not informed.

Considering the vast and ever-increasing population of witches and demons, it seemed an almost hopeless task to exterminate them altogether. Nor indeed was it until after the thirteenth century that the Church attempted the task on any universal scale. If an individual witch was unlucky enough to fall into priestly hands, her fate was likely to be unhappy—but in the early days of the faith the priest felt himself capable of triumphing over her by less material weapons. Only, as priests could not be everywhere, and the number of witches so largely exceeded their own, means were provided whereby even the layman might withstand them. Thus burning sulphur was very efficacious in the driving out of devils, the subtlety (!) of its odour having great power of purification. The gall of a black dog put in perfume was another acknowledged recipe, as was the smearing of his blood upon the walls of the infested house.

It is noteworthy, and a fact that vouches strongly for the sincerity of the early Church, that although she thus practised what was nothing less than sanctified witchcraft, she never attempted one of the most frequent and popular of witch-practices—the foretelling of the future, so far, at any rate, as this world was concerned. It is true that the Christian's earthly future, being but an uncomfortable preliminary to posthumous joys, might be more happily left unforetold. Yet many of them did not altogether despise the pleasures of this life, and were very willing to pay for an anticipatory glimpse of any likely to be encountered.

Familiarity in some measure breeding contempt, the public in these early days thus regarded neither witch nor daemon with the dread and hatred so manifest in the fifteenth century and onwards. For one thing, faith in the power of the Church was more implicit. To dally with the forbidden had all the fascination of a sport with a spice of danger in it, when you knew that at any time a power vastly greater than those of evil was ready to step in to protect you from the consequences of your over-rashness. Before the name of a fairly efficient saint the most powerful demon must bend his head, especially with holy water anywhere in the neighbourhood. If you fell under the power of a witch it could only be through neglecting to take proper precautions or to employ someone else to do so for a moderate fee. Our own Anglo-Saxon forefathers showed a very nice spirit of prudence in such matters—as in the famous meeting between Ethelbert King of Kent and Saint Augustine, held, by royal command, in the open air, lest the missionary, being under a roof, might practise unlawful arts upon the King. The witch, in a word, was everywhere, but so were the necessary antidotes—some of them of the simplest. Thus, in the story of Hereward we learn how the Wise Woman of Brandon, near Ely, anathematised the hero from a wooden scaffolding. To be really efficacious her curses must be thrice repeated, but before she had time to do this the scaffold was set on fire by Hereward's followers, and the Wise Woman perished miserably. The witch, in fact, like her gossip the Devil, always comes off second best in folklore where she is matched against the truly virtuous—a comforting reflection for everybody, however ominous for their friends.

She was still to some extent a shadowy personality, of shifting and indefinite attributes. Although in 696 the Council of Berkhampstead decreed that any person sacrificing to the Devil should be punished—a clear enough reference to witches—it was not until some centuries later that the conception of the witch definitely crystallised into its modern form of a woman carrying out an actual compact with Satan, working miracles by his power, and frequently transported through the air to pay him homage at Sabbath gatherings. Until then the Church may be said to have been obtaining and sifting evidence, building up a formidable mass of precedent and tradition, to be employed with deadly effect when witchcraft was definitely branded as heresy.

Whether or not the sins of witch and sorcerer be definitely codified, it is the duty of the lawgiver to provide for all contingencies; and just as Justinian devoted part of his code to dealing with witchcraft, so Charlemagne, two centuries and a half later, enacted new and stringent laws for the abatement of sorcery—as in the Capitular of 789, wherein supernatural meteorology is forbidden. More direct, though perhaps less efficacious, were such deterrent methods as those of the pious

Bishop Barbatus, who in the seventh century cut down and uprooted a certain nut-tree famous as a meeting place for witches. It may here be noted that trees were at all times much favoured by the evil sisterhood, more especially as meteorological offices. Numerous witch-oaks throughout Germany served for this purpose—one, at Buckenhofen, was used as a swing by witches attending the Walpurgisnacht. It is something of a paradox that while a grove of oaks—the sacred tree of the Teutons, as is the linden of the Slavs—is a protection against magic, particular trees should be famous as gathering-points for witches.

As the year 1000 approached, the generally optimistic outlook upon things in general suffered a decline. Famine and pestilence grew always more commonplace; the price of corn increased unprecedentedly; starvation became the normal condition of millions throughout Europe; cases occurred in which children were killed and devoured by their famished parents; dead bodies were disinterred and used for food. Old prophecies had placed the end of the world in the year 1000, and to the miseries of hunger and disease were added those of universal terror. The forward movement in the Church seemed to have died away, and Christian fervour gave place to increased insistence on forms and ceremonies, regarded by the commonalty as tiresome, if necessary, duties. Small wonder that they sought for something which, instead of the hopeless contemplation of inherent sin, should provide some ray of present comfort. Here was the opportunity of the witch, the sorcerer, and the alchemist—and here also began the bitterest contest between priesthood and witchcraft. Hitherto the Church had been able to regard such rivals, if not with tolerance, at least with contempt. Now it had to fight against weapons forged in its own furnaces, appealing to that abysmal ignorance ordained by the priest upon his flock. If the monopoly in knowledge be power, its application is double-edged; the Church was forced to seek some new means of inspiring the fear of celestial wrath to come into those who could imagine no circumstances more dreadful than what they already daily endured. The time had come to prove that those who tampered with the forbidden must expect a double share of punishment—in this world as well as the next—and that the earthly penalty was quite as much to be dreaded as the best infernal efforts.

In 1025, Burckhard of Worms inserts the significant question in the confessional:—"Have you believed that there are women who can turn love into hate and hatred into love, or who can harm their neighbours and seize their goods for themselves? Have you believed that godless women blinded by the Devil ride abroad at night with the demon Holda, obeying her as goddess?" Followed in due course Ethelred's decree of banishment against witches, soothsayers, and magicians, and that of Canute, which included love-witchcraft as a branch of heathendom.

Though the anathemas of the Church might for a time stem the increasing tide of witch-popularity, they were fundamentally only incentives towards a cult which did not include anathemas or persecution—except, indeed, those within the control of the humblest individual. In the twelfth century, moreover—the century of the Crusaders—many new influences were at work. To counteract the general lethargy into which the Church was sinking, the Popes availed themselves of their knowledge of human nature. Epidemical frenzy was aroused by remission of penance, absolution of all sins, past, present, and to come, and the assurance of eternal felicity for all who took the cross. Sham miracles and prophecies stimulated the popular enthusiasm, and more potent than either was the knowledge among millions that any change they might experience must be for the better. But however promising at the time, the great "revival" was fraught with danger to the Church that provoked it. New conditions evolved new ideas. Asia provided greater luxury for body and mind than any hitherto known to its European invaders. The new world thus opened before them might be sinful; it was at least very pleasant. Future damnation presents few terrors to the well-fed, and the discovery that millions existed, and in comfort, who had never taken off their hat to a priest in their lives—however shocking it might seem at first—was bound to give furiously to think.

Among the forbidden institutions upon which the Crusader found reason to reconsider his ideas, witchcraft took a prominent place. Anathema though it might be, it had a multitude of Oriental exponents, who, whatever they might have to look for in the next world, had little cause to complain of this. Such abominations cried for intelligent investigation, if only that they might be refuted, with the result that the Crusader returned home with the knowledge of many novel features that might be profitably added to the Western ritual of magic. Meanwhile in his absence his own native practitioners had not been idle. Faithful wives were anxious to know something of their lords' whereabouts, safety, or, it may be, fidelity. Those who were not faithful had even more need of tidings as to his probable return and of means for delaying it. In such emergencies the services of the witch were indispensable—and priestly prohibitions only served to advertise her powers and to increase the number of her suppliants. These various causes, and more particularly the last, combined to give witchcraft an importance in social life hitherto denied to it, and to draw down upon it more and more the wrath of Mother Church. She had, indeed, other no less pressing calls upon her attention. The long slumber of orthodoxy was at an end; many heresies disturbed the minds of the faithful. The revival of Latin literature stirred thoughts and feelings long blurred by Church teaching. The Crusaders were not the sole importers of Oriental ideas; Greek traders also, along with the drugs and perfumes of the East, brought new doctrines, received with dangerous tolerance. The vigorous Innocent III. quickly perceived the danger, and entered upon a systematic persecution of heretics. In 1208 a Papal Legate having been murdered by Raimond of Toulouse—against whom the Church had already serious cause of complaint, Innocent at once proclaimed a crusade, and the heretical Albigenses were involved in the ruin of their most powerful protector, suffering a persecution of almost unprecedented severity. The establishment of the Inquisition now became a logical necessity if the spread of heresy was to be saved, and little time was lost in its creation.

By this time Satan had assumed a definite form and personality in the public mind, and the idea that the witch obtained her powers through a compact with him, long sedulously inculcated, had taken root. It is true that even yet the "Sabbath" was but a harmless servile carnival, frowned upon, indeed, and discouraged wherever possible. Coincidentally with the rise of the general heresy hunt, Europe was overrun by a number of devastating epidemics. Leprosy, epilepsy, and every form of skin disease raged almost unchecked. They were attributed to many causes, from lack of faith to the consumption of various Eastern drugs introduced by home-faring Crusaders—though lack of food and cleanliness were doubtless the most active agents in spreading them abroad. Dirt had long been accounted almost a mark of holiness—and one so easy of attainment that few cared to disregard it and arouse suspicion as to their orthodoxy by too frequent ablutions. Medical science was at its lowest ebb; the priests, with keen common sense, declared skin eruptions to be divinely-inflicted punishments, and therefore not amenable to holy water. In despair the unhappy sufferers turned to the witch for aid, who, by her knowledge of herbs and simples, was qualified to alleviate, if not to cure. Everything seemed to conspire in thrusting forward the witch into dangerous prominence.

The ecclesiastical measures of repression grew always more severe. Canon Law decreed that soothsayers be subjected to excommunication, and enjoined upon the bishops to leave no stone unturned for their repression. By the fourteenth century the Sabbaths, under the penetrating eye of the Inquisition lost their harmless character and became forcing grounds of the Black Mass. The practice of medicine by women, however beneficial, grew more and more into disfavour, and year by year the attributes of the witch grew more infernal as the material Devil became more and more familiar in men's minds. No doubt the increase of witches was real as well as theoretical. Love of notoriety is of no modern growth—and the reputation of possessing infernal powers satisfactorily filled the position of the modern newspaper paragraph. This in more senses than one—for not only could you obtain notoriety for yourself, as does the modern Apache who murders for the *réclame* it will bring him, you could also satisfy a grudge against a neighbour, with no risk to yourself, by anonymously accusing her to the local clergy. Witchcraft, again, was open to all, without licence, examination, or entrance fee. Poverty, the desire of solitude, a nice taste in invective, and a black cat or so were all the stock-in-trade required to start in business.

The convenience, from the Church point of view, of catching witch and heretic in the same net was too obvious to be disregarded. By the fourteenth century their connection was well established in the eyes of church and law. In France, so early as the thirteenth century, prosecution took place for "vauderie," an omnibus-word which covered at once witchcraft and the heretical practices of those Vaudois from whose name it was derived. In Ireland, in 1324, proceedings for witchcraft taken against Dame Alice Kyteler and others in the Court of the Bishop of Ossory, brought about a conflict between Church and State, such cases, according to English law, being tried by a secular tribunal.

The substitution of linen for wool in dress was an efficient factor in abating the ravages of skin-diseases, but their place was taken by the more terrible Black Death, and, in 1350, epileptic dancings, known as the Dance of Saint Guy, broke out with especial virulence in Germany and Flanders. These and other diseases, constant wars, bad harvests, and other troubles brought about a series of class-wars, the Jacquerie in France, and Wat Tyler's insurrection in England, for example; the Devil and the witch between them shared the blame in the eyes of respectable Europe. The greater pestilences were attributed to the Devil's personal intervention, while minor diseases, and especially poisonings, fell to the witch's share—this latter accusation being, perhaps, not altogether without cause. The public—or that portion whose lives were cast in places sufficiently pleasant to prevent them desiring such consolation as magic might afford them—were now fully aroused to their iniquity. Against the agents of so grisly a horror as the mediæval devil no measures could be too severe, no torture too dreadful. Scholasticism vied with the Church in deploring the increasing evil; John XXII.'s publication of the first Bull against witchcraft was capped by the University of Paris, which, in 1398, laid down rules for the judicial prosecution of witches, expressing at the same time regret that the crime of sorcery should be growing more common than in any former age. In England, from the Conquest onwards, commissions were issued from time to time empowering the Bishops to seek out sorcerers. In 1406 such a mission was delegated to the Bishop of Lincoln. It was not, however, until 1542 that penalties more severe than fine and imprisonment were inflicted by the Ecclesiastical Courts.

The ever-increasing prestige of witchcraft in time raised it to a point where it could be made an apt weapon for political intrigues. The burning of Jeanne d'Arc as a witch is a case in point, her tormentors by their choice of indictment dimming for long centuries the halo which surrounded her efforts towards the freeing of her country, while at the same time it provided ample opportunity for those who, having been among the first to hail the rising popular star, are also first to enjoy his fall from greatness. Another case, even more definitely political, was that of Eleanor Duchess of Gloucester, in which the charge of witchcraft proved a serviceable weapon in the hands of Cardinal Beaufort. The Duchess, although accused of no less a crime than procuring a wax image of Henry VI., manufactured by the Witch of Eye, with nefarious intent, escaped the death penalty indeed, but was condemned to public penance, followed by life-long banishment.

As the Reformation grew, nearer, public opinion veered round to some slight extent in the direction of leniency. The Inquisition was itself becoming so unpopular that its victims were bound to excite some secret sympathy. The Renaissance, throwing wide the door to all the intellect of classical days, already shook the dominion of the Church to its foundations. The time had come for desperate measures if Orthodoxy was to hold her own. In 1484 the Witch-Bull of Innocent

VIII. definitely handed the witch over to the care of the Inquisitors—and thus gave the signal for a series of persecutions of unexampled horror, enduring through more than two centuries, and the last echoes of which have scarcely died away even to-day.

X. THE WITCH-BULL AND ITS EFFECTS

I have elsewhere in this volume attempted to show that, even in our own days, there is nothing particularly incredible about a witch—and that the disrespect into which she has fallen is due rather to our modern lack of any sense of proportion in our beliefs, than to any fault of her own. Certainly we have no cause to pride ourselves on any intellectual superiority to the great divines and scholars of past ages who devoted themselves to the dissection or condemnation of witchcraft—rather we should deplore our lack of faith and of imagination. For them there existed no possibility of doubt, no relative standard of fact or theory. The premises were absolute. The spiritual world was based upon the word of God as expressed in the Bible and translated by the Church. To argue the absurdity or inadmissibility of any particular tenet of Christian doctrine was to suppose a paradox—the fallibility of the infallible. Eminent jurists, as was Bodin, or learned physicians such as Wierus, both writing towards the close of the sixteenth century, arguing with great mental dexterity on opposite sides, alike accepted the initial axiom, cramp and confine them though it might. They had, indeed, no alternative—as well might two modern astronomers in disputing over the whereabouts of an undiscovered planet deny the existence of the sun. The humane Wierus, a friend of Sir Philip Sidney, by the way, preaches from the same text as does the judicial Bodin—though he delivers a different sermon. Bodin, supporter of the old conventions, makes a formidable onslaught on Wierus—not for any scepticism as to the existence of witches—no ground was given him for such an accusation—but for maintaining against the view of the Church that witches were victims rather than disciples of the Devil. Nor, in the face of the very explicit injunction, "Thou shalt not suffer a witch to live"—and the suggestion was still to be mooted that "witch" in the original stood for "poisoner"—can we accuse those who obeyed it of having acted from any other motives than those of earnest Christians. It is true that they carried zeal to the point of enthusiasm—but zeal has always been accounted a mark of grace.

As we have seen the severest period of witch-persecution commences from their definite classification as heretics by the Bull of Innocent VIII. issued in 1484. The Bull itself was not lacking in directness:—"It has come to our ears," it commences, "that great numbers of both sexes are not afraid to abuse their own bodies with devils that serve to both sexes. And with their Inchantments, charms and sorceries to vex and afflict Man and Beast with inward and outward pains and tortures....Therefore with the authority apostolic we have given power to the Inquisitor ... to convict, imprison and punish." The Inquisitor, Sprenger, lost little time in making use of this delegated authority—and such was his zeal and so many his opportunities of acquiring knowledge that within two years after the issue of the Bull he gave to the world his famous "Witch's Hammer," for the direction and guidance of those upon whom should fall the duty of exterminating so vile a heresy. This "Malleus Maleficarum" contains minute accounts of every description of witch, with suggestions for counteracting and exterminating their influence. Like most of his predecessors—and successors—Sprenger blames the whole existence of witchcraft upon the notorious frailty of women. The very word "foemina," he declares, in the accents of authority, is derived from "fe" and "minus"—because women have less faith than have men. From this unhappy constitution of the sex countless ills have sprung—among them innumerable varieties of witch. Of these, thirteen are exhaustively described, that all may recognise them. Worst are those who slay and devour children. Others raise hail, tempests, lightning and thunder, procure barrenness in man, woman and beast, make horses kick until they throw their riders, or pass from place to place through the air, invisible. Others can render themselves taciturn and insensible under torture, can find things hidden or lost, foretell the future and alter men's minds to inordinate love or hate. They can draw down the moon, destroy unborn children, raise spirits—in a word, there is no department of devilry, major or minor, in which they are not adepts, if we may trust their enthusiastic historian, whose work at once became an authority—almost a ready reckoner of witchcraft, by which anyone with a knowledge of Latin had at his fingers' ends the best possible method of recognising, convicting and destroying any variety or variant whatsoever.

It is pleasant to reflect that so careful and conscientious a work earned for its author the affection and admiration alike of his contemporaries and of posterity. Later writers based their theories and arguments upon his discoveries as upon a firm rock, while during his lifetime he directed public opinion upon the evil he had set himself to combat so successfully that not one old woman in fifty could be sure of dying in her bed for generations. It is a pregnant sign of the genuine horror in which witches were held that all the ordinary legal conventions were suspended at these trials. Contrary to the usual procedure, witness might be borne against them by excommunicated persons, convicts, infants, dishonest servants and runaways. Presumption and conjecture were accepted as evidence, an equivocal or doubtful answer was regarded as a confession and rumour or common report sufficient to ensure a conviction. It is true that such improvements in legal procedure cannot be altogether attributed to the exertions of the Inquisitor—dating, as many of them do, from centuries before the publication of his magnum opus—at least he devoted a splendid enthusiasm to the object he had set before him, and on his death-bed was able to look forward with confident humility to the reward merited by a well-spent life.

The effects of the Witch-Bull were immediate and in every way satisfactory to its authors—a perfect frenzy of witch-finding resulting. Forty-one women were burned in one year—commencing in 1485—by the Inquisitor Cumanus. A colleague, not to be outdone, executed a hundred in Piedmont—and was perfectly willing to continue the good work, had not public enthusiasm waned in view of the inevitable monotony in this form of amusement. A little later a tempest devastated the country around Constance. The inhabitants recognising that—in face of the recent Bull—it were blasphemous to attribute such a storm to natural causes, seized two old women, obtained confessions in the usual way, and burned them. About 1515, some five hundred persons were executed in Geneva as "Protestant witches"—an instance of the alliance between heresy and witchcraft. In Lorraine the learned and enthusiastic Inquisitor Remigius put to death nine hundred persons in 15 years. Hutchinson, indeed, writing in 1718, puts the number at eighteen hundred, but even the smaller—and more correct—total shows that Remigius did his duty nobly. Italy, naturally enough, was determined not to be outdone by foreign holocausts, and accordingly we find that more than a thousand executions took place in Como in 1524, and an average of more than a hundred was maintained for several years.

Mere lists of figures such as these are apt to

pall, especially when, as in such a case, it is almost impossible for a modern reader to realise their actual meaning, as that every day throughout a whole year, three unhappy women, old, poor, and defenceless, should be inhumanly tortured, and afterwards publicly murdered in the most painful way imaginable in one district, not only without a word of protest being raised, but with the approval of all Europe. That it should have actually taken place vouches for the earnestness with which our forefathers regarded their religion, if for nothing else.

Nor is it to be supposed that Protestants were in any way less attentive to this branch of their religious duties than were their Catholic neighbours. They might differ upon every other point—on this at least there was no room for disagreement. Martin Luther, with his usual decision, makes his attitude perfectly clear, "I have no compassion on these witches. I would burn them all." Perhaps one reason for this uncompromising attitude may have been his contempt for Satan's snares, of which he had considerable experience. So accustomed did he grow to the assaults of the Devil that, having been once, as it is related, awakened at dead of night by an alarming clatter, "he perceived that it was only the Devil and so went to sleep again" Calvin, again, says of Psalm v., 6, "If there were no charms of sorcery, this were but a childish and absurd thing which is here written." It is true that Protestant and Catholic regarded the witchcraft question from diametrically opposite standpoints. Whereas the Roman Church regarded heretics as a variety of witch, the Reformers were inclined to regard Catholic rites and forms as among the most virulent of the black arts. At a somewhat later date, during the New England persecutions, a girl was deposed to have been allowed, by the Devil, to read "Popish Books"—such as "Cambridge and Oxford Tracts" —while good Protestant works, as "The Bible Assemblies' Catechism" or Colton's "Milk for Babes" sent her, being in the power of the Devil, into violent convulsions!

However enduring might be the enthusiasm of the judges, the commonalty in time grew sated with the spectacle of their own and their friends' aunts and grandmothers being burned to ashes for the glory of God. Witch-trials and witch-burnings, however dramatically exciting, were lacking in variety—and were expensive as well as entertaining. While the energy of the Inquisitors was stimulated by the forfeiture—in their favour—of the witch's worldly goods—the community had to lose them, such as they were, besides suffering complete disorganisation of daily business routine. There were even those—difficult of belief as it may seem—who so far risked their chance of Paradise as to sicken at the continuance of such useless bloodshed and to grow sceptical as to the singlemindedness of its promoters. Such a one was the humane and learned Dr. Wierus, who, in 1563, published at Basel his famous volume, "De Præstigiis." At the time, indeed, this plea for the witch as the victim rather than the ally of Satan, served only to fan the flame of persecution, by the bitter controversy to which it gave rise, though subsequently quenching it in no small degree. Although, needless to say, a firm believer in the reality of the black art, Wierus branded it as the direct rather than the indirect work of the Devil. As helpless victims, thereoffore, his agents should not be punished for crimes in which their human frailty was alone guilty. He adopted, in a word, towards the witch, the modern attitude towards the dangerous lunatic—that she should be restrained rather than punished. He even displays a certain contempt for her powers—understanding, in the light of his own medical knowledge, that many so-called cases of bewitchment or demoniacal possession, were the result of purely natural causes. Like his contemporaries, Wierus concludes that the Devil chooses women rather than men to do his will as being easier to influence. Naturally malicious and impatient, they are unable to control their affections and are all too credulous—qualities of which Satan takes every advantage. Particularly does he appreciate stupid, weak old women, the shakiness of whose wits places them the more surely in his power. Wierus parts company from his contemporaries in urging that this very frailty should arouse compassion—that they should be pitied rather than treated as stubborn heretics—and that if punished they should be treated less severely than were men, because of this infirmity of their sex.

Not content with stirring up doubt as to the spiritual nature of witchcraft, Wierus has the audacity to question the motives of some of its judges. He quotes an example of the profitable side of the witch-mania as having happened in Wurtemburg. The skins of animals that died by mischance there became the property of the executioner. This functionary evidently possessed a spirit far in advance of his age, for coincidently with the rise of a local witch-mania, a fatal epidemic—attributed, of course, to witchcraft—broke out among the sheep, pigs, and oxen of the neighbourhood. The executioner grew rich—and had not the wisdom to conceal it. The jealous suspicions of his neighbours were aroused, he was put to the torture, confessed to having poisoned the animals, and was condemned to be torn to pieces with pincers.

Wierus had studied the natural history of the witch no less closely than his predecessor, the Inquisitor Sprenger. Indeed, judging from some of the charges brought against them at contemporary trials, we may agree with him that they were more suited to the attentions of a physician than of a judge. Thus, among the commonest of their crimes—as frequently proved by their own confession, it is to be remembered—were the dishonouring of the crucifix and the denial of salvation, the absconding, despite bolts and bars, to attend the Devil's Sabbath and the partaking in choral dances around the witch-tree of rendezvous. Remigius tells us that many confessed to having changed themselves into cats, to having belaboured running water with rods in order to bring about bad weather—more particularly hailstorms—and other doings of the kind customary to witches of all the ages. Wierus, who was held to be a disciple of that prince of sorcerers, Cornelius Agrippa, was naturally as expert in all things relating to the Devil and his kingdom as to his earthly slaves. No modern revivalist could exceed the minuteness of his knowledge, nor, indeed, the thoroughness expressed in his detailing of it. He even seems to have taken a census of the more official population in the under-world, enumerating seventy-two princes of evil, who rule over seven million four hundred and five thousand nine hundred and twenty-six devils of inferior rank.

Fifteen years after the publication of "De Præstigiis," appeared Jean Bodin's counterblast. The eminent jurist was well qualified to speak, having done some persecuting on his own account and thus gained first-hand experience of the ways and customs of the witch. To him the theories of Wierus appeared as those either of a very ignorant or of a very wicked man. The suggestion that witches and sorcerers should be pitied rather than punished appeared to him to aim a blow at the very framework of society, human and divine, and he felt it his duty to refute Wierus and all his works, "not through hatred, but primarily for the honour of God." He also gives detailed accounts of the various kinds of witches, but unlike Wierus discreetly refrains from setting down the spells and invocations to the Devil with which he is acquainted, lest, falling into the hands of the evilly disposed, improper use be made of them. For such crimes as those habitually committed by witches he can find no penalty severe enough, while as to Wierus' plea that allowance be made for the weakness of women he quotes approvingly the law, that "the punishment for witchcraft shall not be diminished for women as is the case in all other crimes."

England was in no way singular from the rest of Europe in her method of approaching the question, though her persecutions were on a smaller scale. The Act of 1541 whereby various kinds of sorcery, such as the destruction of a neighbour's goods or person, the making of images or pictures of men, women, children, angels, devils, beasts and fowls for magical purposes, were declared felony without benefit of clergy, was repealed in the reign of Edward VI. Another, distinguishing the various grades of witchcraft, was passed in 1562. By it, conjurations, invocations of evil spirits, the practice of sorceries, enchantments, charms and witchcrafts whereby deaths resulted were declared felony, without benefit of clergy, and punishable with death. If only bodily harm ensued, the penalty for the first offence was a year's imprisonment and exposure in the pillory, and for the second, death. Notwithstanding such laws, the highest in the land were not averse to personal dealings with followers of the black art. Queen Elizabeth herself so far exercised her royal prerogative as to have been—unless rumour lie—on excellent terms with Dr. John Dee, the eminent crystal-gazer, whose "black stone" is now in the British Museum. In Scotland the principal Act was passed in 1563. By it the practice of witchcraft, sorcery and necromancy, the pretence of possessing magical knowledge, and the seeking of help from witches were declared capital offences.

It says much for the common sense of the English nation that it should, at such a period, have produced so enlightened a writer on the subject as was Reginald Scot. As against his contemporary, Holland, who, writing in 1590, urges that since witches were in the Bible, "shall Satan be less cruel now?", Scot, in "The Discoverie of Witchcraft," scoffs at "Sprenger's fables and Bodin's babies"—a conceit that must have afforded him infinite satisfaction. "I denie not," he argues, "that there are witches or images, but I detest the idolatrous opinions conceived of them." And again: "I am well assured that if all the old women in the world were witches, and all the priests conjurers, we should not have a drop of rain the more or the less for them." The suggestion of priests as conjurers is, of course, a hit at "Papish practices," and another description of witches as "Papists" betrays his religious attitude. It must be said that the Anglican Church was inclined towards tolerance —the severe witch-persecutions in these islands, which I detail elsewhere, being chiefly due to that Puritan spirit which dwelt with more satisfaction on the sins than the virtues of mankind. For just as it has been said that the only antagonist more redoubtable on the battlefield than a swearing Irishman is a praying Scotsman, so the Puritan was a deadlier persecutor of witches than the most zealous Inquisitor. This with good reason, if we remember that the Catholic offered the chance of Heaven to anyone who was not an obstinate heretic; while the Puritan was of much the same opinion as the old Scotswoman, who, having with her brother seceded from the local kirk, and being asked by the minister whether she seriously believed that no one but her brother and herself would be saved, replied that she had grave doubts about her brother.

James I., although upon his succession to the English throne he found the Episcopacy well suited to his theories of kingship, yet preserved the Puritanical sense of other people's sinfulness in his heart. To this no less than to his desire for literary laurels, is to be ascribed his painstaking—not to say pedantic—"Dæmonologia," published in 1597, which the loyal Hutchinson excuses in his "Historical Essay on Witchcraft"—excuses on the ground of his youth and inexperience.

James, needless to say, saw no need of apology for the benefit he was conferring on mankind in general and his subjects in particular. In his love for police-court details, indeed, he showed himself altogether at one with his subjects, if we may judge from the taste of their present-day descendants. He had, again, every right to consider himself an authority on his subject, as one who had himself suffered from magical machinations. A Protestant King seeking a Protestant bride, he suffered all the terrors and discomforts of a temptuous crossing from Denmark, brought about through his earthly agents by Satan, filled with wrath and consternation at the alliance of two such powerful enemies of his kingdom. As he might have expected, his plans were brought to nought, and his servants, Agnes Simpson and Dr. Fian, suffered the appropriate penalty, the last-named especially being subjected to perhaps the most sickening torture on record. King James showed so close an interest in the minutiæ of the black art that had he moved in a less exalted sphere he might well have come under suspicion himself. Thus on one occasion he sent for Grellis Duncan, a performer on the Jews' harp, and caused her to play before him the identical tune to which Satan and his companions led the brawl at a Sabbath in North Berwick churchyard. It is true, as against this, that many witches executed in his reign quoted infernal pronouncements that the King was *"un homme de Dieu"* and Satan's greatest enemy—a form of homage which so whetted the

Royal ardour that few juries ventured, with the fear of his displeasure before them, to acquit any of their unhappy victims.

In the "Dæmonologia" James shows every sign of keen enjoyment. He writes after the manner of the most eminent—and tedious—divines, dividing his matter into firstlies, secondlies, and thirdlies—divisions and sub-divisions, headings and sub-headings, with royal prodigality. He is fearfully and wonderfully theological—and occasionally indulges in touches of elephantine lightness such as might well have given pause to the most obstinate sorcerer. His preface, eminently characteristic of the whole, opens thus:—"The feareful abounding at this time in this countrie of these detestable slaves of the Divil, the witches or enchaunters, hath moved me (beloved reader) to dispatch in post this following Treatise of mine, not in any wise (as I protest) to serve for a shewe of my learning and ingine, but only (moved of conscience) to preasse thereby, so farre as I can, to resolve the doubting heart of manie; both that such assaults of Sathan are most certainly practised, and—that the instruments thereof merit most severely to be punished. . . . And for to make this Treatise the more pleasant and facill, I have put it in forme of a Dialogue"—an unwonted concession to the public taste, this last, on the part of one who believed so firmly in the Divine Right of Kings.

In common with most dogmatists on the subject, James declares that the great majority of witches are women, woman being the frailer vessel, and therefore, like Eve, more easily entrapped by the Devil than those of his own sex. He recapitulates many of their commonly-quoted misdeeds, and relates how Satan teaches them "to make pictures by wax or clay," which, being roasted, utterly destroy the person they represent. To some he gives powders such as cure certain diseases, to others poisons, and so on and so forth. For the practice of such infernal arts the English Solon declares that witches and magicians should be put to death without distinction of sex, age, or rank.

Such august patronage of their efforts served the ever-increasing tribe of professional witch-finders in good stead, and the Act of 1563 was enforced more stringently than ever. The trials were sometimes held in the ordinary courts, more often before special tribunals, set up, as a rule, on the petition of a presbytery or of the Grand Assembly. For the greater convenience and protection of the public, boxes were placed in many churches to receive anonymous accusations, giving magnificent opportunity to slanderers and backbiters. To such a pitch had matters come by 1661 that Parliament directed the judges to visit Dalkeith and Musselburgh, two notorious centres of the art magical, twice a week to try those accused. In these trials any evidence was relevant, especially if put forward by professional witch-finders or witch-pinchers, while the ordinary methods of torture were aggravated when confessions were sought for, in view of the Devil's penchant for protecting his own.

The close of the sixteenth century saw the commencement of a series of persecutions fiercer and more general than perhaps any which had preceded them, which did not finally die out before the rising sun of common-sense until almost our grandfathers' time, and which were carried to almost greater extremes in the New World than in the Old.

XI. THE LATER PERSECUTIONS IN ENGLAND

The law—especially in this country—gains half its terrors from its pomp and circumstance. An English prisoner, condemned to death by a wigless judge, might well regard himself as murdered—and few Englishmen that have attended an American court of law but have felt scandalised by its lack of ceremonious decency, even if they have accepted its decrees as just. Indeed, it is scarcely too much to hold that the firm belief in the corruptibility of the American judge and the one-sidedness of American justice, which every Englishman cherishes as his birthright, was originally based upon his distaste for this lack of appropriate ceremonial.

If this judicial dignity be needed even for the

trial of an ordinary fellow mortal, how much more must it be needed when Satan himself and his human agents are at the bar. Accordingly, we find the inquisitor or judge always ultra-punctilious in bringing all due form and ceremony to bear upon a witch-trial. No detail was without its special significance, no circumstance too trivial for august consideration, the more so that from its very nature a witch-trial could not exactly follow ordinary procedure. The power of Satan—in the seventeenth century at any rate—was more than a match even for the trained legal intellect, and special precautions were necessary to provide for the safety of the judge and the conviction of the witch. So exhaustive were these precautions, indeed, that we can find no trace that any judge in England or elsewhere was ever injured by the assaults of the Devil, when in court, while but very few witches, once put on trial, succeeded in escaping conviction—the accusation being, to all intents and purposes, tantamount to a verdict of guilty.

A host of precautionary measures to be taken by the judge when the witch was brought into court, have been recorded. On no account must he allow her to touch him, especially, as Reginald Scot has it, "upon his bare." He must wear about his neck "conjured salt, palms, herbes, and halowed waxe." The prisoner must approach the judge backwards—just as she approaches Satan's throne at the Sabbath, by the way—and he must make the sign of the cross frequently the while. As we have seen, any evidence, even of those debarred from testifying in ordinary cases, might be given against a witch. This, of course, provided an excellent opportunity for the dishonest servant, who, having stolen his mistress' property and with it levanted, need only accuse her of witchcraft to escape any unpleasant consequences to himself. It was, however, the only means by which the law could escape from the horns of a serious dilemma—as none that are honest can detect a witch. Again, she must be denied any chance of proving her innocence—or the Devil will certainly take full advantage of it on her behalf, and once arrested, she must on no account be allowed to leave the prison or go home. Popular suspicion, presumption, and conjecture are sufficient to ensure a conviction, for in such a case Vox populi is emphatically Vox Dei. Confession must, however, be extorted at all costs. As the great Inquisitor, Sprenger, from whose authoritative pronouncements I have already quoted freely, has it: "If she confess nothing she must be dismissed according to the law; therefore every care must be taken *to* ensure confession."

Before burning the witch, it was, however, necessary to catch her. Here—and more particularly in England—private enterprise stepped in to supplement public effort. Witch-finding offered a respectable and lucrative career for anyone gifted with the requisite imagination, and provided a safe opening for those who had failed in other walks of life. Enterprise, imagination, the form of facile expression, the instinct of sensationalism, and so forth—were all necessary for the finished witch-finder, it is true. The names of many have come down to us, but none more fully earned the prophetic title of the Napoleon of witch-finding than Matthew Hopkins, who alone gained, by his eminent services to the public, a "handle to his name"—that of "Witch-Finder General." Hopkins, who flourished in the mid-seventeenth century, gauged the public taste in witch-sensation to a nicety—and elevated his trade to an exact science. Yet curiously enough, he only entered it by accident, owing to an epidemic of witchcraft in his native town of Manningtree. His public spirit leading him to take a prominent part in the discovery and punishment of the culprits, it became plainly evident in which direction his talents could be best employed, and what had been a hobby became his life-work. His position having been legalised, he adopted the manner of a judge, taking regular circuits through the four counties which he more particularly took under his protection, or giving his services to any towns applying for them at the extremely modest charge of twenty shillings and expenses. More than a hundred witches were brought to punishment by his painstaking exertions, though perhaps his greatest triumph was achieved in the case of the Reverend Mr. Lewis, the "reading" parson of Framlingham. Mr. Lewis was a churchman, and as such regarded as a malignant by the Puritan Government, and, needless to say, by Mr. Hopkins, himself a Puritan of the most orthodox type. Mr. Lewis, being eighty-five years of age, was tortured after Mr. Hopkins" recipe, and was so brought to confess that he had made a compact with Satan, that he kept two imps, and that he had sunk several ships by his magic arts. He was duly hanged, though it is satisfactory to know that at his death he withdrew the confession his human weakness had extorted from him and died with a dignity becoming his age and cloth.

As was only to be expected in this imperfect world, Mr. Hopkins" just severity and proper disregard for sickly sentimentality brought him many enemies, some of whom no doubt were inspired by envy of his professional success. Although cheered by the understanding sympathy of the superior class, including among them no less a person than Sir Matthew Hale, Lord Chief Justice of England, he was continually attacked, both publicly and privately, by people who ought to have known better. One of the most virulent of these was one Mr. Gaule, minister of Great Stoughton, in Huntingdon, who not only wrote and preached against Hopkins and his methods, but refused him permission to conduct a witch-hunt at Stoughton. Stung to the heart by such ingratitude, Mr. Hopkins set forth his side of the argument in a letter which Mr. Gaule himself subsequently gave to the world. It is sufficiently characteristic to bear re-quotation:

"My Service to your Worship presented. I have this day received a letter not to come to a Toune called Great Stoughton, to search for evil-disposed persons, called Witches (though I heare your Minister is farre against us through Ignorance:) I intend to come the sooner to heare his singular Judgment in the Behalfe of such Parties; I have known a Minister in Suffolk preach as much against this Discovery in a Pulpit, and forced to recant it by the Committee in the same Place. I much marvaile such evil Members should have any, much more any of the Clergy, who should daily preach Terrour to convince such Offenders, stand up to take their Parts, against such as are complainants for the King and Sufferers themselves, with their Families and Estates. I intend to give your Toune a visit suddenly. I am to come to Kimbolton this Weeke, and it shall be tenne to one, but I will come to your Toune first, but I would certainly know afore whether your Toune affords many sticklers for such Cattell, or willing to give and afford as good Welcome and Entertainment as other where I have beene, else I shall wave your Shire (not as yet beginning in any Part of it myself) and betake me to such Places, where I doe, and may, persist without Controle, but with Thanks and Recompense. So I humbly take my leave and rest.

> Your Servant to be Commanded, Matthew Hopkins."

Mr. Gaule, however ill-advised, proved himself no despicable antagonist. He turned the batteries of ridicule against the worthy witch-finder:, and his methods, which he describes as follows: "Having taken the suspected Witch, she is placed in the middle of a room upon a stool or table, cross-legged or in some other uneasy Posture, to which if she submits not she is then bound with cords; there she is watched and kept without Meat or Sleep for the space of Four and Twenty Hours (for they say within that time they shall see her

Imp come and suck). A little Hole is likewise made in the door, for her Imp to come in at—lest it should come in some less discernible shape. They that watch her are taught to be ever and anon sweeping the Room, and if they see any Spiders or Flies, to kill them, and if they cannot kill them, then they may be sure they are her Imps."

But however earnest in their errors might be Mr. Gaule and those who supported him, it was long ere they could find many supporters in their crusade against one who had so struck the public imagination. Hopkins" methods of torture might be severe, but they produced results—such as the following:—" One Penitent Woman confessed that her mother, lying sick, and she looking at her, somewhat like a Mole ran into the bed to her, which she being startled at, her mother bade her not fear it, but gave it her, saying, "Keep this in a Pot by the fire and thou shalt never want." And so on and so forth.

In the end, however, as too often happens, envy triumphed over modest merit, and Hopkins had to pay the penalty that usually awaits the popular idol. Either his severity outran his discretion, or he showed too openly his belief that the chief object of a profession is to provide a handsome income; or perhaps his inventive faculties did not keep pace with the public desire. Be that as it may, his fall, when it came, was heavy. It is even said, on reputable authority, that Hopkins was himself, at the last, accused of witchcraft, that he was tried by one of his own methods, that of "swimming," and that like many of the old women he had tried, he "swam," was accordingly found guilty, and executed. It may be agreed that, like the story of Phalaris destroyed in the fiery bronze bull of his own devising, or of Dr. Guillotin, first to suffer on the guillotine he had invented, this end of Hopkins has too much of poetic justice about it to be altogether credible. But in all that has to do with witchcraft, faith is a matter of opinion, so there we may leave it.

That Matthew Hopkins initiated new methods of witch-finding by no means implies that there was any lack of such before his time. Where the simple rule-of-thumb torture failed to extract the requisite confession, a further range, subtler and more exquisite, came into play. No witch could say the Lord's Prayer—a possible enough contingency under great nervous strain even for a good Christian. Thus Fairfax relates how Thorp's wife, accused of bewitching his children, being put to this test, could not say "Forgive us our trespasses" and thus convinced the justices of her guilt. Another method much practised by Hopkins was the searching for the Devil-marks. These marks, as we have said, were the corporeal proofs of her contract with Satan, borne by every witch upon some part of her body, and were further the places whereat her imps came to suck her blood. Few witches—which is to say, suspects—were ever found to pass this test satisfactorily—a fact the less surprising in that any blemish, birth-mark, or even insect-bite was accepted by special legal injunction as sufficient evidence. The witch-mark was believed to be insensible to pain, whence arose the popular and lucrative profession of "witch-pricking." The witch-pricker, having blindfolded the witch, proceeded to prick her in suspected places with a three-inch pin, afterwards telling her to point out to him the places where she felt pain. If the suspect, half-crazed with shame and terror, was unable to do so with sufficient exactitude, the spot was declared insensible, and her conviction followed. Before the actual pricking, when the witch had been stripped of her clothes, she was shaven, lest she should have concealed in her hair some charm against confession under torture. Great care was taken at the same time lest the Devil, by sucking blood from her little finger or left foot, should make it impossible for her to confess. Further, as a witch was notoriously unable to shed tears, another test of her guilt was to call upon her to weep to order—very much as Miss Haversham in "Great Expectations" commanded Little Pip, "Now, play!"

Most popular test of all, as taking place in the open and thus providing a general holiday, was witch-ducking or "swimming." So near was it to the great heart of the British public that its celebration continued informally well into the nineteenth century. In Monmouth, so late as 1829, several persons were tried for the ducking of a supposed witch; while in 1857 the Vicar of East Thorpe, in Essex—perhaps the most noted witch-stronghold in England—was compelled to mount guard in person over the door of a suspected witch to prevent her from undergoing a similar fate. The procedure was of the simplest. The thumbs and great toes of the suspect were tied across, and she was thus dragged in a sheet to a pond or stream. If she floated, she was pronounced a witch; if she sank, she was in all probability drowned. Even if by a lucky chance she escaped both these perils, the nervous shock—to say nothing of what was probably the first cold bath she had ever experienced—acting upon her advanced age, gave her little chance of final triumph over her accusers. Another well-known and popular test was that of weighing the suspected witch against the Church Bible. Had the authorities provided one of more than common weight which outweighed her skin and bone, woe betide her! for her guilt was proved beyond further question.

Such forms of extraneous evidence were, however, held in less store than was the obtaining of a definite confession, which had the double advantage of justifying the judges to the full as well as of convicting the accused. Of how it might be obtained Reginald Scot gives us a vivid example. "The seven words of the Cross" he says, "be hanged about the witch's neck and the length of Christ in wax be knit about her bare bodie with relikes of saints." If torture and other means of persuasion cannot obtain a confession, the jailer must pretend to leave her, and some of her friends must visit her, promising that if she will but confess they will help her to escape from prison. Friday, according to the same writer, was the most auspicious day for the purpose. As to the actual torture, the prisoner must first be stripped lest the means of witchcraft be sewn into her clothing, the instruments of torture being so placed that she has an uninterrupted view of them. The judge then exhorts her that if she remains obstinate, he bids the attendants make her fast to the strapado or other chosen instrument. Having been tortured, she is taken aside and again urged to confess by the promise of thus escaping the death-penalty. As the Church conveniently absolved the faithful from the necessity of keeping faith with heretics or sorcerers, this promise was never kept. To put it briefly, every possible avenue of escape was denied the accused. Even an alibi, however complete, was unavailing, seeing that in her absence her place was always filled by a demon.

However much we may sympathise with the victims of such judicial proceedings, it would be less than fair to blame the general public for its attitude towards them when such men as Blackstone or Sir Matthew Hale were convinced of their reasonableness. Blackstone, indeed, one of the greatest of English lawyers, went so far as to declare that "to deny the possibility, nay, the actual existence of witchcraft is at once flatly to contradict the revealed Word of God." The attitude of Sir Matthew Hale, Lord Chief justice, an enlightened and God-fearing man, may best be gathered from an account of one of the trials in which he was concerned. In 1664, at St. Edmundsbury, two women, Amy Duny and Rose Cullender, were tried before him upon the usual charges. The first witness was Dorothy Durent, whose child was under the care of Rose Cullender. Dorothy had for some time suspected Rose of bewitching her child —a fact which throws some doubt upon the witness's maternal care in confiding her offspring to such a nurse. Eventually the witness consulted a witch-doctor, a proceeding which, had she known it, rendered her liable to conviction as well as Rose, under the statute of James I.* The doctor advised her to hang up her child's blanket in the chimney, which she did. On taking it down some time later, she was horror-stricken to find a toad in it. This toad she had "put it into the fire and held it there, though it made a great and horrible noise, and flashed like gunpowder and went off like a pistol, and then became invisible, and that by this the prisoner was scorched and burnt lamentably." Other witnesses, Mr. Pacy and Edmund Durent, deposed that Rose Cullender and Amy Duny came to them to buy herrings, and, on being refused, went away grumbling. Further, it appeared

---

* "If any person, or persons, shall use, practise, or exercise any invocation or conjuration of any evil and wicked spirit, or shall consult, covenant with, entertain, employ, find, or reward any evil and wicked spirit, to or for any intent or purpose, or to take up any dead man, woman, or child out of his, her, or their grave, or any other place where the dead body resteth, or the skin, bone, or any part of any dead person to be employed or used in any manner of witchcraft, sorcery, charm, or enchantment, or shall use, practise, or exercise any witchcraft, enchantment, charm, or sorcery whereby any person shall be killed, destroyed, wasted, consumed, pined, or lamed in his or her body, or any part thereof, every such offender is a felon without benefit of clergy." (This Act was not repealed until 1736.)

that Amy Duny had told Cornelius Sandwell's wife that if she did not fetch her geese home, they would be destroyed. She also told Cornelius that if he did not attend to a rickety chimney in his house it would fall. John Soan deposed that he had three carts wherein to carry corn. One of them "wrenched Amy Duny's house, whereat she scolded him. That very day his cart overturned two or three times, and his children had fits" Probably such damning evidence would have sufficed by itself. It was driven home by that of Sir Thomas Browne, who declared with dangerous moderation that "the fits were natural, but heightened by the Devil co-operating with the malice of the Witches, at whose Instance he did the villainies." This was too much for the Lord Chief Justice. He "was in such fears and proceeded with such caution that he would not so much as sum up the evidence, but left it to the Jury, with prayers that the great God of Heaven would direct their hearts in this weighty manner." Needless to say, the jury returned a sentence of "Guilty." Amy Duny and Rose Cullenden were hanged at Cambridge accordingly, obstinately refusing to confess, and no sooner were they dead than the afflicted children were cured of their fits and returned to the best of health. Which can have left no further doubt in the mind of Sir Matthew

Hale, Lord Chief Baron of the Court of Exchequer, as to the justice of his sentence, even had he any before.

It would be both tedious and unprofitable to trace out the whole long history of witch-persecution in the sixteenth and seventeenth centuries. Their details are invariably nauseous, and differ only in the slightest degree; having heard one, the recapitulation of the rest can be of interest only to the moralist. Some of the more famous examples may be briefly considered, however, as typical of the rest. I have already referred to the case of the Knaresborough witches, accused of bewitching the children of Edward Fairfax, the scholar—a case the more remarkable that the six women accused, although tried before two successive assizes, were finally acquitted. The lonely moorlands and grim wastes of the Northern counties were, naturally enough, regarded with suspicion as offering very eligible lurking-places for Satan's agents, and accordingly we find that the majority of the earlier persecutions concerned that part of the county. Ten years before the Knaresborough trial—in 1612—twenty witches were tried "at the Assizes and Generali Gaole-Delivery, holden at Lancaster, before Sir Edward Bromley and Sir James Eltham." They came from Pendle Forest, a wild district on the eastern extremity of the county, and the most prominent among them was Elizabeth Southernes, more generally known as Mother Demdyke, who, by her own confession, had been a practising witch for nearly half a century, having been led astray thereto by one Tibb, a spirit or devil in the form of a boy wearing a parti-coloured coat of brown-and-black, whom she met upon the highway. She and her fellow-prisoners were charged with murders, conspiracies, and other damnable practices, upon evidence fully borne out by their own confessions. Nevertheless, of the twenty only twelve were hanged, one, Mother Demdyke herself, cheating the gallows by dying in prison, while the remaining seven were acquitted—for the time. That so large a proportion should have escaped speaks ill for the abilities of the prosecution, for an example was badly needed. "This remote country," says Scot, "was full of Popish recusants, travelling priests, and so forth, and some of their spells are given in which holy names and things alluded to form a strange contrast with the purpose to which they were applied to secure a good brewing of ale, or the like." One such charm, quoted at the trial, was used by Anne Whittle, *alias* Chattox, one of the twenty, in order to remove a curse previously laid upon John Moore's wife's brewing, and ran as follows:—

> *Three Biters hast thou bitten,*
> *The Host, ill Eye, ill Tongue;*
> *Three Bitter shall be thy boote,*
> *Father, Sonne, and Holy Ghost,*
> *A God's name.*
> *Five Paternosters, five Avies,*
> *And a creede,*
> *For worship of five woundes*
> *Of our Lord.*

Which would seem to show that whether or not Anne Whittle was a witch, she was certainly a Papist, so we need feel little surprise that she was among the twelve executed.

The second great persecution in Lancashire, in 1633, rested almost entirely on the evidence of a boy of eleven. His name was Edmund Robinson, and he lived with his father, a very poor man, in Pendle Forest, where no doubt he heard many legends of the redoubtable Mother Dem-dyke and her colleagues. Upon All Saints' Day, when gathering "bulloes" in a field, he there saw two greyhounds, one black, the other brown, each wearing a collar shining like gold. They fawned upon him, whereafter, "seeing no one, he took them, thinking to course with them. And presently a Hare did rise very near before him. Whereat he cried, 'Loo, Loo, Loo'; but the Doggs would not run. Whereupon he, being very angry, took them, and with the strings that were about their collars, tied them to a little bush at the next hedge, and with a switch that he had in his hand he beat them. And instead of the black greyhound, one Dickenson's wife stood up, a Neighbour, whom this Informer knoweth. And instead of the brown one a little Boy, whom this Informer knoweth not." Dickenson's wife offered him a shilling as the price of his silence, but he answered, "Nay, thou art a witch." Whereupon she put her hand into her pocket and pulled out something like a Bridle, "that gingled," and put it over the little Boy's head, upon which he turned into a white horse. Mrs. Dickenson then seized upon the Informer, set him before her on the white horse, and carried him to a new house called Hoarstones, about a quarter of a mile away. Here he saw about sixty persons, some by the door, others riding towards the house on horses of different colours. In the house was a fire with meat roasting before it. A young woman offered him "Flesh and Bread upon a Trencher and Drink in a Glass," but after the first taste he would have no more of it. On going into the adjoining Barn, he there saw six persons kneeling and pulling at Ropes fastened to the top of the Barn. Whereupon "there came into the Informer's sight flesh smoking, butter in lumps, and milk as it were syling (streaming) from the said Ropes. All of which fell into basins placed under the said Ropes. And when these six had done, there came other six which did likewise, and during all the time of their said pulling they made such ugly faces as scared the Informer, so that he was glad to run out and steal homewards." They pursued him, but he met two horsemen, whereupon they left him. The foremost of his pursuers was one Loind's wife.

The troubles of the Informer were not yet at an end. "After he had come from the company aforesaid, his Father bade him go and fetch home two kine and he happed upon a Boy, who fought him." The Informer had his ears and face made very bloody in the fight, and looking down he saw the Boy had a cloven foot. With commendable prudence he ran away, only to see a light like to a lantern, which he pursued, thinking it might be carried by a neighbour. But he only found a woman—Loind's wife—standing on a bridge, and running from her he met the cloven-footed Boy again, who hit him and made him cry.

Such was the dread story told in court, and partly corroborated by the boy's father. The wives of Dickenson and Loind, along with some eighteen other persons, were arrested at once, while the informer and his father made a comfortable little sum of money by going the round of the neighbouring churches and there detecting others. The trial took place at Lancaster Assizes, when seventeen of the accused were found guilty, but the judge, not being satisfied with the evidence, obtained a reprieve. Four of the accused were sent up to London, and committed to the Fleet Prison, where "great sums of money were gotten by shewing them." The Bishop of Chester held a special examination of the case, and the informer, being separated from his father, soon confessed that his estimable parent had invented the whole story as a means towards an end. So the trial ended in a lamentable fiasco, from the point of view of that public who were looking forward to the public executions as a holiday.

Although the activities of Matthew Hopkins reached their culminating point in the trial of the Manningtree Witches, held before Sir Matthew Hale at Ipswich in 1645, they were only a part of his bag in that year, as we may gather from a statement in Beaumont's "Treatise on Spirits" that "thirty-six were arraigned at the same time before Judge Corners, an. 1645, and fourteen of them hanged and a hundred more detained in several prisons in Suffolk and Essex." Nearly twenty years later, in 1664, we find the Witch-finder-General at work in Great Yarmouth, where he accused sixteen old women, all of whom were convicted and executed; and in the same year took place the St. Edmunsbury trials already referred to. Nevertheless it must be said for Matthew Hopkins, gent., that by the very enthusiasm he imparted into his business he did something towards checking the tide of persecution even at the full. Although the general public gave little sign of satiety, those in authority and the more educated class in general were growing tired of so much useless bloodshed. Witch-trials continued unabated, but towards the close of the century the judge's directions to his jury were frequently such as to ensure an acquittal; while, even when found guilty, the accused were often reprieved through the judge's exertions. Among these just judges the name of Lord Chief Justice Holt merits a high place, as of one more than usually in advance of his age.

In 1694, before the same Lord Chief Justice, at Bury Saint Edmunds, was tried Mother Munnings, of Hartis, in Suffolk. Many things were deposed concerning her spoiling of wort and harming of cattle, and, further, that several persons upon their death-beds had attributed their destruction to her arts. Thus it was sworn that Thomas Pannel, the landlord, not knowing how to turn her out of his house, took away the door and left her without one. Some time after, he happening to pass by, she said to him, "Go thy way; thy nose shall lie upward in the churchyard before Saturday next." On the Monday following Pannel sickened, died on the Tuesday, and was buried within the week, according to her word. To confirm this, another witness added that a doctor, being consulted about another afflicted person, and Mother Munnings being mentioned, said that she was a dangerous woman, for she could touch the line of life. In the indictment she was charged with having an imp like a polecat, and one witness swore that coming from the alehouse about nine o'clock at night, he looked through her window, and saw her take two imps out of a basket, a black and a white. It was further deposed that one Sarah Wager, after a quarrel with the accused, was struck dumb and lame, and was in that condition at home at the time of the trial. Many other equally dreadful accusations were brought, and things might have gone hard for Mother Munnings had not the Lord Chief Justice been on the bench. He, however, directed the jury to bring in a verdict of "Not Guilty," which they obediently did. "Upon particular Enquiry," says Hutchinson, "of several in or near the Town, I find most are satisfied it was a very right Judgment. She lived about Two years after without doing any known Harm to any, and died declaring her

Innocence. Her landlord was a consumptive spent Man, and the Words not exactly as they swore them, and the whole thing seventeen Years before ... the White Imp is believed to have been a Lock of Wool taken out of her Basket to spin, and its Shadow, it is supposed, was the Black one."

In the same year Margaret Elmore was tried at the Ipswich Assizes before the same judge. "She was committed," says Hutchinson, "upon the account of one Mrs. Rudge, who was Three Years in a languishing condition, as was thought by the Witchcraft of the Prisoner then at the Bar, because Mr. Rudge, Husband of the afflicted Person, had refused letting her a House. Some Witnesses said that Mrs. Rudge was better upon the confinement of the woman, and worse again when her chains were off. Other witnesses gave account that her grandmother and her aunt had formerly been hanged for Witches, and that her Grandmother had said she had 8 or 9 Imps, and that she had given two or three apiece to her children." It was further shown on the evidence of a midwife who had searched her grandmother, that the prisoner had plainer witch-marks than she; while several women who had been on bad terms with her took oath that their bodies were infested with lice and other vermin supposed to be of her sending. But not even the vermin could influence the Lord

Chief Justice, and Margaret Elmore was found "Not Guilty."

Yet another case, tried before Holt, was that of Elizabeth Horner at Exeter, in 1696. Three children of one William Borch were said to have been bewitched by her. One had died, the leg of another was twisted, all had vomited pins, been bitten, pricked, and pinched. Their mother deposed "that one of them walked up a smooth plaistered Wall till her Feet were nine foot high, her Head standing off from it. This," she said, "she did five or six times, and laughed and said Bess Horner held her up." Poor Elizabeth had a wart on her shoulder, which the children said was a witchmark, and was sucked by her toad.

But the Lord Chief Justice seems to have been of another opinion, for he directed the jury to acquit her. Indeed, of all the many cases of witchcraft brought before him, not one prisoner was convicted—a state of things which would certainly have resulted in a question being asked in Parliament had it happened in our time. The last woman found guilty of witchcraft in this country was Jane Wenham, the Witch of Walkerne, in Hertfordshire, who was tried in 1712. The witchfinder was called into requisition, and she was submitted to the usual inane and degrading tests. "They either did themselves or suffered others that were about them to scratch and tear her face and run Pins into her Flesh. They . . . turned the Lord's Prayer into a Charm"—(the Vicar of Ardely was responsible for this part of the performance, by the way). "They turned to Spectre Evidence, they drave her to such Distraction that by leading Questions they drew from her what they called a Confession. They had her to Jail. The witnesses swore to vomiting Pins. The Jury found her Guilty, the Judge condemned her, and those clergymen wrote a Narrative of the Tryal, which was received and read with such Pleasure that in a Month's Time it had a Fourth Edition." But Jane Wenham was fortunate in her judge. Being a man of learning and experience, "he Valued not those Tricks and Tryals, and though he was forced to condemn her because a Silly Jury would find her guilty, he saved her Life. And that she might not afterwards be torn to pieces in an ignorant Town, a sensible Gentleman, who will for ever be in Honour for what he did, Colonel Plummer of Gilston, in the same County, took her into his protection and placed her in a little house near his own, where she now lives soberly and inoffensively, and keeps her church, and the whole county is now fully convinced that she was innocent, and that the Maid that was thought to be bewitched was an Idle Hussy . . . and was well as soon as her sweetheart came and married her." Thenceforward the law of England had no more terrors for the witch, though she was not yet quite out of danger. The Statute of James I. was not repealed until 1736, and long after that the mob was accustomed to take the law into its own hands. Thus, in 1751, a man and his wife named Osborn were ducked at Thring, having been dragged by the mob from the workhouse where they had been placed by the parish officers for safety. The woman lost her life in the process. She was, however, not unavenged, for a verdict of "Wilful Murder" was returned against the ringleader of the mob, a chimneysweeper named Colley, and he was hanged, very much to his own and other people's indignation. There was indeed something to be said for the injured Colley when a man like Wesley, pinning his faith to the Bible, could find no means of evading the direct command, "Thou shalt not suffer a witch to live" The last case in which the blood of a witch was actually shed in this country, so far as I have been able to trace, was in 1875, when a certain Ann Turner, a reputed witch, was murdered by a man, who was, however, declared insane.

XII. PERSECUTIONS IN SCOTLAND

The influence of longitude upon national tendencies in superstition is far too wide a subject to be here discussed in any detail, but speaking generally, it may be said that the superstitions of a people—as their religion—are largely a matter of climate—milder and more genial in temperate districts, carried to fiercer and more terrible lengths amid extremes of heat and cold. The man whose gods are based upon his conceptions of the thunderstorm, the grim northern winter or the tropical sun, evokes sterner and more dreadful images than he whose lot is cast amid mild skies and gentle breezes. How wide is the difference between the grim gods who ruled the inhospitable heavens of Scandinavian and Teuton from the tolerant Bohemians who tenanted the classical Olympus. The gentle dryads and light-hearted fauns of Italy would have perished in the first snows of a Baltic winter, just as the hungry ravens of Woden would have been metamorphosed into Venus' doves in one Italian generation.

Nowhere is the influence of climate upon national temperament more clearly typified than in the island of Great Britain. The Viking, settling amid the lush meadows and pleasant woodlands of England, laid aside his heathen sacrifices for the more climatically appropriate religion of Christ with scarcely a regret. Thor and Woden long held their own in the bare northern fastnesses, not to be finally driven out until they had tinged the Christianity which took their place with' something of their own hopelessness and gloom. Just as the gods of Valhalla ever looked forward to the day of their destruction, so Hell rather than Heaven has always held the leading place in the Scottish imagination. So it came about that the superstitions of the Scot were gloomier than were those of his neighbour over the Border. The conviction of his own sinfulness was always with him; how much deeper and more certain that of his neighbours. And because he had a more imminent sense of sin, his belief in witches and their malignancy was more intimate and more resentful. The Englishman, again, feared the witch chiefly on his own personal account; the Scotsman took up the cudgels on behalf of his Creator as well. The Devil seemed so much more powerful to the dwellers of a bleak Highland glen than to the stout yeoman walking amid his opulent English pastures. In Scotland he was on terms almost of equality with God; it is scarcely too much to say that to the majority he was even more powerful, and his earthly agents all the more to be feared and hated.

As in Rome and Greece, the witch was firmly settled in Scotland centuries before the coming of Christianity. But she was of another breed, as befitted her sterner ancestry. She and her demoniacal coadjutors held all the land under a grip of blood and iron. There was nothing amiable, nothing whimsical, nothing human about the spirits, of one kind or another, that lorded it among the mists and heather. Even the fairies had more in common with Logi than with Oberon, Elfame, their dwelling-place, resembled rather Hell than Fairyland. In place of a Lob-lie-by-the-Fire, who found his highest pleasure in the helping of good housewives without fee, of a Queen Mab, who tormented no one but the idle or the wicked, you had a Kelpie, lurking in lonely places intent upon your murder, or a Banshee, prophesying your coming death or ruin. When at last Christianity came, it had a long, stern struggle against such antagonists—nor, indeed, could it ever altogether overcome them, even though it forced them to adopt new names and new disguises. The missionary saints found their task of conversion increased tenfold by the strenuous opposition of the witches and other evil spirits. St. Patrick, in particular, so enraged them and their master the Devil, by his pertinacity, that he was forced, for a time, to flee before their assaults back to Ireland. One of their most famous exploits was the bombardment with a mountain-top of the vessel in which he was embarked. It is true that their aim, like that of Polyphemus, a member of their own family, was bad, and the mountain-top fell into the sea instead of drowning the saint. But by this very mischance they provided permanent proof of their exploit; for the mountain-top remains to this day to testify unto it, being that upon which Dumbarton Castle was subsequently built.

Among the many legends dealing with these same early Scots witches, I am tempted to quote from one, taken down verbatim from the lips of an old Highland woman, by the late Dr. Norman Macleod and related by him in his "Reminiscences of a Highland Parish." In its modern form it was woven around the imaginary misadventures of a

Spanish Princess—and the real shipwreck of the *Florida*, one of the vessels forming the Spanish Armada, sunk near Tobermory, in Mull, in 1588. Actually, however, the magical passages have some much more ancient history, probably, as we may judge from incidental reference to Druidism, from pre-Christian days. The first part of the legend relates how the Spanish Princess came to Mull, there had a love affair with Maclean of Duart, and was murdered by his jealous wife. The King of Spain, hearing of his daughter's fate, fitted out a war-vessel and despatched it to Tobermory to take summary vengeance. Maclean and his people, feeling unequal to resisting it by ordinary means, sought aid from magic (Druidism, in fact) and by powerful spells and charms gathered all the witches of Mull, the *Doideagan Muileach*, together. He explained the position and begged them to raise a tempest and sink the Spanish vessel, pointing out at the same time that her commander, one Captain Forrest, was himself a magician. The chief witch asked if the Spaniard, when declaring his unfriendly intentions, had said, "With God's help!" On learning that he had omitted that precaution she professed herself ready to undertake the task. This passage is so unsuggestive of the pagan witch's usual attitude that I take it to be a pious interpretation of later date.

In due time the witches began their work of *ŭbag*, *obag* and *gisreag* (charm, incantation and chanting), but with little initial effect. Stronger measures becoming necessary the chief witch tied a straw rope to a quern-stone, passed it over a rafter, and raised the stone as high as she was able. As it rose the wind rose with it, but she could not get it very high owing to the counter-spells of the Spanish captain with the English name. Accordingly she called her sister-witches to help her—witches with very much finer names, by the way, than their English colleagues could boast of. They were nine in all, and the names of five were Luideag (which is to say "Raggie"), Agus Doideag (or "Frizzle Hair"), Agus Cor-rag Nighin Jain Bhàin ("The Finger of White John's Daughter"), Cas a'mhogain Riabhaich à Gleancomham ("Hogganfoot from Glencoe") and Agus Gormshuil mhòr bhàrr na Maighe ("Great Blue-Eye from Moy"). All pulled together at the rope, but could not raise the quern-stone. Some of them then flew through the air and climbed about the ship's rigging in the shape of cats, spitting and swearing. But Captain Forrest only laughed at them. So he did when their number increased to fifteen. At last the *Doideag* got a very strong man, *Domhnull Dubh Làidir*, to hold the rope and prevent the stone from slipping down again, while she flew off to Lochaber to beg the assistance of Great Garmal of Moy, the *doyenne* of Scotch witchcraft, whose powers were more developed than those of all the others put together. Garmal accepted the flattering invitation, and set out for the scene of action. No sooner was she in the air than a tempest began, and by the time she reached Tobermory Captain Forrest realised that he had better retire. But before his cable could be cut Great Garmal had reached the ship, had climbed to the top of the mast in the shape of the largest black cat that ever was seen, and uttered one spell, whereupon the Spanish man-o'-war with all her crew sank to the bottom of the sea.

Against witches of such prowess he must be a powerful man—saint or king—who would gainsay them. Many—if not most—of the earlier Scottish kings had passages with witchcraft, mostly to their own detriment. Leaving aside Macbeth, quite as credible an historic character as the rest, we have King Duff, who, towards the end of the tenth century, narrowly escaped a lingering death at the hands of the witches—they employing the old-fashioned, even in those days, but eminently dependable "waxen image." By good luck only he was enabled to discover the witches and, having burned them and broken up the magic before it was quite melted before their fire, to recover his usual health and spirits.

Not only for its long line of eminent witches does Scotland claim an important place in the annals of the arts magical. In Michael Scot she had one of the most famous wizards known to history, far superior in prowess to the great bulk of his successors, if tradition may be credited, and every whit as eminent, while a great deal more probable, than the British Merlin of Arthurian legend. Thomas the Rhymer, he of Escildonne, chosen lover of the Fairy Queen, was another wizard of repute.

It is an indirect testimony to the high, if evil, place held by magic in Scotland that so many of its followers and practitioners were men and women of the first ranks of life. We have the dread figure of William, Lord Soulis, boiled to death as the only fit punishment for the crimes committed in his feudal stronghold, such as put him on an evil parity with the Marshal de Retz, the French Bluebeard. Or again, in 1479, by which time we are on firm ground, the Earl of Mar, with a whole band of male and female abettors of humbler rank, was burned in Edinburgh for attempts on the King's life by aid of waxen images and spells. Indeed, the whole family of this peccant nobleman proved, on investigation, to be tarred with the same magical brush. Lady Glammis again, burned in 1536 as a witch, was one of the proud Douglasses, granddaughter of Archibald Bell-the-Cat, widow of "Clean the Causeway" Lord Glammis, whom, *inter alia*, she was accused of murdering—young, beautiful, and wealthy. It is true that her death was very necessary to one of the contemporary political parties, though that may have been only a coincidence. Another aristocratic witch was Lady Katherine Fouliss, who, with her step-son, was tried in 1590 for "witchcraft, incantation, sorcery, and poisoning." She, although she seems to have gone about her questionable business with an open-hearted publicity that arouses our admiration, was acquitted through family influence, and her stepson with her, though several of their humbler accomplices paid the penalty in the usual way.

In the following year occurred a witch-trial of interest in itself, and the cause of the great outburst of persecution which for the next century makes the annals of Scottish justice run red with innocent blood—that of Dr. Feane—or Fian, as it is variously spelt. The story of the "Secretar and Register to the Devil" has been often told, but it will bear recapitulation. Fian was a schoolmaster at Saltpans, Lothian; he was further, according to his accusers, a wizard. More exactly, perhaps, he should be described as a male-witch, seeing that he had no control over Satan, but, on the other hand, had sworn allegiance to him, received witch-marks—under his tongue—and otherwise conformed to the etiquette of the lower grade in the profession. This seems, indeed, to have been customary in Scotland, where the distinction which I have endeavoured to lay down between the sorcerer and the witch is often hard to trace. His magic, however, gains its chief interest from its object—no less a person than James I. and VI. This learned and Protestant monarch, being on his way to visit his Danish bride in her native land, the Devil and his Secretary laid a plot to drown him. They put to sea, after the vessel, along with a whole regiment of witches, and there cast an enchanted cat into the sea, raising a fierce storm, which could not, however, prevent the Divinely-protected James from reaching Denmark in safety. On his return journey the plotters tried another plan—to raise a fog whereby the Royal ship might be driven ashore on the English coast. Towards this end Satan cast a football, or its misty semblance, into the sea, and succeeded *m* raising what may be accurately described as the Devil's own fog. But angels guided the ship upon its proper course, and again the King escaped the assaults of his enemies. For these and other crimes Dr. Fian, with a number of women-witches, was tried, tortured, forced to confess, and burned on Castle Hill—though he withdrew his confession before the end and died like a gentleman and a scholar. It is an interesting point about the trial that in it occurs the first Scottish mention of the Devil's mark.

The effects of this outrage upon the Lord's Anointed were not to end with the death of its presumed concocters. If the tribe of witches had grown so bold, it was high time they were extirpated, and gallantly did the King and his advisers set about it. It was in 1563 that the persecution of the witch was regularised as a distinct branch of crime by an enactment of the Estates, "that nae person take upon hand to use any manner of witchcrafts, sorcery, or necromancy, nor give themselves furth to have ony sic craft or knowledge thereof there through abusing the people," and that "nae person seek ony help, response, or consultation, at any sic users or abusers of witchcrafts . . . under pain of death"

Thenceforward, until the last witch-burning in 1727, the fires were seldom allowed to go out, and to be an old and ugly woman was perhaps the most "dangerous trade" in Scottish industry. There was, indeed, one incidental to a witch-burning which may—it is at least to be hoped—have sometimes moved the economical Scotsman in the direction of toleration—the expense. Here, for instance, are the items expended in the execution of one batch of witches in Fife in 1633:—

- For ten loads of coal to burn them £3 s.6 d.8
- For a tar-barrel s.14 d.0
- For towes s.6 d.0
- For harden to be jumps to them s.3 d.10
- For making of them d.8

Or a grand total of £4 11s. 2d., no small sum, seen with thrifty eyes, especially if we consider the greater value of money in those days.

It is, perhaps, only characteristic of the national attitude towards the whole subject that the "White," or amiable, witch was held in as great detestation as her "Black," or malignant, sister. Torture and penalty were the same for either. Thus we find that, in 1597, four women were convicted at Edinburgh for curing, or endeavouring to cure, certain of their neighbours' ills by witchcraft, and were in due course strangled and burned. It is true that they did not suffer the greater penalty of being burned alive, which was reserved for witches of unusual malevolence. The dislike and dread of a "White" witch was not, be it noted, due to ingratitude alone, but rather because it entailed the mutilation of the patient at the Resurrection. While the rest of his body would owe its preservation in this world to God Himself, any limb or organ healed by the Devil—acting through the "White" witch—would belong to him, and thus be unable to rise at the Day of Judgment with the rest. In endeavouring to understand the mental attitude which gave rise to the great persecutions of the seventeenth century, one cannot afford to overlook such points of belief as this. Fear and the instinct of self-preservation, not cruelty, were the driving-power in the witch-murderer. We, who think no shame of shooting partridges for pastime, have little cause to contemn the seventeenth-century Christian who killed witches lest they should destroy him body and soul.

Such is the similarity of the various Scottish witch-trials that too-detailed recapitulation would be tedious and unprofitable. Some, however, stand out from the rest by reason of their grotesque horror and exaggeration. Such is the trial of Isobel Grierson, "spous to Johnne Bull, wark-man in the Pannis" (Preston Pans), tried at Edinburgh in March, 1607. Grierson, by the way, was a name very prominent in witch-circles at the time. One Robert Grierson had taken a leading part as an accomplice of Dr. Fian, above referred to, his being the hand which cast the enchanted cat into the sea in the endeavour to drown King James. He was also, as shown in the confession of another defendant in the same trial, the cause of much disturbance at a Sabbath held in North Berwick Churchyard. Satan, by an unfortunate slip, addressed him by his real name. As etiquette strictly demanded that Christian names should be ignored, and nick-names—in this instance "Rab the Rower"—used instead, the mistake appeared an intentional insult on Satan's part, and was so taken by the assembled witches, who expressed their displeasure with uncompromising vigour, even to the extent of running "hirdy girdy" about the churchyard. But to return to John Bull's wife. She was accused, *inter alia*, of having conceived a cruel hatred and malice against one Adam Clark, and with having for the space of a year used all devilish and unholy means to be revenged upon him. On a November night in 1606, between eleven and midnight, Adam and his wife being in bed, Isobel entered the house in the form of a black cat, accompanied by a number of other cats, and made a great and fearful noise, whereat Adam, his wife, and maid-servant were so frightened as almost to go mad. Immediately afterwards the Devil appeared, in the likeness of a black man, seized the servant's nightcap and cast it on the fire, and then dragged her up and down the house. Who thereby contracted a great sickness, so that she lay bed-fast, in danger of her life, for the space of six weeks. Isobel was further accused of having compassed the death of William Burnet and of laying on him a fearful and uncouth sickness, by casting in at his door a gobbet of raw, enchanted flesh. Whereafter the Devil nightly appeared in poor William's house in the guise of a naked infant child for the space of half a year. Occasionally he varied the performance by appearing in the shape of Isobel herself, but being called by her name would immediately vanish away. As a result of all which, Adam languished in sickness for the space of three years, unable to obtain a cure, and at last, in great "douleur and payne," departed this life. Another of her victims was Robert Peddan, who remained sick for the space of one year and six months, and then suddenly remembering that he owed Isobel nine shilling and fourpence, and that before the time of his sickness, as he had refused to pay it, she had delivered to him certain writings that she kept in MS., and thereafter, with divers blasphemous speeches, told him he should repent it.

Remembering this, he sought out Isobel and satisfied her the said sum, at the same time asking his health of her for God's sake, saying, "If ye have done me any wrong or hurt, refrain the same and restore to me my health." And within twenty-four hours he was as well as ever before. Yet again, Margaret, the wife of Robert Peddan, lying in bed, Isobel, or a spirit in her shape, entered his house, seized Margaret by the shoulder and flung her upon the floor, so that she swooned with fright, and was immediately seized with a fearful and uncouth sickness. Isobel, hearing that rumours of her ill-doing were abroad, caused Mrs. Peddan to drink with her, whereupon her sickness left her for eight or ten days. But as Mrs. Peddan, learning nothing from experience, declared *hic et ubique* that Isobel was a foul witch, she straightway laid another charm upon her, so that the sickness returned. Isobel, being found guilty of all these and other crimes, was ordered by her judges to be "taken to the Castle Hill of Edinburgh, and there to be strangled at the stake until she be dead and her body to be burnt in ashes, as convict of the said crimes; and all her movable goods to be escheat and inbrought to our sovereign lord's use, as convict of the said crimes." Which was done accordingly.

In 1622 Margaret Wallace was executed on the charge of inflicting and causing diseases. The chief count against her was of having consulted with Christiane Graham—burned as a witch some time before Margaret's trial—how to cure Margaret

Muir, "a bairne," of a disorder, "to which end they went about twelve at night to a yard, and there used their devilish charms, whereby the disease was removed from the bairne."

The next twenty years are filled with a monotonous record of witch-trials, similar in essentials to those already quoted. Perhaps the most outstanding is that of Catharine Oswald, who kept many rendezvous with Satan, and cursed the yard of John Clerk so effectually that for four years neither "kaill, hemp, nor other graine would grow therein." Alice Nisbet, also famous in her day, was likewise convicted of having "took paines off a woman in travell, by some charms and horrible words; among which thir ware some, 'the bones to the fire and the soull to the divill.'"

In 1633 twenty witches were executed, Sir George Home, of Manderston, being the most zealous persecutor, chiefly, it was said, to spite his wife, with whom he was not on good terms, and who had a taste for Black Magic. Ten years later arose another fierce persecution, so that in Fifeshire alone thirty women were executed—the local ministry taking the lead in the prosecution. Two of the accused were domestic servants in service at Edinburgh, and with that love of finery which even now attends their kind. By their own confession they had been introduced to the Devil by Janet Cranston, a notorious witch, and had by him been promised that, if they gave themselves bodies and souls to his allegiance, "they should be as trimlie clad as the best servants in Edinburgh." Janet Barker, one of the twain, admitted having the Devil's mark between her shoulders, and when a pin was thrust therein it remained there for an hour before she noticed it. Needless to say, both were "wirriet" (strangled) at the stake and burned. Agnes Fynnie was convicted on no fewer than twenty counts of different offences, chiefly of harming the health of personal enemies. Her defence was more vigorous than was customary, but although she pleaded that of all the witches already burned not one had mentioned her name, she was found guilty and executed.

It must not be supposed that Satan did not make occasional efforts to befriend his own. Thus we may learn from Sinclair's "Invisible World Discovered" that he directly interfered, endeavouring to save the wife of one Goodail, "a most beautiful and comely person," for whom he had a particular regard, much to the jealousy of less well-favoured witches. He even visited her prison and endeavoured to carry her off through the air. so that "she made several loups upwards, increasing gradually till her feet were as high as his breast." But James Fleming, the gaoler, was a man of might. He caught hold of her feet, so that it was a case of "Pull Devil, pull Gaoler" and the better man—which is to say Mr. Fleming—won, and the prisoner was saved for subsequent execution. On another occasion Satan actually released a witch from the church-steeple of Culross, where she was confined. Unfortunately for her, before they had gone far upon their aerial flight, she happened, in the course of conversation, to mention the name of the Deity—whereupon he dropped her.

Political ups and downs, whomever else they might affect, made no difference in the hard lot of the witch—save,—indeed, that she was regarded as belonging to the opposite- party by that in power. That did not, however, gain for her the sympathy of the defeated. Thus the death of Charles I., according to many, could only have been compassed by the Powers of Darkness themselves. Even the brute creation seemed to have realised this, if we may judge from the reputed fact that some of the lions in the Tower of London died from the smell of a handkerchief dipped in the martyred monarch's blood. "Old Noll" was declared, by Royalists anxious to explain away their defeats, to be Satan's direct agent, if not the Devil incarnate, the Commonwealth representing his Kingdom upon Earth. Thus although the Republicans had done their utmost in the way of witch-harrying, their efforts were but feeble compared to those of the Royalists upon the glorious Restoration. Obviously a witch must be a friend to crop-eared Roundheads—and fearfully did she pay the penalty. Somewhere about 120 were executed in the year 1661, immediately following the King's entering upon his own again—the majority owing their arrest to the exertions of John Kincaid and John Dick', witch-finders as eminent, though less famous, than Matthew Hopkins himself. And now it was the turn of the victorious Cavaliers to be regarded, by Presbyterian and Parliamentarian, as owing their success to the help of Satan and his agents. Their Bishops were reported to be cloven-footed and shadowless, their military commanders to be bullet-proof by enchantment, and to possess horses that could clamber among inaccessible rocks like foxes; the justices who put fugitives on trial for treason were seen in familiar converse with the Fiend, and one of them was known to have offered up his first-born son to Satan.

A representative example of the trials held in the latter part of the seventeenth century is that consequent upon the death of Sir George Maxwell, of Pollock, slain, as was supposed, by the malice of "some haggs and one wizard." A full account of it is given in the "Memorialls" of

Robert Law, writer, edited from his MS. by Charles Kirkpatrick Sharpe. To put it briefly, Sir George, having been ill for some time, having great pain in his side and shoulder, a dumb girl called at the house and explained by signs that his waxen "picture" was being melted before the fire in a certain woman's house, who had a grudge against him. Search being made, his image was found up the chimney. Two pins being found stuck in the figure's shoulder were removed, whereupon Sir George recovered, and the woman was laid by the heels and found to have several witch-marks. But very soon the baronet was again taken ill. The witch's house, now inhabited by her son, was again searched, and a second "portraitour," this time of clay, found under the man's bolster. Arrested, he confessed that the Devil had visited him, in company with four witches, had made the image himself, and stuck pins in the appropriate limbs. The four witches were apprehended, and, with the young man, burnt at Paisley; but this did not prevent their victim's death. A few months later he died, "being worn to a shadow," owing, according to the dumb girl, to the existence of yet another "picture" which his friends had "slighted."

The last Scottish execution of a witch took place in 1722. The prisoner was accused of having turned her daughter into a pony, shod by the Devil and so ridden upon her—whence the girl was ever afterwards lame. Found guilty, this last of a long line of martyrs was burned at Dornoch, and scandalised the spectators—the weather being chilly—by composedly warming her hands at the fire that was to consume her.

In 1735, English and Scottish statutes against witchcraft were alike repealed, much to the horror of the seceders from the Established Kirk, who, in their annual confession of National and Personal Sins, gave a prominent place to "The Penal Statutes against Witches having been repealed by Parliament contrary to the express Law of God."

XIII. OTHER PERSECUTIONS

The universality of the belief in witchcraft carried in its train international belief in the efficacy of persecution as its cure. When one nation led the others were bound to follow, and accordingly we find that every European country—to say nothing of non-Christian peoples—lent itself vigorously to this form of legalised murder. But so similar are the details of these proceedings that witchcraft might claim to have preceded Volapuk or Esperanto as an international bond. Everywhere the persecution followed the same, or parallel lines, differing only in minor national idiosyncrasies. So far as Catholic countries were in question this was natural enough—seeing that all alike drew their inspiration from the same source

—Innocent VIII.'s Bull; while the Protestants, however much they might object to Papal persecution of their peculiar tenets, heartily agreed with both the purpose and the method of those directed at the common enemy of all.

In France, as elsewhere, the seventeenth century saw the witch-fever rise to its most extravagant height. Though it is difficult to compare them in degree—where all alike rose to the highest level of bloodthirstiness—the French may be said to have excelled their ancient rivals in thoroughness. Thus the direction of the campaign was in the direct control of either Church or State, rather than being submitted to the ordinary process of the law; they were official rather than local, and witchcraft a religious and political rather than a merely criminal offence. Thus, in 1634, Urbain Grandier, who had satirised Richelieu, was accused, at the Cardinal's direct instigation, of practising the Black Art upon some nuns at Loudun, and was in due course burned at the stake; and many similar cases are recorded. A point in which the French practice differed from the English in the matter of witch-finding was that, while in England the affair was usually entrusted to the care of such comparatively humble persons as Matthew Hopkins, the French Commissioner was an official of importance, and usually, as in the case of Pierre de Lancre, of education. This gentleman, sent as we have seen at the instance of the King, according to his own account, by the Parliament of Bordeaux to investigate the charges of wholesale witchcraft against the inhabitants of the Labourt district in 1608, has himself provided us with illuminating insight into such an official's frame of mind. This is shown even more clearly in his introductory argument than in his book—already frequently referred to—written to prove the inconstancy of devils and bad angels. Towards this end he sets out to prove the inconstancy of the natives of Labourt and their peculiar liability to Satan's snares. Then he argues that Labourt must, on the face of it, breed an unsettled and inconstant race, being both mountainous and situated on the borders of three kingdoms, France, Spain, and Navarre. Its language, being likewise varied—a mixture of French, Spanish, and Basque—is in itself another powerful argument. Its inhabitants, again, are for the most part sailors, when they might with better reason be farmers, because they prefer the inconstant sea to the firm, unchanging land. Their long absences, he finds, tends to make their wives unfaithful—another powerful impetus towards witchcraft. Although the Commissioner—a man of open mind—confesses that their dress is not indecent; he has grave doubts about their dances, being not quiet and respectable, but rowdy in the extreme, and accompanied upon the tambourine, an instrument of baleful significance. They live very largely upon apples—which may also account for their proneness to forbidden things, the Devil's power over the apple having been recognised ever since the days of Eve. De Lancre even puts forward the assertions of heretical Scottish and English merchants, who have visited Bordeaux to buy wines, and have there assured him that they have often seen large troops of daemons heading across the sea straight for Labourt. From all of which the Commissioner concludes that there is scarcely a family in the district but is more or less deeply involved in or connected with witchcraft and its practices.

The same causes which rendered the French persecutions more severe while they lasted, also brought it about that any relaxation of the Governmental attitude diminished them to a greater extent than was the case in England, where witchcraft had a more personal aspect. The armed peasant, who, musket in hand, proved his possession of supernatural powers by defeating the King's best troops led by a Marshall of France, among the bare peaks of the Cevennes, in defence of his detestable heresies, might look for nothing but ruthless extermination as a wizard; but even Governments have human memories, and the humble old woman muttering spells in obscure corners of the kingdom, was apt to be overlooked. Sometimes, too, as the years passed, the Royal Person actually interfered to shield the accused from less official persecution. Thus, when in 1672, a number of shepherds were arrested in Normandy and the Parliament of Rouen prepared for an investigation similar to that previously held at Labourt, the King ordered all the accused to be set at liberty, with salutary effect in dissipating the increasing witch-fever. Some ten years later, however, a Royal edict revived all previous ordinances against sorcery and divination. Many such cases were tried before the "Chambre Ardente," the last being that of a woman named Voisin, condemned for sorcery and poisoning in 1680. The anti-sorcery laws were in force until the mid-eighteenth century, while as proof of the persistence of the superstition we may again quote the case of the Soubervies, in 1850, already referred to.

Germany—the land of sentiment, no less than of common sense—was not different from her neighbours in her method of regarding the witch. The German, though he protested against the methods of the Inquisition, as applied to himself, could have no objection to its treatment of the witch-question. Cases were sometimes heard in the civil court, but were far more frequently left to the tender mercies of the Church. At the end of the fifteenth century the Inquisitors Sprenger and Kramer taught the whole duty of an Inquisitor in the "Malleus Maleficarum," and found many apt pupils throughout the Empire. Persecutions of unprecedented fierceness broke out in many districts, one of the most striking examples being that at Trier in the second half of the sixteenth century. For many years there had been failure of crops and increasing sterility throughout the land, attributed by many to the increase of witchcraft and the malice of the Devil. In time, so ferocious became the popular antipathy that scarcely any who fell under suspicion had the remotest chance of escape. It was perhaps the most democratic persecution recorded in history; neither rank nor wealth was of the least avail in face of accusation. Canon Linden, an eyewitness, relates that two Burgomasters, several councillors and associate judges, canons of sundry collegiate churches, parish priests and rural deans were among the victims. Dr. Dietrich Flade, judge of the secular court and deputy governor of the city, strove to check the persecution and fell a victim to it for his pains. He was accused, tortured into confessing various crimes of sorcery, and burned at the stake in 1589. A Dutch scholar, Cornelius Loos by name, a reputed disciple of Wierus and tenant of a professorial chair at the Trier University, also ventured to enter a protest against the prevalent madness. Failing in his appeal to the authorities he wrote a book, in which his views were set forth at length. It was seized while in the printers' hands and its author cast into prison. He was, however,' released in the spring of 1593 upon uttering a solemn recantation—published in book form six years later by Del Rio. Far from curing the barrenness of the land, the persecution only increased it—and thus provided its own cure—dying down at last when the general poverty prevented the necessary funds being provided for its maintenance.

A pathetic incident is recorded of another formidable outburst of the witch-mania—at Bamberg in 1628. The Burgomaster Johannes Junius, was among those put on trial. In the beginning he denied all the charges against him, but being put to the torture, confessed that he had been present at a witch gathering and a witch-dance and had desecrated the Host. Such a confession, though it spared him further torture, did not, of course, stay his execution. Some little time after, having partially recovered from his first agonies, he was in great distress of mind as to the opinion his dearly-loved daughter should hold of him after his death. With sorely maimed hands he yet managed to scrawl a letter and ensure its reaching her. In it he appeals in agony of heart that she shall not believe the matter of his enforced confession: "Innocent have I come into prison, innocent have I been tortured, and innocent must I die.....I confessed only in order to escape the great anguish and bitter torture, such as it was impossible for me longer to bear." Unfortunately the torturers were never satisfied with a confession unless it implicated other people as well, and the case of Junius and some of his friends and neighbours who also suffered formed no exception to the rule.

The Bamberg persecution was succeeded by one at Wurzburg in the following year. Fortunately the noble Jesuit priest and poet, Friedrich von Spee, was appointed confessor of those sentenced to death, and was inspired to write, in 1631, his "Cautio Criminalis," which, published anonymously, did much to stem the tide of persecution. "Incredible among us Germans," he begins, "and especially (I blush to say it) among Catholics, are the popular superstitions, envy, calumnies, backbitings, insinuations and the like, which being neither punished by the magistrates nor refuted by the pulpit, first stir up suspicion of witchcraft. All the Divine judgments which God has threatened in Holy Writ are now ascribed to witches. No longer do God or Nature aught, but witches everything."

It was a long time, however, before such enlightened views could obtain universal credence, and it was in Germany that the last European execution for witchcraft took place, so lately as 1793.

The international epidemic did not spread to Sweden till the end of the century, when it broke out, in more than usually eccentric form, in the village of Mohra. It was chiefly remarkable for the number of children concerned. "Four score and five persons, fifteen of them children, were condemned, and most, if not all of them, were burnt and executed. There were besides six-and-thirty children that ran the gauntlet and twenty were whipt on the hands at the Church-door every Sunday for three weeks together." The whole proceedings were, indeed, almost a children's drama and no emanation of childish imagination but was eagerly swallowed by a normally sober and sensible community. Most probably, indeed, the whole affair had its foundation in some myth or folk-story more or less popular in all the local nurseries. Indeed, were we of the present generation to return to the earlier belief in lycanthropy and the ceaseless malignancy of ubiquitous were-wolves, it is easily within the bounds of possibility that "Red Riding Hood," a story which quite conceivably owes its origin to the same superstition, might bring about some similar panic. An imaginative child might easily mix up the grandmother in the story with the wolf who devours her: might thus come to the conclusion that his own grandmother occasionally masqueraded in the form of a wolf: might in time convince himself that he had actually seen her thus transmogrified, and might thus in time bring not only his own venerable relative but those of half the other children in the school that he attended under unpleasant suspicion and not improbably to a more unpleasant death.

The mainstay of the Mohra panic was the sudden belief—propagated by the children themselves—that some hundreds of them had been brought under the power of the Devil by local witches. The whole community took the alarm, the Government was appealed to, and a Royal Commission embodied to investigate the charges —with sanguinary results. It was declared that the witches instructed the children to go to the crossways, and there to invoke the Devil, begging him to carry them to the Blockula, the favourite local mountain meeting-place for Sabbaths. Satan, in answering their prayers, appeared in many forms, the most original being that of a man with a red beard, wearing a grey coat, red and blue stockings, a high-crowned hat adorned with ribbons of many colours, and preposterous garters. So attired he must have wanted only a magic pipe to serve as double to the Pied Piper of Hamelin, the Teutonic legend most nearly recalled by the whole circumstance. He provided the children with mounts and anointed them with unguent composed of the scrapings of altars and the filings of church-clocks. Another account says that the witches accompanied the children, riding with them to the Blockula on men's backs—the said men, upon arriving there, being propped against the wall, fast asleep. Now and again they preferred to ride upon posts, or goats transfixed upon spits, and they flew through walls, chimneys, and windows without either injuring themselves or breaking the glass and bricks.

The actual transportation of the children gave rise to many weighty arguments. All the time they asserted they were at the Blockula, their parents declared that they had held them asleep in their arms. It was finally concluded that their nocturnal travels might be either in the flesh or the spirit, according to circumstances. So firmly did many parents credit their children's assertions that a local clergyman determined to watch his little son throughout the night, holding him tightly in his arms; but even this ocular demonstration did not serve to convince the mother.

Upon the Blockula was declared to be a fine house, having a gate painted in very gay colours. Within it were a large banqueting-hall and other rooms. The food served at the banquets consisted of such nourishing fare as coleworts, bacon, and bread, butter, milk and cheese—all of them, be it noted, familiar to childish palates, as was the feast of the Lancashire witches—quoted elsewhere—to the "Informer." Those who attended the Blockula gave birth to sons and daughters, who were married in their turn to each other, their children being toads and serpents. They built houses, but so badly that the walls fell upon them, making them black and blue; they were beaten, abused, and laughed at—yet when on one occasion they thought the Devil was dead, the place was filled with wailings and lamentations. As usually happened in such persecutions, the bloodshed at last brought people to their senses—perhaps the execution of fifteen children gave their parents pause. At all events, the Commission was in due course dissolved, and the persecution came to a sudden end, though prayers continued to be offered weekly in the church against any other such horrible visitation—as indeed they well might!

It is not my intention to give more than a general idea of the most outstanding historic persecutions—for, as I have said, they differ only in minor degrees in different times and places. There are, however, yet one other group too striking to be ignored—those which raged in the New England Colonies. It might have been supposed, by one unconversant with human nature, that the memory of their own sufferings would have softened the hearts of the colonists when they themselves were in power. The reverse was the case; their enmity against their former oppressors was diverted towards this new channel, gaining force in the process. There is indeed some excuse to be found for their mental attitude. Springing in the most cases from the humbler class, they had many privations and sufferings to endure before they could gain any respite in their newly-settled country to think of progressive education. Their warfare against the Indians might well have given both sides reason to think that the Devil was indeed arrayed upon the side of their enemies—and in time the gloomy superstitions of the natives served to buttress the imported beliefs of Europe.

From the beginning of the seventeenth century to the end the settlers had been forced to devote most of their thoughts to means of subsistence alone, and there had been no opportunity for speculative thought to modify ideas which, standing still, became more and more stereotyped. The precarious existence of the infant State also gave its leaders every ground for taking the severest measures towards anything considered to be dangerous to its welfare. As early as 1648, Margaret Jones of Charlestone was accused of practising witchcraft. The charge was "that she was found to have such a malignant touch as many persons, men, women and children whom she stroked or touched in any affliction or displeasure, were taken with deafness or vomiting, or other violent pains or sickness." Governor Winthrop, in whose Journals the account is found, also adds that "in prison there was seen in her arms a little child which ran from her into another room, the officer following it, it vanished."

Margaret Jones was found guilty of the crime of witchcraft, and was hanged according to the law. Soon after her execution her husband wished to go to Barbadoes in a vessel lying in Boston Harbour. He was refused a passage as being the husband of a witch, and thereupon the vessel began to roll as though it would turn over.

Instead of the phenomenon being attributed to the refusal to take an innocent man on board, it was reported to the magistrate, and an officer was sent to arrest Jones. On his exhibiting the warrant for the arrest, the vessel instantly ceased to roll.

Jones was thrown into prison, but there is no evidence of his ever having been tried.

In 1655, Ann Hibbins was hanged at Boston for witchcraft; there were witch-executions in different places at ever-decreasing intervals. One of the most interesting cases of witchcraft was that of the Goodwin family in 1688. A full account of this case is given by Cotton Mather, "Minister of the Gospel," in a book which purported to contain "a faithful account of many Wonderful and Surprising Things that have befallen several Bewitched and Possessed Persons in New England." In his own words, in 1689, "There dwells at this time in the South part of Boston a sober and pious man, whose name is John Goodwin, whose Trade is that of a Mason, and whose Wife (to whom a good Report gives a share with him in all the characters of Virtue) has made him the Father of six (now living) children. Of these children all but the eldest, who works with his Father at his calling, and the youngest, who lives yet upon the Breast of its mother, have laboured under the direful effects of a (no less palpable than) stupendous WITCHCRAFT." After explaining the godly and virtuous tendencies of the children and the excellence of their upbringing and religious education, Mather says:—"Such was the whole Temper and Courage of the children that there cannot easily be anything more unreasonable than to imagine that a Design to Dissemble could cause them to fall into any of their odd Fits."

In 1688 the eldest daughter, on examining the linen, found that some of it was missing, and questioned the daughter of the washerwoman with regard to it. 'The washerwoman—as might have happened in much later times—used very bad language in her daughter's defence, whereupon poor Miss Goodwin "became variously indisposed in her health, and was visited with strange Fits, beyond those that attend an Epilepsy or a Catalepsy, or those that they call the Diseases of Astonishment." Shortly afterwards one of her sisters and two of her brothers were seized in a like manner and "were all four tortured everywhere in a manner so very grievous that it would have broken a heart of stone to have seen their agonies." "Physicians were of no avail. Sometimes they would be Deaf, sometimes Dumb, and sometimes Blind, and often all this at once. One while their Tongues would be drawn down their throats, another while they would be pulled out upon their chins to a prodigious length. They would have their mouths opened into such wideness that their Jaws went out of joint; and anon they would clap together with a force like that of a Strong Spring-Lock. The same would happen to their Shoulder-Blades, and their Elbows and Hand-wrists and several of their Joints. They would at times ly in a benummed condition, and be drawn together as those that are tyed Neck and Heels, and presently be stretched out, yea, drawn Backwards to such a degree it was feared the very skin of their Bellies would have crack'd." There were many other symptoms which Mather relates with zealous satisfaction.—At last the distracted father told the Magistrates of his suspicions of the washerwoman Glover. On being examined, she gave such a poor account of herself that she was committed to prison. It was found that she could not say the Lord's Prayer, even when it was repeated to her clause by clause, and when she was committed it was found that all the children "had some present ease." The supposed witch was brought to trial, but, being an Irishwoman, there were difficulties in her understanding the questions, which told very badly against her. Orders were given to search her house, and several small images—dolls, perhaps—made of rags and stuffed with goat's-hair, were found. The old woman then confessed "that her way to torment the objects of her malice was by rubbing of her Finger with her spittle, and stroaking of those little Images." When one of the images was brought to her, she took it in her hand, and immediately one of the children fell into fits before the whole assembly. Witnesses were easily found against her, one of whom said that Glover had sometimes come down her chimney. After her condemnation the worthy Mather visited her in prison, "but she entertained me with nothing but Irish, which language I have not Learning enough to understand without an Interpreter." On her way to execution she declared that her death would not end the sufferings of the children, as there were more in it besides herself; and so it proved. The children would bark like dogs and purr like cats, and they would fly like geese. "Such is Satanic perversity that if one ordered them to Rub a clean table, they were able to do it without any disturbance; if to rub a dirty Table, presumably they would, with many Torments, be made uncapable." Mather relates that owing to their Bewitchments, holy Books caused them horrible agonies. One girl told him that if she went to read the Bible, her eyes would be strangely twisted and blinded, and her neck presumably broken, but also that if anyone else did read the Bible in the Room, though it were wholly out of her sight, and without the least voice or noise of it, she would be cast into very horrible agonies. "*A Popish Book*" says Mather, "she would endure very well and also books such as the Oxford Tests"—

Mather must be forgiven for being a partisan—but "my grandfather Cotton's catechism called 'Milk for Babes' and the Assemblie's Catechism would bring hideous convulsions on the child if she look'd into them." With a certain unconscious jocularity, Mather hopes that he has "not spoilt the credit of the books by telling how much the Devil hated them."

At last Cotton Mather and some devout neighbours kept a day of prayer on behalf of the afflicted children, and gradually "the liberty of the children increased daily more and more, and their vexation abated by degrees," though demons and spirits continued to trouble Boston for some time after.

In 1692 Salem village was the scene of a fierce outbreak against witchcraft, which lasted some 16 months. Cotton Mather attributes it to the Indian "Paw-Maws," but Hutchinson, with his usual common sense, probably hits upon at least one of the real causes. Mather had published a book on witchcraft in 1689. It was strongly recommended in England by Richard Baxter, who a short time later published his own "Certainty of the World of Spirits" This contained a testimony to Mather, and he, in his turn, caused it to be widely circulated in New England. The witch epidemic at Salem occurred but a short time after this and Hutchinson attributes it to "Mr Baxters Book" and "his and his fathers" (i.e., Mather's book and that of his father) and the false principles and frightful stories that "filled the people's mind with great fears and dangerous notions."

The witchcraft scare in Salem began in the house of Mr. Parris, minister of the place, and several other people soon began, to act in an unusual manner. "They crept into holes and under chairs and stools. They used antick gestures and spake ridiculous speches and fell into fits. After some time and a day of prayer kept, the afflicted persons named several that they said they saw in their fits afflicting them, and in particular an Indian woman." The Indian woman, Tihuba was her name, was disposed to have used charms, at the beginning of the outbreak, for the discovery of the witches, but the fact of her being an Indian would probably have been sufficient to cast suspicion upon her. On being beaten and threatened by her master, she confessed to being a witch, and said the Devil urged her to sign a book. Two other women, Osborn and Good, were accused by the Parris children of having bewitched them, and warrants were issued for their arrest. All three were sent to the jail in Boston. Good's little daughter, Dorcas, aged five, was called upon to testify against her mother and her evidence amounted only to this: "That her mother had 2 birds, one black and one green and these birds hurt the children and afflicted persons." Sarah Good was sentenced to be hanged. The Rev. Mr. Voyes told her as she stood on the scaffold, "You are a witch and you know you are a witch." She replied, "You are a liar. I am no more a witch than you are a wizard, and if you take my life God will give you blood to drink." Sarah Osborn died in prison, and the bill of the Boston jailer for the expenses of both women runs thus:—

- To chains for Sarah Good and Sarah Osborn s.14
- To keeping Sarah Osborn from the 7th March to 10th May, when she died, being nine weeks and two days £1 s.3 d.5

Tihuba was kept in prison for 13 months and was then sold to pay her prison fees.

The arrest of these three women was followed almost immediately by many more accusations. The arrival of Governor Phips in May, armed with a charter which empowered the general court to erect and constitute judicatories and courts of record, or other courts of which the Governor was to appoint the judges, gave a great impetus to the persecution. Finding the prison full of witches he gave orders for their immediate trial. All through June and July the cases crowded one upon another, and such was the pitch of superstitious terror to which the people of Salem had arrived, that two dogs were put to death for witchcraft. The cases of Martha and Giles Carey, and of Rebecca Nurse, are so well-known that we will rather turn to the trial of Susanna Martin, held in the court of Oyer and terminated at Salem on June 29th, 1692.

Cotton Mather relates of her that:—"Susanna Martin, pleading 'Not Guilty' to the indictment of witchcraft brought in against her, there were produced the evidences of many persons very sensibly and grievously bewitched, who all complained of the prisoner at the bar as the person they believed the cause of their miseries."

At the examination the cast of Susanna's eye was supposed to strike the afflicted people to the ground whether they saw it or not.

Magistrate. Pray what ails these people?
Martin. I don't know.
Mag. But what do you think ails them?
Martin. I don't desire to spend my judgment upon it.
Mag. Don't you think they are bewitched?

Martin. No, I do not think they are.

Mag. Tell us your thoughts about them then.

Martin. No, my thoughts are my own when they are in; but when they are out they are another's. Their master-

Mag. Their Master? Who do you think *is their Master?*

Martin. If they be dealing in the Black Art, you may know as well as I.

Mag. Well. What have you done towards this?

Martin. Nothing at all.

Mag. Why, it is you or your appearance.

Martin. I cannot help it.

Mag. Is it not *your Master?* How comes your appearance to hurt these?

Martin. How do I know? He that appeared in the shape of Samuel, a glorified Saint, may appear in anyone's shape.

John Allen, of Salisbury, testified that he having refused because of the weakness of his oxen to cart some staves at Susanna Martin's request, she was angry and said, "It had been as good that he had, for his oxen should never do him much more service." The witness answered her, "Dost thou threaten me, thou old witch? I'll throw thee into the brook!" to escape which she flew over the bridge and escaped. From that time various misfortunes happened to his oxen and they ended by swimming out into the sea. Of fourteen good oxen only one was saved, the rest were cast up drowned in different places.

John Atkinson also testified to the bewitching of cattle by Martin, and Bernard Peache said, "that Being in Bed, on a Lord's Day night, he heard a Scrubbing at the Window, whereat he then saw Susanna Martin come in and jumped down upon the floor." She took hold of witness's feet and drew his body up into a heap. For two hours he could neither speak nor stir, but at length he caught her hand and bit three of her fingers to the bone. Whereupon she went down the stairs and out of the door. Snow was lying on the ground and drops of blood were found upon it, as also in a bucket on the left-hand side of the door. The marks of her two feet were found just without the threshold, but there was no sign of them any further off. Another accusation against Susanna was that after a long walk her feet were dry when other people's would have been wet. John Kembal had wished to buy a puppy of Martin, but as she would not let him choose the one he wanted he bought one elsewhere. "Whereupon Susanna Martin replied, 'If I live I'll give him puppies enough.' Within a few days after this, Kembal coming out of the woods, there arose a little cloud in the N.W. and Kembal immediately felt a force upon him that made him not able to avoid running upon the stumps of trees that were before him, albeit that he had a broad plain cartway before him; but though he had his ax also upon his shoulder to endanger him in his Falls, he could not forbear going out of his way to tumble over them. When he came below the Meeting House there appeared unto him a little thing like a Puppy of a Darkish colour, and it shot Backwards and forwards between his Leggs. He had the courage to use all possible Endeavours of cutting it with his ax; but he could not Hit it; the Puppy gave a jump from him and went, as to him it seem'd, into the ground. Going a little further, there appeared unto him a Black Puppy, somewhat bigger than the first, but as Black as a Cole. Its motions were quicker than those of his ax; it flew at his Belly and away; then at his Throat and over his Shoulder one way and then over his Shoulder another. His heart now began to fail him and he thought the Dog would have tore his Throat out. But he recovered himself and called upon God in his Distress; and naming the Name of Jesus Christ, it vanished away at once. The Deponent spoke not one word of these accidents for fear of affrighting his wife. But the next morning

Edmund Eliot going into Martin's house, this woman asked him where Kembal was? He Replyed, 'At home abed for aught he knew.' She returned, 'They say he was frighted last night.' Eliot asked, 'With what?' She answered, 'With Puppies.' Eliot asked when she heard of it, for he had heard nothing of it; she rejoined, 'About the Town'; altho' Kembal had mentioned the Matter to no creature Living."

Susanna could do nothing against such evidence as this. She was found "Guilty" and executed on July 19th.

In sixteen months nineteen persons were hanged, one (Giles Corry) was pressed to death and eight more were condemned. More than fifty confessed themselves to be witches, a hundred and fifty were in prison and two hundred others were accused. But people were growing weary; and it was thought time to cease the persecutions. By about April, 1693, all those imprisoned were set at liberty, and others who Had fled the country were allowed to return home. It is a striking comment that Mr. Parris, in whose house the supposed witchcrafts had begun, was accused by his congregation "that he hath been the beginner and procurer of the sorest afflictions, not to this village only, but to this whole country that did ever befall them," and he was dismissed.

XIV. PHILTRES, CHARMS AND POTIONS

Were it not that dogs and horses have frequently been observed to express their fear of ghosts, an apt definition for man would be "the superstitious animal." Certainly no human feeling is more universal or more enduring. If, as I have endeavoured to prove, the first mother was the first witch, she must have brought superstition with her as a legacy from the unknown world. Not only is it universal in mankind, it is also essential to mankind, if only that it is the one barrier between them and the tyranny of fact. As many-headed as a Hydra, it is to be found in one form or other, in the composition of every human being, from the sage to the savage. Dr. Johnson's idiosyncrasy for touching every post he passed upon his walks abroad, Napoleon's belief in his star, the burglar's faith in his lump of coal as his surest safeguard against discovery, and the bunch of bells which every Italian waggoner hangs about his team to scare away errant demons, are all alike variations upon the one theme—humanity's revolt against the tyranny of knowledge. Our boasted education avails nothing against the rock upon which superstition is securely based. The Girton girl who wears a bracelet hung with lucky-pigs, or rejoices when she finds white heather growing upon a brae-side, may not perhaps consciously accept them as capable of influencing her fortunes, any more than does the card-player believe with his head that if he wins when not playing for money that his next gamble will result in loss, or the race-course punter that a horse whose name includes some particular word such as gold, or love, or black will, for that reason, win races. But all alike have in their hearts this unexpressed belief, and though they may not admit it, does any unexpected good fortune befall them, their mascot has some share of their thanks. Few of us but hold that a certain colour, as, for instance, green, or a certain stone, as the opal, is unlucky. Many of us would not pass under a ladder if we could help it, even though we know that we are thus upholding a superstition based upon a former connection between a ladder and a gallows. In Paris, fashionable people carry little images of their special friends and in case of their illness mutter prayers or charms over the part affected. Indeed, those who protest most strongly their freedom from such degrading weakness thereby show themselves the more believing—he who resolutely walks under every ladder he passes as a mute protest is but acknowledging the faith he seeks to outrage.

All these modern forms of civilised superstition are, of course, survivals from a former age. Some of them, as, for instance, that of spilling salt or sitting thirteen at table, can be traced back to religious or other sources. Others, again, have endured from the earliest days of the human race. Many directly emanate from the art of witchcraft. A full-fledged witch must have her regular recipes and prescriptions—the first witch as much as the last. With the genius that made her a witch, she must seize and formulate the shadowy conceptions that form so large a share of her *clientèle's* beliefs; with her power of organisation, she must elaborate and adapt them to individual needs; in answer to the primitive appeal, she must return the full-fledged spell or charm. As we have seen, her magical powers were exercised in various directions; her methods were consequently as variant. In her capacity as healer, and conversely as disease-inflicter, her various spells must cover all the ills that flesh is heir to. She must be able to cure the disease she inflicts; more, those who combat her must have their own ammunition of the like kind. To the Greek Abracadabra the Church must oppose the sign of the Cross or the mention of the Trinity. Thus in time arose an enormous store of such early methods of faith cure—a store which has since accumulated to such vast proportions as make it hopeless to do more than enumerate a few gleaned from various ages and countries as examples of the rest.

A great number of these charms are given by Wierus, who is severely reprobated by Bodin for propagating such iniquities. Toothache being a common and distracting complaint, there were various recipes for its cure. To repeat the following was found to be very efficacious:—

Galbes, Galbat, Galdes, Galdat.

Or it was equally good to write the following on a piece of paper, and then to hang it round your neck:—

Strigiles, falcesque, dentatæ.
Dentium, dolorem persanate.

Another and more religious means was to quote John, ch. ix., concerning the curse of the blind man, and Exodus, ch. xii., where it is written that no bone of the Passover shall be broken; and then to touch your teeth during Mass, by which time it was more than probable that your pains should cease. Ague, another common complaint, had several remedies. You might either write Abracadabra triangularly and hang it round your neck, or visit at dead of night the nearest crossroad five different times, and there bury a newlaid egg (this has never been known to fail), or emulate Ashmole, the astrologer, who wrote in 1661

> *I took early in the morning a good dose of elixir and hung three spiders about my neck; they drove my ague away.*

Against mad-dog bite there were more complicated methods than mere Pasteurisation, and what is more, you had a large choice. A cure was effected by writing on a piece of bread the words:
—

Irioni Khiriori effera Kuder fere.

then swallowing it; or writing on a piece of paper or bread the words:—

> *Oh, King of Glory, Jesus Christ, come in*
> *peace in the name of the Father +*
> *max in the name of the Son + max*
> *in the name of the Holy Ghost, prax,*
> *Gaspar, Melchior, Balthasar + prax*
> *+ max + God imax +.*

Some people were known to have been cured by a man who wrote

> *Hax, pax, max, Deus adimax*

on an apple, which he gave the patient to eat; but this, says Wierus, was very impious.

According to Cato, bones out of joint could be put back into place by the charm:—

> *Danata, daries, dardaries, astataries.*

Divers were but little distinguished from one another, and we find a number of cures for fevers included under one generic form. Several cures are given by Wierus:—

> *Wash your hands with the patient and say Psalm 144. "Exaltabo te, Deus meus Rex."*

Or:—

> *Take the invalid's hand and say "Acque facilis tibi febris hæc fit, atque Mariæ Virgini Christi partus."*

Or:—

> *Take three holy wafers, and write on the first, "So is the Father, so is Life"; on the second, "So is the Son, so is the Saint"; on the third, "So is the Holy Ghost, so is the remedy." Take these three wafers to the fever patient and tell him to eat them on three consecutive days, neither eating nor drinking anything else; also say fifteen times daily the Pater and the Ave.*

A similar prescription is found in the following:

> *Cut an apple, in three places and write on the first, "In-creatus Pater"; on the second, "Immensus Pater"; and on the third, "Aeternus Pater then let the patient eat them fasting on three different days.*

The following savours little less of religion:—

For fever wryt thys words on a lorell lef + Ysmael + Ysmael + adjuro vos per angelum ut soporetur iste Homo. And ley thys lef under hys head that he mete not thereof and let hym ete Letuse oft and drynk Ip'e seed smal grounden in a mortar and temper yt with ale.

A cure for epilepsy was contained in the following words:—

> *Gaspare fert myrrham, thus Melchior,*
>   *Balthasar aurum*
> *Hæc tria cui secum portabit nomina*
>   *regum*
> *Soluitur a morbo Christi pietate caduco.*

Another remedy was to take the hand of the patient and say in his ear:—

I conjure you by the Sun, the Moon, the Gospel of the Day, given of God to Saint Hubert, Gilles, Corneille and Jein, that you get up without falling again, in the name of the Father, the Sonn and the Holy Ghost. Amen.

For the cure of headache Pliny recommends a plant growing on the head of a statue (*i.e.*, that has never touched the ground), gathered in the lappet of any one of the garments, and attached to the neck with a red string.

Against the King's Evil, vervaine, plucked with the root, wrapped in a leaf, and warmed under cinders, was considered efficacious. This might at first sight seem to differ little in character from a medical prescription, whether useless or no, but to be efficacious certain conditions must be complied with. It must be applied, that is to say, by a young and fasting virgin, and the patient must receive it fasting. While touching his hand the virgin must say, "Apollo, let not the plague increase which a virgin has allayed." And thereafter she must spit three times.

Pliny also provides us with a recipe against accidents in general, originally taken from the Druids of Gaul:—"Carry about your person the plant selago gathered without the use of iron and with the right hand passed through the left sleeve of the tunic, as though committing a theft. When you gather it your clothing must be white, your feet bare and clean, while a sacrifice of bread and wine must be offered previously."

There were also many specific cures for different accidents. An incantation for thorn-pricks is found in the recorded case of one Mr. Smerdon:— "When our Saviour Christ was on earth He pricked His forefinger on the right hand with a black thorn, or whatever it may be, and the Blood sprang up to Heaven, nor moath, nor rust, nor canker did corrupt, and if Mr. Smerdon will put his trust in God his will do the same. In the name of the Father and of the Son and of the Holy Ghost." This is to be repeated three times, and at the end Amen and the Lord's Prayer are to be said.

A once-popular "prayer" for a "scalt" is the following:—

> *Their was two angels came from the East. One carried Fire, the other carried Frost. Out Fire. In Frost. Father, Son and Holy Ghost.*

A more modern version runs thus:—

> *There were three Angels came from East and West,*
> *One brought Fire and another brought Frost,*
> *And the Third it was the Holy Ghost.*
> *Out Fire. In Frost, &c., &c.*

A simple way of extracting an arrow is:—

> *Say three times, while kneeling-, the Pater and Ave, and then + add these words:—"A Jewish soldier*

evilly inclined struck Jesus Christ + Lord Jesus Christ I pray Thee + by this iron + by this lance + by this blood + and by this water, draw out this iron + in the name, &c., &c.

There are several charms useful for stanching blood. One runs:—

Jesus that was in Bethlehem born and baptized was in the flumen Jordane, as stinte the water at hys comyng, so stinte the blood of thys Man N. thy servaunt throw the vertu of Thy Holy Name.—Jesu—and of Thy cosyn swete Saint Jon. And sey thys charme fyve tymes, with fyve Paternosters in the worschip of the fyve woundys.

Another runs:—

In nomine Patris et Filii et Spiritus Sancti, carat, Cara, sarite, confirma oonsana imabolite.

And another:—

Sepa + sepaga + sepagoga + Blood cease to flow. All is consummated in the Name of the Father + podendi + and of the son + pandera + and of the Holy Spirit + pandorica + peace be with you. Amen.

The following simple charm may be found efficacious against the assaults of stinging-nettles:—

Nettle in, Dock out,
Dock in, Nettle out,
Nettle in, Dock out,
Dock rub, Nettle out!

The famous Nothhemd, or *"chemise de necessité"* had such magical qualities that it was worn alike by men to protect them against arrows and other weapons in battle, and by women to assist them in their delivery. It was spun by virgins upon a night in Christmas week. On the breast were two heads: on the right side that of a bearded man wearing a morion, that on the left being hideously ugly and having a crown like that of Beelzebub. By a curious confusion of thought, a cross was placed on either side of these heads.

From spells and charms against disease and accident we may turn to those intended to protect against injury from outside agencies, as, for example, caterpillars, serpents, and particularly thieves.

Were your cabbages or roses suffering from the over-attentive caterpillar you had no need to approach the chemist for a remedy. In Thuringia, for example, they might be banished from the cabbage-patch if a woman could be found to run naked round the field or garden before sunrise on the day of the annual fair. In Cleves it was sufficient to say:—"Beloved caterpillar, this meat that you are having in the autumn profits you as little as it profits the Virgin Mary when, in eating and drinking, people do not speak of Jesus Christ. In the name of God. Amen."

Yet another infallible cure was to pick a switch in the neighbourhood of an adulterer's house, or, by a curious contrast, that of an upright magistrate, and to strike with it the infected cabbages. Provided you walk straight through and across the cabbage-bed, the caterpillars will faint and fall away, but if you turn round you lose all chance of getting rid of them.

A good way of exterminating serpents, toads, lizards, and other vermin was to obtain a supply of the herb called "serpentine." When making use of it you must draw three rings on the earth, and say:—In nomine Patris an + et Filii elion + et Spiritus sancti tedion + Pater Noster." Then say three times:—"Super aspidem et basilicum ambulabis et conculcabis leonem et draconem."

The numerous aids towards discovering thieves seem to indicate that the difficulty of distinguishing between meum and tuum is of no modern growth. Many religious formulæ were, of course, pressed into the detective service, perhaps the most famous being the curse of Saint Adalbert. Such value was placed upon it that the Church only permitted its employment with the licence of the Bishop under pain of excommunication. It is of interminable length, and commences as follows:—"In the authority of all-powerful God, Father, Son, and Holy Ghost and of the Holy Virgin Mary, mother of our Lord Jesus Christ and of the holy angels and archangels, and of Saint Michael and of John the Baptist, in the name of the apostle Saint Peter and of the other apostles, of Saint Sylvester, Saint Adalbert, and of all Confessors, of Saint Aldegonde, of holy virgins, of all the saints which are in Heaven and on the earth to whom power is given to bind and unbind, we excommunicate, damn, curse, and anathematise and forbid the entrance into Holy Mother Church of these thieves, "sacrilegists," ravishers, their companions, coadjutors, and coadjutrices who have committed this theft, or who have taken any part in it," &c., &c.

Another method combines an invocation with the use of a crystal:—

> *Turn towards the East, make a cross above the crystal with olive oil, and write the name of Saint Helen below this cross. Then a young- boy of legitimate birth must take the crystal in his right hand, while*

you kneel down behind him and say three times devoutly, "I pray you, holy Lady Helen, mother of King Constantine, who have found the cross of our Lord Jesus Christ, that in the name and favour of this very holy devotion and invention of the cross; in the name of this very holy cross; in favour of this joy that you experienced when you found this very holy cross; in consideration of the great love you bore your son, King Constantine; in short, in the name of all the good things you enjoy for ever, may it please you to show in this crystal what I ask and am longing to know." Then the boy will see the angel in the crystal, and you will ask what you want, and the angel will reply. This should be done at sunrise and when the sun has risen.

A simpler and more homely means runs thus—

Go to a running river, and take as many little pebbles as there are suspected people. Carry them to your house and make them red-hot; bury them under the threshold over which you most commonly pass into the house, and leave them there three days. Then dig them up when the sun is up, then put a bowl of water in the middle of the circle in which there is a cross, having written upon it: "Christus vicit, Christus regnat, Christus imperat." The bowl having been set and signed with the cross, with a conjuration by the passion of Christ, by his death and resurrection, &c., throw the pebbles one after the other in the water, each one in the name of the suspects, and when you come to the pebble of the thief, it will make the water boil.

Wierus sagely adds the comment that it is not "difficult for the Devil to make the water boil in order to convict the innocent."

A means of getting a little private revenge upon the thief or the witch, even if the harm they have done you has ceased, is as follows:—

Cut on Saturday morning, before sunrise, a branch of nut-tree a year old, saying, "I cut you, branch of this summer, in the name of him whom I mean to strike or mutilate." Having done that, put a cloth on the table saying, "In nomine Patris + et Filii + et spiritus sancti." Say this three times with the following, "Et incute droch, myrroch, esenaroth, + betu + baroch + ass + maarot." Then say "Holy Trinity punish him who has harmed .me, and take away the harm by your great justice + eson elion + emaris ales age"; then strike the cloth.

The numerous proverbs dealing with the tender passion seem to imply that it is inclined to go by contraries, which perhaps accounts for the particular nastiness of the ingredients composing love-philtres. Another constant feature is that they are all double-edged, so that the slightest deviation from the prescribed course may turn love into hate, or *vice versa*, and thus bring about a catastrophe, whereby, doubtless, hang several morals. The "louppe" of a colt is a powerful philtre. It must be ground to powder and drunk with the blood of the beloved. Other specific means are the hair on the end of a wolf's tail, the brain of a cat and of a lizard, certain kinds of serpents and fish, and the bones of green frogs which have been eaten inside an ant-heap. The frogs' bones must be treated thus:—"Throw the bones into water, so that one part floats above water and the other sinks to the bottom. Wrap them in silk, and hang them round your neck, and you will be loved; but if you touch a man with them, hate will come of it."

Another prescription hard to equal runs thus:

—

> *Take all the young swallows from one nest; put them into a pot, and bury them until they are dead of hunger. Those which are found dead with open beaks will excite love, and those with closed beaks will bring hatred.*

If two people hate each other, write the following words, "Abrac, amon, filon," on a consecrated wafer, and if it be given them to eat they will always be friends.

The use of images to work death and destruction upon your enemies has been the subject of tales from time immemorial. Some kinds of images are, of course, much more deadly than others, according to their differences of construction; and whereas some may only subject the victim to great discomfort, others have far more awful results. In any case, a victim will do well to take every means of discovering his enemy should he suffer such pains for which he can in no wise account. Happier still is he who gives no provocation for the use of this deadly and secret means of vengeance.

Images were sometimes made of brass or the dust of a dead man, as well as of wax. The limbs were often interchanged and inverted, a hand being in place of a foot, and *vice versa*. The head was also turned backwards. The worst kind was given the form of a man with a certain name—Wierus hesitates to give it—written above the head and the magic words, "Alif, lafeil, Zazahit mel meltat leuatam leutare," then it should be buried in a sepulchre.

Reginald Scot gives the following variation:—

> *Make an image in his name whom you would hurt or kill, of new virgine wax; under the right arme poke whereof a swallowes hart, and the liver under the left; then hang about the neck thereof a new thread in a new needle, pricked into the member which you would have hurt, with the rehearsalle of certain words (which for the avoiding of superstition are omitted).*

This was probably taken straight from Wierus' book, with which it corresponds almost exactly, and the following instructions are, with some changes in the magic words, identical with those given above. This does not, however, by any means exhaust Wierus' list, as will be seen by the following:—

> *Take two images, one of wax and the other of the dust of a dead man. Put an iron, which could cause the death of a man, into the hand of one of the figures, so that it may pierce the head of the image which represents the person whose death you desire.*

Charms for taciturnity under torture, or against feeling the pangs of torture itself, were obviously very freely bestowed by Satan upon his servants. As an enlightened and advanced thinker Wierus remarks that the merit of the spells does not lie in the words which compose them, but is merely a piece of Devil's work. One of these spells against the torture runs thus:—

> *To three unequal branches, three bodies are hung, Dismas, Gestas, et Divina potestas, which is in the middle. Dismas is condemned, and Gestas has flown to Heaven.*

Scot's version of this is:—

> *Three bodies on a bough doo hang,*
> *For merits of inequalitie.*
> *Dismas and Gestas, in the midst*
> *The power of the Divinitie.*
> *Dismas is damned, but Gestas lifted up*
> *Above the starres on hie.*

Paul Grilland, a jurisconsult, tells a story of a thief who had concealed in his hair a little paper on which he had written, "+ Jesus autem + transiens + per medium illorum ibat + os non comminuitis ex eo +." He was marked with the cross, and was thus immune from torture.

Much of this is, of course, mere gibberish, in which the original idea may or may not be traceable. The divorce of the sense from the words gradually led people to believe that the words themselves contained peculiar merit, and that absurd reiteration of meaningless sounds sufficed to give them their heart's desire. This attitude accounts, of course, for the many spells which recall the patter song in character. Their main feature consists in the repetition or rhyming of certain syllables, as in the cure of toothache, "Galbas galbat, galdes, galdat"; or against mad-dog bite, "Irioni Khiriori effera Kuder fere." This characteristic doubtless made them easy to remember, while the confusion of meaning no doubt added to their value in the eyes of the faithful. Witches, too, were probably as susceptible to the fascination of jingle and alliteration as is the poet of to-day.

It will have been noticed that religion and magic are curiously mingled in many of the spells —Wierus, indeed, states specially that numbers of those given by him were taken secretly from the book of a priest. By degrees, however, they became so much used and altered that the witch herself might frequently use spells which had originally been formulated by the Church. There are, of course, spells against the witch herself. A preventive against witchcraft was to carry a Bible or Prayer-book; mistletoe, four-leaved clover, and a rowan that is found growing out of the top of another tree, are esteemed exceedingly effective. In Mecklenburg, herbs which protect people against witches are gathered on midsummer night. "If you wish to hang a witch by the hair," says Wierus, "take an effigy made of the dust of a dead man's head, and baptise it by the name of the person you wish to hang, perfume it with an evil-smelling bone, and read backwards the words:—'Domine, dominus noster; dominus illuminatio mea; domine exaudi orationem meam; Deus laudem meam ne tacueris.' Then bury it in two different places." If you meet a witch you should take the wall of her in town or street, and the right hand of her in lane or field, and when passing you should clench both hands, doubling the thumbs beneath the fingers. Salute her civilly before she speaks to you, and on no account take any present from her. Finally, the dried muzzle of a wolf is recommended by Pliny as efficacious against enchantments.

Certain stones and vegetables were part of the stock-in-trade of the witch or wizard. The power of mandragore as a philtre was unequalled; cinquefoil was used for purification; while olive branches are so pure that if planted by a rake they will be barren or die. Jasper is powerful against apparitions, and coral, worn by infants or mounted in bracelets, protects against charms. Perfume made of peewits" feathers drives away phantoms; antirrhinum worn in a bracelet ensures against poison; a lemon stuck full of gaily-coloured pins, amongst which are no black ones, brings good luck; while the horseshoe has long been used for the same purpose. Against chafing of the thigh while riding Pliny recommends that a sprig of poplar should be carried in the hand.

On the whole, the means of enchantment were very easily procured, and they were generally most efficacious when most nasty. While some of them, such as hellebore, which secured beneficial rest, had real medicinal value, others were adopted for some trivial reason of growth, form, or time of year. As much stress was laid on the words that accompanied them as on a doctor's* prescription, and the strength of the appeal to the imagination was only equalled by the openness of the imagination to that appeal.

One other point is to be remembered ere we close the chapter: that these charms and philtres very often served their purpose. Though there may have been little value for thief taking in the monotonous repetition of a meaningless jingle, it by no means follows that it would be equally useless in the cure of, say, toothache. Only get your patient to believe, or believe yourself, that the pain is on the point of vanishing and—but are not Faith Healers and Christian Scientists a power in the land to-day. So, again, if a young woman should get to hear that a young man was so impressed by her charms as to seek diabolical assistance in gaining her smiles, he would in all probability assume a position in her thoughts more prominent than that held by his rivals—with a possible sequel in matrimony. Let us laugh at the folly of our forefathers by all means—no doubt they set us the example—but it does not therefore follow that our means to an end are always the more efficacious through being presumably more sensible.

XV. THE WITCH IN FICTION

To those who deny the existence of the witch in fact, any mention of the witch in fiction as a separate entity may seem superfluous. Nevertheless even the enlightened must admit a distinction between the witch as she appeared to Bodin or Pierre de Lancre and the "very repulsive-looking old witch whose underlip hung down to her chin" of Hans Andersen's "Tinder-box." Indeed, this latter can scarcely be considered a witch at all in the true sense of the word, seeing that despite her underlip she seems to have had no occult powers of her own, except, indeed, that her checked apron had the faculty of quieting savage dogs. For the rest, though, she seems to have been entirely dependent upon the old tinder-box left by her grandmother underground, and of which she sent the soldier in search. The only detail, indeed, wherein she resembled the more orthodox witch of history was that when the soldier cut off her head without any provocation whatever, he not only incurred no blame, but even thereby paved his way to marrying a king's daughter—a moral such as would certainly have appealed to Mathew Hopkins. Again, the wicked stepmother of "Snow White" in Grimm's story of that name, although regarded as a witch and in the end suffering appropriate punishment for her crimes, has no more claim to take her place beside Circe or Mother Damnable in the pages of history than is due to the apparently fortuitous possession of a magic looking-glass and some knowledge of toxicology.

The witch in fiction might serve a more serious purpose than does the heroine of a problem novel, for not only has the perusal of her incredible pranks served to enlighten many a weary hour; she is also a standing proof of the *bonâ fides* of the real personage upon whom she is based. Just as in fiction, dealing with less recondite characters, we find that their doings are for the most part exaggerated caricatures of the happenings of everyday life in the real world, and that their potentialities of action are limited, not by hard fact, but only by the furthest bounds of the novelist's imagination, so the witch of fiction caricatures her historical prototype to the point of verging on the incredible. For your real witch, whether she be Diana or Mother Demdyke, Joan of Arc, or the Witch of Endor, has always—like less gifted human beings—conformed to one of several types, varying from them only in the degree proper to human nature. Whether young and beautiful, or old and repulsive, whether hag or heroine, goddess or gude-wife, she remains constant to her type, and has done so from the beginning of things. The witch of fiction, on the other hand, like the problematic heroine, doth as her creator wishes in defiance of all laws of possibility. As any inquisitor could tell you, in a court of justice, once a witch always a witch; in the pages of Grimm a witch is quite as likely to be a fairy godmother or a benevolent old lady, with a: magic golden apple, or, for that matter, a benevolent old lady pure and simple. Sometimes, it is true, as with characters in a realistic novel, the witch of fiction may pass for an impressionistic study of the real witch. Thus in the famous story of Hansel and Gretel she is so far realistic as to desire the capture of small children. But, instead of acting thus in the service and for the honour of her master the Devil, she is moved by no nobler impulse than the desire to eat them, and thus shows herself not a witch at all—for your true witch is always altruistic—nothing better, indeed, than a greedy old cannibal. Her methods, again, however creditable to their inventor, are by no means such as would have commended themselves to the economical tastes of her Satanic employer. The real witch was never yet provided with the capital necessary to build herself houses of "sugar and spice and all that's nice" either as residence or decoy. She lived notoriously in hovels—unless, indeed, she had private means—and the profits of her infernal bargain, even when she received them, were never sufficient to provide her with more than the barest living. Grimm's cannibal, with her roof of chocolate and walls of marzipan, might have been a sorceress; she certainly was no witch.

More realistic, and thus all the more misleading, are the weird sisters in Macbeth. Did we take them as representative types of witchdom, we should be as much deceived as were he who, reading nothing but newspapers, believed that English life was made up of murders, divorces, political speeches and judicial witticisms. They give us, indeed, an excellent impressionist idea of the witch as she appeared in the public eye, some valuable recipes for potions, apt illustrations of divinatory methods and so forth, but no suggestion whatever of that quiet home life wherein the witch, like the British public, passed most of her existence. No doubt she occasionally took part in social reunions, in caverns or on blasted heaths, with Hecate as the guest of the evening; no doubt she there interchanged ideas as to the surest means of drowning sailors or ruining kingdoms. But these were only paragraphs in the story of her life, very much as being tried for murder or presented at Court are outstanding incidents in the life-story of the average Briton. For the most part, she spent her time in the quiet seclusion of her hovel, adding to her stock of every-day poisons or giving interviews to the local peasantry. Of this Shakespeare tells us nothing; to judge from the witches in Macbeth they might have spent the whole of their time waiting about on Scottish moorlands on the chance of making history.

Much nearer to the truth are the lives of Mother Demdyke, Mother Chattox, and the rest of the "Lancashire Witches" as portrayed for us by Harrison Ainsworth. It is true that for purposes of dramatic effect the author exaggerates their characteristics; but such is the privilege of the historical novelist. Nobody supposes—or is expected to suppose—that the Queen Elizabeth of "The Faerie Queene" or the Richelieu of "Les Trois Mousquetaires" corresponds in every respect to the historical personages for whom they stand. In real life Queen Elizabeth was probably insufferable, vain, ugly, with the bad temper that comes from biliousness founded on a *regime* of beer and beefsteak for breakfast; Richelieu an imposing figure only because he was successful. But nobody would think of blaming Spenser or Dumas for having built up an heroic edifice upon a mediocre foundation; had they told us no more than the bare truth, they would certainly have been accused of falsifying history, and, with more justice, of lack of literary artistry. The mission of the historical novelist, as generally understood, at any rate, is, like that of the scene-painter, to provide us with the appropriate setting for figures bathed in conventional limelight. If he draws things as they were he fails in his duty towards people as they are. So it is with the Mother Demdyke of Ainsworth's imagining. The limelight is upon her all the time. She is condemned to be theatrical, if she is to be real; her destinies must be interwoven with those of dispossessed abbots, of aristocratic heroes, and of beautiful ill-used heroines. When composing a curse, she must never forget what is expected of her by the world beyond the footlights; when she interviews her master the Devil, such an interview must always be melodramatic. In actual fact, we know that when the Devil had occasion to visit Lancashire in order to discuss business projects with Mother Demdyke, he did so briefly and without waste of words, for the Devil is above all else a man of business. We know, too, that the real Mother Demdyke was never able to do mischief on such an heroic scale as her bioscopic reflection in the novel. At least, if we make full allowance for her creator's necessities, we may admit that he has given us a sufficiently fair picture, if not of Mother Demdyke as she was, at least of what she was supposed to be.

Of a different order of realism is the witch-world described for us by Goethe. Here, again, had we no further knowledge of witchdom, we should be sadly led astray, though naturally and inevitably. For Goethe, though he gives us some vivid sketches of witch-life, uses them only incidentally. His witches have no greater purpose than to form a background against which the figures of Mephistopheles and Faust may be the better shown up—nay, more, his witches are but part of that background, phantasmagorically confused with Menelaus, Paris, Oberon, Ariel, Titania, and a hundred other figures of mythology or fairy-lore. It is true that by moments he gives us studies of the witch as a personal entity, as, for instance, when Faust and his mentor visit the Witch Kitchen, there to interview not only a very witch, but with her a miscellaneous collection of her familiars, cats, kittens, and the like. It may be noted as a subtle touch of realism that the witch does not at first recognise her master owing to his temporary lack of a cloven hoof and attendant ravens, cursing him roundly before she realises the mistake. But in this the poet overdoes his realism, seeing that in real life the witch had so many opportunities of meeting Satan in unexpected forms, as a tree-trunk, a brazen bull, or a greyhound, that any minor modification of his anatomy would certainly not have caused any such mystification. Even in the original, then, we have to make great allowances for poetical or other licence before we can admit that the witches of Faust are at all true to life. When we come to the acting editions of the play as performed in England by ambitious actor-managers, we find that the unfortunate witch becomes little more than a caricature. On the Brocken she is elbowed out of place by miscellaneous mythological, so that the audience gains no truer idea of an ordinary Sabbath than does the visitor of London who only sees it on a Bank-holiday. In the Witch-kitchen scene again, not only is she quite lost in a world of red fire and scenic effects, but she is represented as resembling rather the pantaloon in a pantomime than a junior partner of the Devil. At least the witch has so much cause of gratitude to the poet, that he and his imitators have given her a new, even if rather meretricious, popularity at a period when it is badly needed.

Properly to appreciate the difference between the witch of fiction and her prototype in real life, we must seek her in what is, after all, her stronghold, the fairy-story. It would seem, indeed, as if, having been driven to take refuge in the nursery, she has there caught something of the vitality of its more familiar occupants. For just as we find that the real witch has more than one seeming, so the witch of fiction may belong to any of many types—if not to several of them at once. As already noticed, she makes a habit of exceeding the bounds of possibility; she is also as frequently as not a dual personality. In real life the witch is always the witch first, the queen, or duchess, or gude-wife only incidentally. Were it not for her occult powers she would cease to exist, would be degraded, indeed, to the ordinary level of queen or beldame. But in fiction, and especially in fairy fiction, this does not hold good; that is to say, there are certain ranks and positions which carry with them almost of right the being considered a witch. Thus if you happen to marry a king, who has a beautiful daughter, or a particularly eligible son, it is almost a foregone conclusion that you are a witch; this, not because widowed monarchs are particularly given to making bad marriages, but rather, it would seem, on some such principle as that by which the wife of the Egyptian Pharaoh became a goddess by marriage. It is true that to be a witch in fairyland, you need not have entered into any agreement with the Devil, nor possess any supernatural power whatever. As in the already quoted story of the Tinder-box, the possession of any magic article sufficiently bewitched to do mischief is all that you require. You need not have bewitched it yourself, in many cases you have inherited, in others purchased it, in others had it thrust upon you. You need not, again, be ugly; in most cases you cannot be, for no one can suppose that a royal widower would feel himself called upon to mate with a hag *en secondes noces*. Sometimes, of course, you may only assume an attractive appearance for the purpose of catching your monarch, but this is rare. The stepmother witch in "Snow White" for example, we know to have been beautiful on the authority of her magic mirror, for did it not in reply to her queries tell her before the irruption of Snow White that she was the fairest woman in the world? Nor have we any cause to doubt that the mirror was truthful, seeing that it sacrificed both expediency and politeness to veracity by maintaining later that "Snow White is fairest now, I ween."

It is impossible not to feel a certain sympathy with this unfortunate royal lady in her subsequent fate, that of being condemned to dance herself to death in red-hot iron shoes; seeing that the sin of envy, for which she suffered, was entailed upon her by all the conventions of stepmother-hood, and that, had she failed in it, the story could never have been written.

That the stepmother witch might and frequently did possess magical powers on her own account we may learn from the story of "The Wild Swans," as related by Hans Andersen. In that instance the wicked queen, by merely making a pass in the air, is able to turn her eleven stepsons into wild swans as easily as Circe herself turned the companions of Ulysses into swine. Strictly following earthly precedent again, we find that her spells sometimes fail, as when she bids her familiars, three toads, place themselves upon Eliza's head, forehead, and heart, so that she may become as stupid, as ugly, and as evilly inclined as themselves. In this they fail altogether, being unable to make headway against the virtuous innocence of Eliza, very much, as upon earth, all evil spells were rendered impotent when confronted with holy words or the sign of the cross. She does not, it may be noted, disdain such more commonplace methods of annoyance, as anointing her stepdaughter's face with walnut-juice and driving her from home. Yet another point in which the story of "The Wild Swans" shows itself in accordance with the traditions of the real witch-world is where the good princess, now become queen, being accused of consorting with witches in a churchyard, is herself accused of witchcraft by the local archbishop, and would inevitably have been burnt but for the timely intervention of her brothers. It was fortunate for her that she lived in fairy-land and not under the jurisdiction of Innocent VIII. or James I., when it is much to be feared that a whole army of brothers would not have sufficed to save her—as a matter of fact they would probably have been among her warmest accusers. This the more so, that she was attended in prison by three familiars in the shape of mice, who would certainly have provided damning evidence in the eyes of any self-respecting inquisitor.

In seeking for the witch in fairy-land, we must often look for her under some other name—as a fairy, for instance, and especially as a fairy-godmother. One of the most embarrassing attributes of the fairy-godmother is that if you offend her she at once changes into a witch, without giving you any warning whatever. She may have officiated as godmother to half a dozen of your children, treating them always as a real fairy should. But should you once offend her, and especially should you forget to invite her to a christening, she at once becomes a witch of the utmost malignancy. This is a curious perversion from the habits of the real witch, whose interests are entirely against the baptising of children under any circumstances. It may be supposed that, having for the nonce laid aside her evil doing, and adopted the civilised veneer of fairyism, she is quick to take offence at any implied non-recognition thereof, very much as might a black man if anyone said to him, "I suppose you don't wear trousers at home?" A famous example of the beneficent fairy godmother occurs, of course, in "Cinderella"; a cynic might, indeed, argue that her beneficence towards Cinderella, her provision of fine dresses, six-horse coaches, and glass slippers, were induced rather by the desire to spite the ugly sisters than out of any actual love of Cinderella herself. Another common type of the double-edged godmother occurs in the story of Prince Hazel and Prince Fair. With characteristic perversity, while pretending that each prince will have an equal chance, she yet makes everything smooth' for the one, while placing irresistible temptation in the path of the other, basing her action upon her preconceived idea of their disposition.

The witch-fairy need not be a godmother. In the "Sleeping Beauty" for instance, her sole cause of irritation is at not receiving an invitation to the christening. In consequence, as every child knows, she condemns the future Beauty to prick her finger at the age of fifteen and thereafter to fall asleep—she and all her entourage—until a casual prince shall have sufficient curiosity to make his way through the surrounding thorn-thickets. It may be noted in this connection that the everyday inhabitants of fairy-land have never shown themselves able to learn from experience. Scarcely a royal christening could take place without some important witch-fairy being forgotten, always with disastrous results, yet no steps seem ever to have been taken to guard against the recurrence of such disastrous negligence.

The witch-princess differs from the witch-queen stepmother in that she is usually herself under a spell, which, being removed, usually by the intervention of some adventurous lover, she at once resumes all the lovable qualities inherent to beautiful princesses. Thus, in "The Travelling Companion" the princess is at first made to appear in the most unamiable light possible, though her beauty and her mantle of butterflies" wings none the less turn the heads of the wooers whose skulls are destined to adorn her garden—a phenomenon not unknown on solid earth. Nevertheless, when a suitor arrives with the necessary qualifications to overcome the spell, she settles down to a life of the domestic virtues, perhaps on the principle that the reformed rake makes the best husband. The witch-princess, be it noted, is so far of earthly origin as to be directly descended from that unhappy heroine, Medea.

I have hitherto refrained from reference to what are perhaps the most vividly convincing characters in witch-fiction: "Sidonia the Sorceress" and "The Amber Witch" the creations of the German Lutheran clergyman, Wilhelm Meinhold. They can, however, more especially the "Amber Witch," scarcely be regarded as absolute fiction, seeing that they provide not imaginary portraits, but actual photographs of the witch as she was supposed to live. So carefully did the author collate his facts, so exact to truth were the details of the trial, tribulations, and final escape of the unhappy girl suspected of witchcraft, that at the time of its publication in 1843, "The Amber Witch" was generally accepted as an actual record of a witchcraft trial in the time of the Thirty Years' War. Perhaps, indeed,

Maria Schweidler deserves a better fate than to

be included as a witch under any heading whatever, seeing that not only was her innocence finally made manifest, but that the accusation was originally aroused against her for no better cause than her own kindness of heart and practical benevolence. It is true that many of the names enshrined in the annals of witchcraft would never have been there if guilt or malevolence were the sole rightful claims to this form of immortality.

As might be expected, the wizard, no less than the witch, has appealed to the picturesque imagination of the romancist in many times and countries. What is more, he has, if anything, been taken more seriously. This is perhaps due to the fact that his creator has generally conformed more closely to his original. The great alchemists of history have been pressed into the service of many writers, much as have the Rosicrucians, the Cabalists, and other members of magico-secret societies. Even when we find the wizard, magician, or sorcerer in his purely romantic guise, he conforms more closely to his original than does the witch. In the "Arabian Nights," for example, are many magicians, to say nothing of djinns, but there is scarcely one among them who transcends the powers of his real-life prototype. Merlin, again, despite his ambiguous origins, wherever he appears, whether in Arthurian legend or Maeterlinckian variation, is always recognisable and true to type. Prospero, in the "Tempest" is a magician of no mean power, but he is none the less a man with human affections and human aims, taking the side of good in the age-long struggle against evil, as represented by Caliban. No one meeting Prospero in the society of, let us say, Albertus Magnus, need have found anything to cavil at in his verisimilitude. Even when you find a magician in fairy-lore, as in the already quoted story of "The Travelling Companion" he is, if unamiable, not unreal, unless, indeed, in his preference for cushions made of live mice, eating each others' tails.

Thus in fiction, as in fact, we find the caste distinction between the witch and the wizard rigidly observed, the one approached with something like reverence, the other regarded with dislike and half-contemptuous fear. This may be largely due in both worlds to the fact that there are "to ten thousand witches but one wizard" and that familiarity breeds contempt. Nevertheless, it should serve but as another claim upon our sympathy for the much-abused witch, even while it exemplifies the truth of the proverb that nothing succeeds like success. The magician, after having led the Devil by the nose throughout a long and ill-spent life, not only succeeds nine times out of ten in cheating him in the end, but also preserves to a remarkable degree the sympathies of mankind, whether as devotee or novel-reader.

The unfortunate witch, having devoted her industrious days to carrying out faithfully the terms of her bargain, is condemned to the flames both in this world and the next amid universal execration. Truly he does not always bear the palm who best merits it.

XVI. SOME WITCHES OF TO-DAY

No study of witchcraft—however slight—could be considered complete did it ignore its importance in the world of to-day. Dispossessed though she may be, in a small intellectual district of the Western World, the witch still queens it over the imagination of the vast majority of mankind. What is more, as I have tried to show in an earlier chapter, there are many indications that her reconquest of her lost territories cannot be long delayed. With the close of the nineteenth century—in which the cult of neo-materialism reached its widest sway—the reaction against the great conspiracy may already have begun. The Russo-Japanese war, with its defeat of an Occidental, or semi-Occidental, Power at the hands of the

Orient, may also be held to typify the approaching victory of witchcraft over science. It is true that the true Russian—the moujik, as apart from the germanised, official class—has always preserved his faith in magic; true also that the Japanese victories were won by a free adaptation of European methods. But this can only obscure, without changing, the great underlying phenomenon—that the lethargic East, the great home of witchcraft and witch-lore, has at last aroused itself from its long trance, and, by whatever methods chastised the fussy West that sought, professedly for its own good, to change its lotus-dreams to nightmares. It only remains for China to rise up and chastise the inconstant Japanese for their treachery to a common ideal, to make the certainty of the witch's victory more certain.

The position of the witch is, indeed, unassailable. Whatever the result of the racial Armageddon of to-morrow, she can lose nothing. If white civilisation stand the test of battle, she is in no worse position than before; if it go down before the hosts of Asia, the witch and her devotees will reap the fruits of victory. It may suit the present Asiatic purpose to drape its limbs with tawdry European vestments—but the patent-leather boots worn by the Babu cannot make an Englishman of him. He may be a "failed B.A. of

Allahabad University" a persistent office-seeker, a bomb-throwing Revolutionist and a professed Atheist, but he is none the less a believer in a million gods and ten times as many witches. In his native village he has an hereditary official magician, who controls the weather, wards off evil spells, performs incantations and the like at fixed charges—and commands the implicit confidence of educated and uneducated alike. What is more, the Indian cult of witchcraft has flourished the more widely beneath the contemptuous protection of the British Raj. In the old times there were certain inconveniences attendant upon the witch or wizard-life in India as elsewhere. Dreaded they were, as they are still, but there were times when an outraged community turned under the pressure of their malignant spells and meted out appropriate punishment full measure. Witch-tests very similar to those employed by Matthew Hopkins were everywhere in use. Among the Bhils, for example, and other allied tribes, a form of "swimming" prevailed, in many ways an improvement upon the fallible British methods. A stake being set up in a shallow tank or lake, so that it protrudes above the surface, the suspected witch must lay hold of it and descend to the bottom, there to remain while an arrow is shot from a bow and brought back by a runner to the firing-place.

If the suspect can remain under water until then, she is declared innocent; if she rises to breathe, she is a confessed witch. This method offers so many opportunities of manipulation, either by the suspect's friends or enemies, that it may well take precedence even of the ordeal by fire, water, or ploughshare favoured among us in feudal days, while the inventiveness of the English witch-finder is put to open shame. Needless to say, Indian witchcraft had and has all the material incidentals proper to a cult. There are substances susceptible to spells, much as is the case with electricity; there are others, as, for example, the boughs of the castor-oil plant, very effective in its cure—so that to flog a witch with such rods is the best possible way of rendering her harmless. There are proper ways of punishing her, too, as, for example, to rub red pepper into her eyes. But unfortunately for those susceptible to spells, the British Government has now stepped in to protect, not the persecuted ryot, but the witch who persecutes him. It is a crime to destroy, even to torture, a witch, however notorious; and however strongly we may object to such iniquitous laws, it is advisable to obey them, or to break them only very secretly indeed. Owing to this unfortunate state of things, the witch riots unchecked throughout Hindustan, and everywhere increases in importance. For, if you are forbidden to suppress her, the only alternative is to seek her favour, and if you have offended to appease her with gifts, or pay some rival practitioner to weave yet more potent counter-spells. Otherwise the odds are heavy that sooner or later, as you are returning home through the jungle one day, she will lie in wait for you in the disguise of a poisonous snake or man-eating tiger, or, failing that, that you will die miserably of typhoid fever or plague.

The witch of Hindustan, though somewhat exalted in importance by the protection extended to her by the British Government, differs but little from her sisters in other parts of the Orient, in the Nearer East, in Further India, China, even in enlightened Japan. Everywhere, indeed, where any regularised form of religion exists, you may find her actively protesting against its decrees, catering for its unsatisfied devotees, or those who agree with that old woman who, discovered offering up prayer to the Devil, explained that at her time of life she thought it well to be in with both sides. Sometimes she takes the place of the Devil; sometimes she provides a way of escape from heavenly and infernal powers alike; sometimes she embodies the whole of the supernatural. The creed of the African native, by him transported to the Americas, may be described as devil-worship—but more properly as witchcraft pure and simple. The African witch-doctor, as with the majority of savage tribes, is himself a god, far more powerful than the devilkins whose destinies he directs. More powerful than the European magician of old times, he can command Heaven as well as Hell—and whether by election, assumption, or descent, he is the sole arbiter of fate, even though, perhaps out of deference to infiltrated European ideas, he sometimes professes to act only as the mouthpiece of Destiny.

I have already referred to the persistence of the belief in witches in our own and other European countries. Further examples might be quoted, almost *ad infinitum*, all going to prove the same thing, that the elementary school is powerless against the inherited tradition. Those interested may find a striking example of belief in witchcraft and the power of the evil eye in Somerset, including an incantation of some merit, the whole too long for quotation, in "Somerset and Dorset Notes and Queries" for December, 1894. Or again, in "La Mala Vita a Roma," by Signori Niceforo and Sighele, a chapter is devoted to the present-day witches of the Eternal City, showing conclusively that, among a host of fortune-tellers and similar swindlers, the genuine "strege" flourish as of yore, though they are perhaps less easily to be found by strangers in search of them. Instead, however, of quoting further from the experiences of others, I may adduce one or two instances of witches with whom I have personally come in contact. I must admit that, as providing any test of the *bona fides* of the modern witch, they are singularly unconvincing. They may, however, serve as some proof, not only that the witch can still find many to do her reverence in modern Christian Europe, but that, as a profession for women, that of the witch is not without its potentialities in these overcrowded days.

If you cross over the Ponte Vecchio at Florence and, leaving the Via dei Bardi on your left, continue along the Via Porta Romana for about two hundred yards before turning sharply to the right, you will be following a course which has been often trodden by those in search of respite from witch-harrying. If you wish actually to consult the witch you must persevere yet further, through a maze of rather mouldering streets, until you come to a very tall house, painted a pale maroon colour and pock-marked with brown stains where rain has eaten into the plaster. You may recognise the house by the fact that it has two sham windows frescoed on its side wall—it stands at a corner of two malodorous lanes—and that one of them purports to be occupied by a lady who is smiling at you invitingly. Smiled, I should say, for even at the time of my last visit, two years ago, she was fading into the plaster background, and by now she may have disappeared altogether or have been replaced by a scowling gentleman, for all I know to the contrary. I would not swear, for that matter, that even the house still stands where it did, so quick is the march of modern improvement in New Italy. But granted that you find the lane and the house and the painted lady, granted further that Emilia has not changed her address, you may be sure of speaking with a witch whose fame has permeated a considerable portion of Tuscany. You will have to climb a wearisome distance up some incredibly dirty and unpleasantly-smelling stairs to reach her first, though, and it is possible that even then you may have to wait until she has settled the destiny or cured the ills of some client from a distant village. But having overcome all difficulties, you may count upon a not unamiable reception from a stout, elderly woman with a good-humoured eye and a plentiful crop of glossy black hair turning slightly to grey. She will not be at all puffed up by her powers or position, and she will be quite ready to accept any little token of appreciative regard you may be inclined to press upon her; but, to be quite candid, I doubt if you will leave her apartment knowing much more of witchcraft after the modern Italian convention than when you entered it. This partly from a certain diffidence on her part to give away trade secrets, but still more because Emilia's Italian is several shades worse than your own, so that unless you are an amateur in Tuscan also, you will find her altogether unintelligible. Only, if you should prove able to interchange ideas, you must by all means ask her about the Old Religion, how far it still prevails among the Apennines, what are its gods, and what their powers. If, further, you ask her opinion as to the magical powers of certain Christian saints, and especially of Saint Anthony, you will be amply repaid, supposing you to be interested in such matters, for all the trouble you and your nose have been put to in discovering Emilia's abiding-place.

My acquaintance with Emilia commenced in a certain hill-top village within easy walking distance of Florence. I was there honoured by some slight intimacy with a worthy contadine who had one fair daughter, by name Zita. Having a lustrous eye, a praiseworthy figure, and a neat ankle, she had also a sufficiency of admirers, whose fervour was not the less that she was generally regarded as likely to receive an acceptable marriage-portion, as such things go thereabouts. Nor was Zita at all averse to admiration, accepting all that was offered with admirable resignation. Had Zita happened to be the only young woman in the village desirous of admiration I might never have become acquainted with Emilia. As things were, Zita was one day attacked by an illness and took to her bed. There was no apparent cause, and dark whispers began to go abroad of jealousies, witchcraft, and what not. Their justice was proved within three days by the discovery, in Zita's bed, of an ear of grass, two hen's feathers, and a twig tied together by a strand of horsehair. The whole had been neatly tucked away beneath the mattress, where it might have remained undiscovered in a less cleanly household than was the Morettis'. Doubt was at an end—obviously Zita was bewitched, and the worst must be feared unless the spell could be expeditiously removed.

In my ignorance I supposed that the local priest would be the proper person to apply to in such a difficulty. But I was very soon convinced of my mistake. To marry you, usher you into or out of the world, the reverend gentleman may have his uses. But to ward off the ills of witchcraft his ministrations are worse than useless, seeing that they only serve to irritate the demons and thus make the patient's sufferings more intense. All this provided, of course, that he be not himself a stregone, a state of things more common than might be supposed. But just as the priest is the one genuine authority on Heaven, Purgatory, and the simpler issues of Hell, so, to grapple with witchcraft, no one is so capable as a witch. And of all available witches none was so efficient or, be it added, so moderate in her charges as Emilia. She was, in fact, the family-witch of the Moretti family, frequently called in and as frequently being entirely successful in her treatment. She was, for that matter, long since become a valued family friend, and—in fact, Emilia must be called in without delay. I accompanied Zita's elder brother Luigi when he visited Florence for the purpose, and with him and Emilia returned, travelling part of the way by electric tramcar, the conductor being, as it chanced, an acquaintance of my companions, and, as such, chatting pleasantly with Emilia concerning her profession, contrasting it favourably with his own. Exactly what counter-charms she used in Zita's treatment I was not privileged to know; at least, I can testify that they were entirely successful, and that within a very short time Zita was herself again, breaking her usual quantity of hearts round and about the village well, and openly jeering at the rival beauty to whom she attributed her indisposition, for the ill-success that had attended her. If I cannot claim that through Zita's bewitching and its cure I gained much knowledge of Italian witchcraft as presently understood, I may at least instance it as an example of the matter-of-fact way in which its existence is accepted by the modern Tuscan peasant. He regards it indeed with as little, or less, perturbation as the coming of the motor-car. Just as the motor has become a danger on every road, so the evil spirit throngs every field. You may take precautions against him and the ill-deeds done by him at the witch's bidding—just as you look carefully round before crossing a road nowadays—you may string bells or weave feathers on your horse's head-dress as preventatives, or make the requisite sign whenever you have reason to believe yourself within the radius of an evil eye; but accidents will happen—and it is always well to know the address of such a dependable practitioner as Emilia, in case. For that matter, you may sometimes desire to have a spell cast on your own account—it is difficult to go through life without a quarrel or two—and in that case also Emilia—But I am becoming indiscreet.

Another witch with whom I have had personal dealings lives—or did live, for she was reported to be more than one hundred years of age at the time —in a small town, locally termed a city, in North Carolina. I must frankly admit that I learned even less of magical knowledge from her than from her Italian colleague. She was a negress, and having heard of her existence from the coloured coachman of the friend in whose house I was staying, I determined to leave np stone unturned to make her acquaintance. I hoped to glean from her lips some particulars of the extent to which Voodooism—elsewhere referred to in this volume—is still practised by the American negro—a fact of which I was repeatedly assured by Southern friends. I was signally disappointed; the old lady would not, in fact, condescend so much as to open her lips to me at all. She lived with her son, who held a position of some trust in connection with the Coloured Baptist Church, in one of the wooden shanties which make up the Coloured town. They stand at some little distance from the august quarters inhabited by the white gentry, and the approach is rendered almost impossible upon a wet day by oceans of brick-red mud of incredible prehensibility. The old lady I found crouching over a fire in approved witch-fashion, her attention entirely devoted to the contents of a pot set upon the hob. However it might suggest a magical brew, it consisted in actual fact of broiling chickens, very savoury to the smell and speaking well for the worldly prosperity of Coloured Baptist office-holders. So concentrated were her few remaining senses thereon, to the exclusion of all else, that although her son supplemented my own efforts and those of my guide in endeavouring to attract her attention, she would not so much as turn her be-handkerchiefed head in my direction. So concerned was the deacon—if that were his actual rank—at his mother's neglect, that I was driven to console him by accepting him as guide through the beauties of the Coloured cemetery near by. It is true that the cemetery was not without its human—its pathetically human—interest, the grave of each child being watched over by the humble toys it had played with in its lifetime, and those of adults by the medicine-bottles, even down to the last, half-emptied, made use of in their illness—this tribute being intended as mute testimony to the care expended upon them. But it could not console me for the lost opportunity. Nevertheless I can vouch for it that the old lady was a witch, and of no small eminence, for her son told me so himself, instancing examples of her power, and he was a very good Christian.

Less elusive, although in some respects scarcely more enlightening, was an interview I once had with a middle-aged witch of unpleasing exterior in the kitchen of the suburban house tenanted by a relative. To the practice of witchcraft this example added the collecting of old bottles and kitchen refuse as a means of livelihood, and she lived, as the police afterwards informed us, in a caravan temporarily moored on a piece of waste land in the neighbourhood of Hammersmith Broadway. The mistress of the house, having occasion to enter the kitchen, there found her seated at the table, unravelling the mysteries of Fate to the cook and scullery-maid by the aid of a very greasy pack of playing-cards. Whatever her pretensions to knowledge of the lower world, she had obviously been drinking—so much so, indeed, that I was called upon for aid in ejecting her from the premises. A large woman, of determined aspect and an aggressive tongue, this might have proved a task of some difficulty had I not luckily bethought me of adjuring her in German, before which she slowly retreated, cursing volubly in English the while, until she had reached the area-steps, when we were able to lock the back door upon her and so be rid of her. It appeared on subsequent inquiry that she had obtained sums amounting in all to some 17s. 6d. from among the domestics, the greater part being the price of informing the aforesaid scullery-maid that her young man, then serving his country in India, still remained faithful to her memory. This information proved in due course to be well founded, the gallant warrior returning six months later filled with amatory ardour. It is true that the witch forgot to mention that by that time he would be ousted from Griselda's heart by—if I remember aright—a dashing young milkman, and that he would incur a fine of *circa* 40s. for assaulting and battering him thereafter. Nevertheless public feeling below-stairs remained strongly in favour of the ejected sorceress, and no minor domestic mishap could happen for weeks thereafter but it was set down as directly resulting from the witch's departing curses.

One other incursion into the World of Magic lingers in my memory as having taken place in a seaside town that shall be nameless. While there passing a holiday with some friends, I frequently observed large yellow handbills, and even posters, setting forth that a lady, who from her name appeared to be of Oriental antecedents, was prepared to cast horoscopes, read palms, and arrange all kinds of personally conducted tours into the future at fees which could only be described as ridiculous. It so happened that among the members of the party was a young lady who was then in the throes of her last love-affair. Naturally anxious to learn its future course, she, it appears, consulted the seeress, whom I will call, though it was not her name, Madame Fatimah. So remarkable did the results appear that the convert felt it her duty to acquaint the rest of us therewith. The fame of Madame Fatimah was not long in penetrating to my ears, and the day came when I found myself waiting upon the witch's doorstep. She was lodged in a back street some little distance from the centre of the town, in one of those lodging-houses which make a point of advertising that they possess a fine sea view, as indeed they may if you ascend to the roof or extend your body out of window at an acute angle. Certainly no less promising hunting-ground for the witch-finder could be imagined. Madame occupied the first floor, and delivered her prognostications amid an Early-Victorian atmosphere of horsehair and antimacassars that was not altogether unimpressive, though speaking of the past rather than of the future. She was middle-aged, of comfortable rotundity, and dressed in a black silk dress, over which was thrown a Japanese kimono embroidered with wild geese. Doubtless from the long residence in the Orient, to which she took an early opportunity of referring, and where she had studied her art at the fountain-head from the lips of a native gentleman very well known in magic circles, and very likely to the Evil One himself, judging from Madame Fatimah's account of his prowess, but whose name I can only vaguely remember as sounding something like Yogi Chandra Dass—doubtless owing, I say, to her long absence from England, for I understood that she was originally of British birth, though married early in life to a Turkish or Indian magician of some note, she had acquired a habit of either leaving out her aspirates altogether or putting them in the wrong place. She was as businesslike as she was affable, and detailed the various methods by which I could be made acquainted with my past and future, at charges ranging from 2s. 6d. to 10s., with a crisp incisiveness. Having chosen what Madame described as "the crystal" at "s., she at once seized both my hands in hers and gazed narrowly into my face, giving me the opportunity of myself reading her past nearly enough to know that onions had been included in the ingredients of her lunch. Satisfied, I trust, of my respectability, she produced a round ball of glass or crystal and placed it on a black ebony stand upon a table. Then, having darkened the room, made several gestures, which I took for incantations, with her hands, and muttered certain mystic formulæ, she commanded me to gaze into the crystal and tell her what I saw in its depths. I regret to say that my willingness to oblige now led me into an indiscretion. Being in actual fact unable to see anything at all, I was yet so anxious to appear worthy that I imagined something I might expect to see. It took the form of a brown baby, two crossed swords, and what might be either an elephant lying on his back with his legs in the air, or the church of Saint John, Westminster, seen from the north-west, the details being too hazy for me to speak with absolute certainty. Madame Fatimah seemed slightly disconcerted at first, but I am bound to admit that she very soon displayed abundance of *savoir faire*, to say nothing of a sense of humour, for without any further waste of time she announced that I must look forward to a life of misfortune, that whether in business, in love, or in pleasure I could expect nothing but disaster, and that I should inevitably suffer death by hanging in my sixty-seventh year. Let me only add that I paid her modest fee with the greatest willingness, and that I have ever since remained convinced that the modern witch is no whit behind her mediæval predecessor in those qualities which led her to so high a place in the public estimation.

I have instanced these few examples of my personal knowledge of witches and witchcraft not as throwing any light either upon their claims or their methods, but simply as some proof of what I have adduced earlier in this volume, that belief in witchcraft, under one form or another, is as widely prevalent in the modern civilised world as ever it was, and that it is ever likely to remain so. Nor does the fact that rogues and vagabonds not a few have availed themselves of its time-honoured respectability as a cloak for their petty depredations at all detract from its claims to respectful credence. That great faith is yet to be whose fundamental truths cannot be turned to the advantage of the charlatan, the swindler and the sham devotee—the greater the faith, indeed, so much the greater is, and must be, the number of its exploiters, battening upon the devotion of the faithful. Nevertheless, it is not upon questions of credibility or faith alone that the world-empire of the witch is founded. Demonstrably true or proven false, the cult of witchcraft has existed from the beginning and will continue until the end of history. Worshipped or reviled, praised, persecuted or condemned, witchcraft and the witch have endured and will endure while there remains one man or woman on the earth capable of dreading the Unknown. Rejoice or grieve as you will the witch is the expression of one of the greatest of human needs—that of escaping from humanity and its limitable environment—of one of the greatest of human world-movements, the revolt against the Inevitable. She does and must exist, for the strongest of all reasons, that constituted as it is humanity could not exist without her.

BIBLIOGRAPHY

The principal authorities made use of in this volume, and not referred to in the text, are given in the following list. The dates do not necessarily refer to the original year of publication, but to the edition made use of:—

Adams, W.H. "Witch, Warlock and Magician." 1889.
Ainsworth, H. "The Lancashire Witches."
Andersen, Hans. "Fairy Tales."
Augustine. "De Civitate Dei."
Beaumont. "Treatise on Spirits."
Blackstone. "Commentaries."
Blau, Dr. Ludwig. "Das altjüdische Zauberwesen." 1898.
Bodin, J. "De la Démonomanie des Sorciers." 1580.
Boulton, Rich. "A Compleat History of Magick, Sorcery and Witchcraft." 1715.
Brand, J. "Popular Antiquities of Great Britain." 1905.
Budge, E. A. "Egyptian Magic." 1899.
Burr, G. "The Witch Persecutions." 1897.
Casaubon, M. "Of Credulity." 1668.
Cassel, P. "On Popular Rhymes and Charms." 1890.
Davies, T. W. "Magic and Divination among the Hebrews." 1898.
Fairfax, E. "Dæmonologia." 1622.
Frazer, J. G. "The Golden Bough." 1900.
Gomme, G. L. "Handbook of Folklore." 1890.
Gould, S. Baring. "Old English Fairy Tales." 1895.
Gould, S. Baring. "The Book of Were Wolves." 1865.
Grimm. "Deutsche Mythologie."
Harrison, F. (Edit.). "The New Calendar of Great Men." 1892.
Holland, H. "A Treatise against Witchcraft." 1890.
Horace. Sir Theodore Martin's Translation. 1861.

Hughes, T. P. "Dictionary of Islam." 1896.
Hutchinson, F. "Historical Essay on Witchcraft." 1718.
Inman. "Ancient Faiths Embodied in Ancient Names."
Innes, J. W. "Scottish Witchcraft Trials." 1880, &c.
James I. "Dæmonologia." 1597.
Jastrow, M. "Religion of Babylonia and Assyria." 1895.
John, C. H. W. "The Oldest Code of Laws in the World." (Hammurabi.)
King, L. W. "Babylonian Magic and Sorcery." 1896.
Lancre, Pierre de. "Tableau de l'Inconstance des Mauvais Anges." 1612.
Lane, E. W. "Arabian Nights" Translation. 1901.
Law, R. "Memorialls of the Memorable Things that fell out Within this Island of Brittain from 1638-1684."
Lecky, W. E. "History of Rationalism." 1869.
Leland, C. G. "Aradia, or the Gospel of the Witches." 1899.
Linton, E. Lynn. "Witch Stories." 1861.
Maspero, G. "The Dawn of Civilization." 1901.
Mather, Cotton. "Memorable Providences relating to Witchcraft." 1689.
Mather, Cotton. "The Wonders of the Invisible World." 1693.
Maury, A. "La Magie et l'Astrologie." 1860.
Melton, J. "Astrologastra." 1620.
Meinhold, W. "Maria Schweidler, die Bernstein-Hexe." 1843.
Meinhold, W. "Sidonia von Bork." 1848.
Michelet, J. "La Sorcière."
Middlemore, Mrs. "Spanish Tales." 1885.
Mitford, A. "Tales of Old Japan." 1876.
Müller, W. Max. "Die Liebespoesie der alten Ægypten." 1897.
Nevins, W. S. "Witchcraft in Salem Village." 1892.
Nares, R. "A Glossary." 1857.
Pearson, K. "The Chances of Death and other Studies in Evolution." 1897.
Pitcairn, R. "Criminal Trials in Scotland." 1833.
Plato. "Laws."

Pliny. "Natural History."
Plutarch. "Lives."
Scot, R. "The Discoverie of Witchcraft." 1584.
Scott, Sir Walter. "Demonology and Witchcraft."
Sepp, J. N. "Orient ŭnd Occident." 1903.
Sharpe, C. K. "History of Witchcraft in Scotland." 1884.
Sinclair, Geo. "Satan's Invisible World Displayed."
Smith. "Dictionary of the Bible."
Sprenger. "Malleus Maleficarum." 1486.
Saladin. "Witchcraft in Christian Countries." 1882.
Theocritus. Translation Bion and Moschus.
Wiedemann, A. "Religion of the Ancient Egyptians." 1897.
Wierus, J. "De Præstigiis." 1563.
Wright, Thomas. "Narrative of Sorcery and Magic."
Also many pamphlets, chap-books, &c., &c., chiefly of the seventeenth and eighteenth centuries.

Copyright © 2025 by Alicia EDITIONS
Credits: www.canva.com; Alicia EDITIONS.
Sabbat de sorcière sur le mont de Brocken (B. Berg);
Germanisches Nationalmuseum Nuremberg, Michael Herr
(1650)
https://commons.wikimedia.org/wiki/File:Witch-scene2.JPG
ISBN E-Book: 9782384555444
ISBN Paperback: 9782384555451
ISBN Hardcover: 9782384555468
All rights reserved.
No part of this book may be reproduced in any form or by any electronic or mechanical means, including information storage and retrieval systems, without written permission from the author, except for the use of brief quotations in a book review.

www.ingramcontent.com/pod-product-compliance
Lightning Source LLC
LaVergne TN
LVHW092012090526
838202LV00002B/105